PURSUING PEACE ACROSS THE ALLEGHENIES

THE RODEF SHALOM CONGREGATION

PITTSBURGH, PENNSYLVANIA

1856–2005

The publication of the volume

has been made possible

through the generosity

of

Lillian Goldstein ל"ז

and

Dr. Henry Goldstein ל"ז

RODEF SHALOM ARCHIVES SERIES

Pursuing Peace Across the Alleghenies - The Rodef Shalom Congregation 1856 - 2005, Walter Jacob (ed.), 2005, xii, 370 pp.

OTHER BOOKS ON RELATED TOPICS

Essays in Honor of Solomon B. Freehof, Walter Jacob, Frederick C. Schwartz, Vigdor W. Kavaler (eds.), 1964, *x*, 333 pp.

J. Leonard Levy, Prophetic Voice, Solomon B. Freehof, Vigdor W. Kavaler (eds.), 1970, *xiv*, 233 pp.

Spoken and Heard, Sermons and Addresses by Solomon B. Freehof, (with a bibliography), 1972, *x*, 264 pp.

World Problems and Personal Religion, Sermons, Addresses, and Selected Writings of Samuel H. Goldenson, M. L. Aaron (ed.), 1975, *ix*, 279 pp.

An American Rabbinate – A Festschrift for Walter Jacob (with bibliography), Peter S. Knobel and Mark N. Staitman (eds.), 2000, *xiv*, 324 pp.

PURSUING PEACE ACROSS THE ALLEGHENIES

The Rodef Shalom Congregation

Pittsburgh, Pennsylvania

1856–2005

Walter Jacob, Editor

Rodef Shalom Press
Pittsburgh, Pennsylvania

Published by the Rodef Shalom Press
4905 Fifth Avenue
Pittsburgh, PA 15213
U.S.A.

Rodef Shalom Congregation
4905 Fifth Avenue
Pittsburgh, PA 15213

ISNB 0-929699-15-7 (Hardcover)

Walter Jacob 1930–

CONTENTS

ACKNOWLEDGMENTS

The publication of this volume would not have been possible without the generosity of Lillian and Henry Goldstein. Their support for many projects of the congregation through the decades along with so much else throughout the Jewish and general community has endeared them to all. Few have been so consistently devoted and helpful.

I remain grateful for the patience of the contributors to this volume. It has been delayed by the three year reconstruction of the Temple facilities and another three years due to the change in the rabbinate.

I want to acknowledge with thanks the dedication of Nancy Gross Berkowitz for her help with this volume and others earlier. I am grateful to Barbara Bailey for her kind, continued assistance with the typescript and Hanna Gruen, Irene Jacob, and Martha Berg for their efforts with proof reading. I want to express my gratitude to the Rodef Shalom Congregation, which sponsored the 1996–1997 symposia at which these papers in an earlier form were presented.

The essay by David Glick has been reprinted with the permission of the *Harvard Law Review*. The interview with Dr. Freehof has been reprinted with the permission of the *Journal of Reform Judaism*.

The photographs included in this volume come from many sources. Many were assembled before the creation of the archives through considerable effort. A large number come from my personal collection. In addition I would like to thank Martha Berg of the Rodef Shalom Archives, Susan M. Melnick of the Rauh Jewish Archives, Barbara Goldman, Lee Hershenson, Frances Aaron Hess, Burton L. Hirsch, Irene Jacob, and Richard Rosenzweig for their contribution. The cover picture, entitled "Laurel Autumn," is by Donald Robinson and I am grateful to him.

PREFACE

One hundred fifty years are a blink in Jewish history but represent a major portion of American Jewish life. Rodef Shalom, as the oldest and largest Jewish congregation in Western Pennsylvania, has played a major role in the development of the Pittsburgh Jewish community and can be given the traditional designation – *ir va-em b'yisrael* – a mother community among the people of Israel.

American Jewish histories have been written, but the history of the development of American congregations has not. American congregations are more difficult to describe as they are multifaceted and different from all those that preceded. These essays treat some aspects of the congregation with emphasis on the early and middle years. The authors treat the role of the congregation in the community, its buildings, its programs, and a few outstanding personalities. The last few years have been only casually mentioned by most of the authors; a degree of balance has been created through photographs of events and personalities of these years.

We are close enough to the beginnings to have personal reminiscences of the early growth, such as my conversations with Mrs. J. Leonard Levy, who was more than one hundred years old at the time. She recalled riding a train in the 1880s to Sacramento, her husband's first American pulpit. It stopped while huge herds of buffalo passed. Another, almost equally old religious school superintendent, Nora Levy, who continued to live on the Northside, where many congregants lived in 1900, recalled the atmosphere of Sunday School in the early twentieth century.

We are also sufficiently distant for records to have been lost and significant personalities to be half forgotten. Events may have been verbally noted but rarely photographed. Matters that interest us were also not seen as significant by an earlier generation.

For this reason the earliest period is sparsely represented; additional material is awaiting discovery in numerous ethnic newspapers as well as diaries and papers of individuals outside the congregation. Whether such research will change our views remains to be seen. As this is the first in a series of volumes, we hope in the future to treat the role of the congregation in the Pittsburgh community, its contributions to national and international Jewish life, the liturgical and musical variations through the decades, the developments within its religious education, and related topics.

Rodef Shalom provided for the changing religious needs of its members. Internal Jewish developments such as Zionism were hotly debated. As the leading congregation, it represented Judaism in the broader community and participated in the issues that faced the Pittsburgh community. The immigrant experiences remained significant as wave after wave of newcomers arrived. The problems of the outside world, such as the rise of Nazism, demanded attention.

It is my hope that these essays will add to the mosaic of American Jewish congregational history. When enough such studies have been written, analytic comparisons and a full history of American Jewish congregations will become possible.

Walter Jacob
January 3, 2005

PITTSBURGH AND THE JEWISH COMMUNITY
1816 – 2005

Walter Jacob

The little river-front community incorporated as Pittsburgh in 1816 was a way station for those settling farther west. The rivers enabled travel south to New Orleans and north to the headwaters of the Missouri. Flatboats were built and provisioned, and the settlers moved on. The steady flow of boat and raft traffic that moved down from Brownsville and other points close to the crossing of the Alleghenies had to be provisioned. Some settlers needed a place to recuperate. Then this changed when coal was found in the hills adjacent to the source of the Ohio and industry began. Among these early settlers, even before incorporation, were a handful of Jews, but we know little beyond their names.

By the middle of the century, industries had sprung up as the four huge veins of coal found in and around the city were exploited. It was "shoveled only twice, once at the mine and then directly into the blast furnace" or the coke ovens. Pittsburgh and neighboring Allegheny rapidly expanded and took new direction in the swift industrialization of the nineteenth century. The cities were no longer just river towns that provisioned onward journeys. The banks of the three rivers were lined with iron and glass works as the raw material came in barges.

A series of coal mines within the city fed its local fuel needs. Ancillary industries sprang up. Clothing manufacture was cheaper than importing the finished goods. Beer was brewed for the laborers and stored in the huge excavations near the rivers. Distilleries sprang up; cheap glass became a major industry. Hogs from, the neighboring farm lands were driven to the slaughterhouses. The area was thriving. A small Jewish community was established in the 1840s as German-Jewish immigrants saw possibilities for dry-goods stores.

Pittsburgh and Allegheny became armories during the Civil War with the fabrication of large cannon. The Allegheny Arsenal explosion of 1862 brought the war home as did earthworks erected as

Lee moved toward Gettysburg. More than 400,000 soldiers moved through the city by railroad and boat during the war; some were the wounded.

The 230,000 inhabitants of 1866 had to deal with a city "curiously hemmed in.... Every street appears to end in a huge black cloud and there is everywhere the ominous darkness that creeps over the scene when a storm is approaching. When the traveler has satisfied himself that the black clouds are only the smoke-covered hills that rise from each of the three rivers, still, he catches himself occasionally...so as to get back to his umbrella.... Pittsburg announced its peculiar character from afar off. Those who approach it in the night see before them...black hills with rows of fire half-way up their sides; and there are similar fiery dots in the gloom as far as the eye can reach...the chimneys and coke-oven, quietly doing their duty during the night, unattended."[1] The city was dirty and would get worse.

The expansion continued as iron works turned into steel mills that covered miles of river front. The Scotch-Irish Presbyterian and German Lutheran population was now augmented by several hundred thousand workers recruited from Eastern and Southern Europe, mainly Catholic and Orthodox Christians. They settled near the mills, mines, and coke ovens. Others were taken to the mills in the nearby counties and West Virginia. The oil boom in Oil City and the North created a new demand for steel as well as much else, and each of these little towns suddenly boasted a Jewish community.

Oil had been known to exist in nearby counties since the 1780s but was not exploited till Drake drilled a well in 1859. A year later half a million barrels were produced, and a new industry was established to play a role in Pittsburgh till the demise of Gulf Oil a century later. George Westinghouse established air-brake, signal, and electric industries, and Charles Hall developed the aluminum industry. These, along with Heinz foods, augmented the industrial base of the region. Although glass making diminished as natural gas found elsewhere made Pittsburgh less competitive, PPG industries survived.

2

Pittsburgh View 1850s

Pittsburgh View 1900

Jews did not participate in any of this development as the Scotch-Irish management excluded them as well as all Catholics; only a handful became laborers. They were peripherally involved in the labor movement and in the major strikes – the railroad riots of 1877, the Homestead steel strike of 1892, the great steel strike of 1919. By the beginning of the twentieth century, a few Jews became involved in steel fabrication and in allied concerns such as Copperweld, which involved a new process initially rejected by the major producers.

Jewish immigrants, who had originally come from the provinces of Germany, arrived in larger numbers from Eastern Europe by the 1870s, fleeing Czarist persecution and conscription. As always, cemetery associations and then congregations representing each immigrant locale were established. These immigrants found work in the smaller industries, such as tailoring, textiles, shoe making and cigar making, or at the periphery of the steel industry in scrap iron and industrial laundries. Jewish stogy makers were exploited, leading to a successful strike organized by the IWW in 1913.

Groceries and dry-good stores demanded little capital; one could settle in an ethnic neighborhood with a knowledge of the local language and make a living. Some managed to expand their enterprises into department stores. Others invested their growing capital in distilleries, and the community began to possess enough wealth to build synagogues and other Jewish institutions.

By the beginning of the twentieth century, Pittsburgh was one of the largest cities in the United States. The positive industrial aspects of the city and the negative social and cultural side were well analyzed in the massive survey of 1907–08. Robert Woods wrote: "There is no city in the country, and probably none in the world where strict Sabbath and liquor legislation is more strenuously enforced.... (Yet) the amount of Sunday work in the steel mills has been appalling. There is an assumed sanctity in the operations of business...."[2] Social services were left to religious groups, and it was in this area that the Jewish community made significant contributions for the general community in addition to taking care of its own.

4

Heinlein Rauh (1779-1856)
whose children settled in
Pittsburgh.

Babette Schonhof (1785-1856),
wife of Heinlein Rauh.

William Frank (1819
Hopfheim, Bavaria - 1891
Pittsburgh), a founder of
Rodef Shalom

Pauline Wormser Frank (1815-
Aldinger, Wurzburg - 1910
Pittsburgh)

5

Cultural life was even slower. In the 1860s it was still possible to say that "a Pittsburg man of business who should publish a poem would find his 'paper' doubted at the bank. 'A good man, sir, but not practical.'"[3] This did not change during the succeeding decades. A university existed but was not nurtured. Cultural growth began as Andrew Carnegie founded the Carnegie Institute in 1901, followed by other families and eventually the Mellons. A symphony orchestra struggled to establish itself; colleges and universities were founded. The symphony, and other institutions began to take shape.

World War I still saw Pittsburgh as a mature industrial giant with a reputation for toughness. It was a beer and sports town with plenty of rough edges, but a genteel life was possible in the growing suburbs. Till the legislation of the 1920s, immigrants continued to arrive, including a fair number of Jews. As there were more limits to upward mobility for Jews in Pittsburgh than elsewhere, the Jewish population did not grow as much as in neighboring Cleveland.

The Depression, the great flood of 1937, and, even more the unwillingness of those in control to modernize and welcome change, meant that the prosperity brought by World War II was temporary. The post-war years began stagnant till a well–orchestrated revival got underway in the 1950s. The inner city was rebuilt; stringent environmental curbs were put into place in the face of powerful industrial opposition; social services and housing were improved, and race relations were given proper attention. As those in charge of the heavy industry base refused to modernize, the steel industry largely disappeared, while other former industrial giants failed because of poor leadership or lack of imagination.

Although the upper class remained, the mobile middle class saw the next generation move to other areas of the country that changed more rapidly. This affected the Jewish community, which saw a major part of the baby–boomer's children move away. In some instances the family ties kept them here while their commercial enterprises flourished elsewhere.

6

Austrian passport for Leiba
Rosenbach, 1892. Born in
Galicia, she came to Pittsburgh
via Berlin.

Berlin work insurance permit for Leiba
Rosenbach 1892

Kaufmann's Department Store
1900

These changes were heart-wrenching, for the working population, which prized its ethnic neighborhoods, was reluctant to move. This meant that a whole series of social services had to be provided for communities that would never fully recover. Much of this was left to the religious communities, which formed alliances across religious lines, such as the East-End Cooperative Ministries, for this task.

It is within this historic setting that the Rodef Shalom Congregation was founded and grew.[4] A start in life, freedom from the restraints of the old world, unhampered by parents or relatives, relieved of any burdens of debt or teenage mischief, religious life was not the first thing on their agenda, but when one among their number died, they wanted a Jewish burial. A small group purchased a plot for a cemetery on Troy Hill, and so Jewish life, after a fashion began in the 1840s. The initial religious services may have centered around the *shivah* for the deceased. Whatever the reason, by 1846 a group of these immigrants from various places in Central Europe established an informal congregation. As the settlers had no roots as yet and frequently left after a short time, the *minyan* dissolved and was replaced by another a little later.

Coming from small communities throughout Central Europe, having little or no formal Jewish education, they conducted services as best they remembered them. The vague Judaism of a fifteen-or seventeen-year old became authentic and led to quarrels about memories of melodies and customs. The little groups without strong leadership or stable settlers lasted for a short time and then disappeared, only to be replaced by more of the same until 1856, when a congregation, Rodef Shalom, was chartered. As they had quarreled, they settled on the name – "Pursue Peace" and hoped for the best.

The newly formed group met in rented rooms and began to function with services on a regular basis. Soon the problem of education arose – not just Jewish education, but general education – as there were no public schools as yet. Expenses beyond the minimal rental now had to be considered.

8

When Isaac Mayer Wise, the founder of American Reform Judaism, arrived in 1862 he found a group ready for some outside guidance. In a short visit, he persuaded most of them to become Reform Jews and thus to adapt themselves to the new land. Not everyone wished to move so quickly, and a group split to form the Tree of Life Congregation. Although the number of Jews in Pittsburgh remained small, they now had two congregations.

Rodef Shalom dedicated its first synagogue, located on 8th Street, which placed Judaism prominently in the center of the city. The building proclaimed that Jews were in Pittsburgh to stay. The little community was led by a series of lay leaders until the arrival of the first rabbi, Lipmann Mayer, in 1885. Under his guidance the congregation undertook more efforts in the broader community.

A steady trickle of German Jewish immigrants continued to arrive; their small beginnings led to prosperity as the city grew and prospered. They joined the two existing congregations. By the 1870s Eastern European immigrants from many different locales began to arrive in greater numbers. A touch of the "Old Country" was provided by the small congregations they established. Each followed the customs of their place of origin. More or less the same thing happened with Catholic parishes. The Jewish immigrants relied heavily on the members of Rodef Shalom for aid in settling and for help when disaster struck.

By the 1890s new Eastern European immigrants began to join Rodef Shalom. A succession of new synagogue buildings, first (1902) on the old location downtown and then (1905) in the more fashionable East End, served the rapidly growing congregation, now under the leadership of J. Leonard Levy, who played a major role in virtually every aspect of Jewish and civic life.

The most successful in the congregation also sought to play a larger role in the general community, but the areas open to them remained limited, in many instances till the end of World War II.

9

The growth of the Pittsburgh Jewish community and the congregation continued through World War I and the twenties under the new rabbinic leadership of Samuel Goldenson, who was concerned with social action. Throughout this time and well into the last quarter of the twentieth century, Rodef Shalom provided the leadership for the entire Jewish community and represented it in the general community on civic and cultural boards. It also shaped its efforts to be part of the larger community and closed its gymnasium and swimming pool in favor of a broader community center.

Interreligious understanding, which had always been cultivated, was further stressed by Rabbi Solomon B. Freehof in face of the atmosphere of the Depression. His book-review series and lectures brought the congregation more into the intellectual life of Pittsburgh. The Jewish community and Rodef Shalom continued to grow into the 1950s, when industrial changes became evident and a gradual exodus began.

The growth of the suburbs and the need for more Reform congregations led Rodef Shalom through Dr. Freehof and later myself to assist four other congregations to establish themselves. The middle of the twentieth century saw Pittsburgh rebuilding itself, a task that was to take the remainder of the century. Rodef Shalom, through its lay leadership, Dr. Freehof, and I, played a significant role.

The broader religious community had changed, so different relationships needed to be worked out; I took part in that alongside Cardinal Wright. Race relations were strained through the riots of the 1960s; I saw to it that Rodef Shalom moved swiftly to help as we could so more easily than other Jewish organizations. I helped to create new ties and to provide a practical outlet through Project Equality, that I served as president along with providing representation on groups which promoted new housing and the retraining of the basic work–force. Direct help through supplying food-banks became part of the congregation's outreach. Much else needed to be done to alleviate the poverty brought by the demise of the steel industry.

As the Jewish community spread into the suburbs, it became clear that an organized rabbinic body that included the Reform, Conservative, and Orthodox rabbinate would be helpful, so a group of us established the rabbinic fellowship, which I served as second president and continue to edit its weekly Torah commentary in the *Pittsburgh Jewish Chronicle*. A closer relationship with the United Jewish Federation was also desirable.

The 1980s brought many immigrants from the Soviet Union; they needed to be warmly welcomed and provided with jobs, housing, furniture, and mentors. Vigdor Kavaler, the Executive Secretary, and I created the structure to undertake this during the period before the broader community became involved. Hundreds became involved and helped to resettle this latest group of immigrants; many joined the congregation.

The Temple which had served the congregation since 1905, needed attention; a major restoration of this national landmark site was undertaken in the 1990s. This project with magnificent lay leadership demonstrated that Rodef Shalom as a significant part of the Jewish community intended to remain in the heart of Pittsburgh in contrast to so many synagogues across North America that had moved to the suburbs. It set a pattern that other synagogues and community organizations followed. After the Temple itself was restored, a reconstruction of the remainder of the facilities was undertaken under the guidance of Dr. Mark Staitman, my successor.

At the beginning of the twenty-first century, Rodef Shalom in its restored and rebuilt facilities, is a vibrant congregation with an emphasis on worship, community service, learning, and leadership development for the broader Jewish and general community.

As Pittsburgh and the surrounding areas rebuild themselves, the future looks bright for the Jewish community. Synagogues, schools, and other organizations are in place with fine facilities and good leadership. The roots of Jewish life, which go back a century and a half, have provided a solid structure along with a firm place in the broader religious, cultural, and civic community. Families who have lived in Pittsburgh for four or five generations continue to provide a warm welcome to those who would join us to build our future.

Notes

1. James Parton, "Pittsburgh in 1866," in *Pittsburgh,* ed. Roy Lubove (New York: Franklin Watts, 1976) p. 11.

2. Robert A. Woods, "Civic Frontage," *Pittsburgh:An Interpretation,* in Frank C. Harper, *Pittsburgh: Forge of the Universe* (New York: Comet Press, 1957) p. 43.

3. Parton, *Pittsburgh,* p. 15.

4. For a resume of the early history of the Jewish population in Pittsburgh and the surrounding communities, see Jacob S. Feldman, *The Jewish Experience in Western Pennsylvania, 1755-1945* (Pittsburgh: The Historical Society of Western Pennsylvania, 1986). For an insight into some portions of this period, see Alion Shilo ed., *By Myself I'm a Book* (Waltham: National Council of Jewish Women, Pittsburgh Section and the American Jewish Historical Society, 1972), and Ida Cohen Selavan ed., *My Voice was Heard* (New York: National Council of Jewish Women, Pittsburgh Section 1981).

SHOWING THE WAY – THE RODEF SHALOM PULPIT
1854 – 1998

Walter Jacob

American Jewish congregations and their membership
have changed drastically from their nineteenth-century
beginnings. The initial congregants were rustic village lads and now
are college educated. Rodef Shalom[1] followed this pattern. The
leaders and rabbis who served this changing congregation provided
religious services and sermons, religious school classes, adult
education, pastoral care, communal outreach, interfaith efforts, and
philanthropic leadership. Some were concerned with scholarship as
well. Of all these tasks at Rodef Shalom, the pulpit became and
remained primary. Some of the rabbis excluded virtually everything
outside the pulpit, others sought a balance but all emphasized the
pulpit.

The role of the rabbis and earlier teachers was defined, as
always, not only by the changing nature of the congregation, but also
the surrounding world. The close–knit immigrant congregation of the
nineteenth-century sought a touch of their former European home and
a bit of America. The early twentieth-century community embraced
America and upward mobility. In the roaring twenties the people
focused on themselves and needed to be reigned in. The Depression
and World War II brought America and the congregation into the
world arena, and the membership now found dozens of Jewish
organizations vying for their allegiance and time. In the post-World
War II years the highly mobile middle class rarely saw all their
children live in Pittsburgh and continue their traditions. The new
focus of the community was on Israel and Russia and its concern,
intermarriage. Industrial Pittsburgh declined, and the younger
generation moved or had national business and professional interests,
with Pittsburgh as its bedroom community. It left a more conservative
older group behind. Throughout the twentieth century, the pulpit had
to compete with the growth of the media as movies, radio, and
television led to different expectations and brought a distinctive new
rhythm to life. These were some of the constraints.

Rodef Shalom emphasized complete freedom of the pulpit. The effective use of that freedom depended on the personality of the preacher and the possibilities presented by the era. Each understood the task differently and shifted the emphasis. The strong–willed young men who formed the congregation in the 1840s may have sought arbitrators, but they soon got leaders who spoke their mind and followed the tradition of the recently revived sermon.

The early nineteenth-century sermon provided a voice for the new religious leadership of Western Europe. The great rabbis of the period built on ancient traditions[2] and took on the new challenges of battling anti-Semitism, broadening the struggle for civil rights, finding a path to express their Italian, French, and German nationalism, coping with the industrial society and the rapidly changing cultural world. As Orthodox Judaism refused to deal with these and other issues, the Reform movement was created. It demonstrated a willingness to interact with the times as Judaism had done through the ages. The modern sermon represented a part of this effort.

By the 1840s, Reform Judaism had become a major factor in the life of all western European Jewish communities. The rabbinic role as judge and interpreter of Jewish law had given way to the rabbi as religious, political, and social leader. As he combined Jewish learning with a university education, he was well equipped for this new role.

The problems and issues that the new immigrants to America faced were similar to those of Europe, but Jewish leadership was almost entirely lacking and the immigrant communities floundered. Made up largely of under educated teenagers from rural backgrounds, they built on their memories mixed with youthful enthusiasm and stubbornness. The result was a series of explosions as small congregations arose and collapsed. Leadership eventually was left to the slightly better educated. When university–trained rabbis became available, they were by far the best-educated members of the community. The growth of the community beyond immigrant status, Americanization, the changing economy, and social pressures presented

Minute Book of the Bes Almon, Troy
Hill Cemetery, 1875. Earlier minutes
have not been preserved.

the agenda for the rabbis. Their efforts at pulpit leadership needed to be placed in the context of the times, but only the pioneering studies of Charles I. Cooper and Jacob Feldman[3] have been available. Little has been written on the American Jewish pulpit, so comparisons with other rabbis are not possible. Nor is there an analytical history of Pittsburgh or the contemporary Christian pulpit, which would enable a broader assessment.

When the small group of Jews who wandered to Pittsburgh and Allegheny considered this home, they established a cemetery[4] and formed a number of congregations that rose and fell. Eventually, in 1856, they chartered a congregation. Their past communal conflicts were reflected in the name Rodeph Scholem. In 1854, its predecessor congregation had engaged William Armhold as its reader; he continued to serve as the first reader and teacher of Rodef Scholem. He followed a number of others[5] who had been engaged by predecessor congregations that had collapsed either because of personal conflict or as its members left to settle farther West.

THE PIONEERS

WILLIAM ARMHOLD (1829–1920)
(AT RODEF SHALOM 1856–1865)

William Armhold was selected principally as a teacher and secondarily to lead religious services. He served the congregation during a period of economic expansion. By 1852 the railroad had reached the city; the Jewish population grew from thirty families to sixty by 1858.[6] In 1853, the community organized the Hebrew Benevolent Society to provide for indigent immigrants and to protest against discrimination. The Hebrew Ladies Aid Society followed in 1855. The congregation was sufficiently strong to build a synagogue in 1861; it was dedicated by Rev. Morris Raphael of New York along with William Armhold and Josiah Cohen. The Civil War expanded the economy and led to a moderate increase in the Jewish population. It also brought the pain and sorrows of war; the Jewish community responded through its aid societies.

16

William Armhold

Louis Naumburg

There was no pattern for American congregational life west of the Alleghenies. The neighboring communities were larger (the reasons for that remain unclear)[7] but were equally raw, and they were too distant for effective support. In 1863, following a persuasive visit by Rabbi Isaac Mayer Wise, under Armhold's guidance the growing congregation, proud of its new synagogue, became Reform. The more traditional element left to form the Tree of Life Congregation, which eventually became left-wing Conservative. The split brought greater harmony to Rodef Shalom. These considerable efforts were gratefully remembered, so Armhold was warmly welcomed when he came from Philadelphia to Pittsburgh to participate in the Pittsburgh Platform deliberations of 1885.

Armhold instructed his classes in German while Josiah Cohen, an English immigrant destined to play a major role in the congregation and in the Pittsburgh community, taught in English.[8] The services and sermons were in German, and Armhold preferred that language for formal occasions throughout his life.[9] No record of his preaching has survived.

Armhold provided stability and established a congregation with a synagogue, which meant that it had a recognized place in the Pittsburgh community. By turning Rodef Shalom to Reform Judaism, he eliminated internal ideological struggles and helped create a second congregation that provided for those who sought a more traditional approach.[10]

LOUIS NAUMBURG (1813–1902)
(AT RODEF SHALOM 1865–1870)

The Civil War was over and Pittsburgh's economy troubled when Louis Naumburg arrived. The congregation was ready for a rabbi but none was available, and the temporary economic decline posed its problems. During the few years in which Naumburg led the congregation, the synagogue was refurbished and the school continued to do well.[11] He, too, preferred German to English for his teaching and preaching. By 1870, the congregation felt that it needed

18

more leadership than Naumburg was able to provide. From time to time, he continued to serve as cantor. He participated in the deliberations that led to the Pittsburgh Platform of 1885. He undoubtedly remained indirectly involved in the life of the congregation, as his daughter married Judge Josiah Cohen, one of the most influential leaders of the community and the first Jewish judge in the county. Cohen began as a teacher in the congregation and eventually became its president. Josiah Cohen, active in the Republican party and public education, was the representative of the Jewish community on the broader Pittsburgh scene. Nationally he was a founder of the Union of American Hebrew Congregations.

Naumburg provided the necessary direction and guidance while the congregation sought a rabbi who would take it further. The improvement in the synagogue facilities and the steady growth of the congregation demonstrated his leadership abilities.

LIPPMAN MAYER (1841–1904)
(AT RODEF SHALOM 1870–1901; EMERITUS 1901–1904)

Pittsburgh was recovering and rapidly becoming a major industrial center when the German-born Rabbi Lippman Mayer took up his rabbinic position after a year in Selma, Alabama, where he presumably learned English. With a Ph.D. he was by far the best-educated person in his congregation.[12] He belonged to the second generation of German Jewish immigrants that arrived after the failed Revolution of 1848. They were generally urban middle class, with a Gymnasium (high school) education and a love for German literature.[13] The congregation had built its synagogue in 1861; it was dedicated by Rev. Morris Raphael of New York along with Rev. William Armhold and Josiah Cohen. It had status in the community, but that needed to be expanded beyond architecture both within the Jewish community and into the larger community.

At Rodef Shalom Mayer insisted on a consistent approach to Reform, and the congregation adopted the prayer book edited by David Einhorn with its German translation. Mayer emphasized the

19

principles of Judaism,[14] not its outer forms in which he was a disciple of David Einhorn, the radical American reformer. He eliminated the second day of the holidays and the wearing of hats during services. The family pew had already become customary. His sermons presumably followed the same path. His participation in the various Reform meetings of the nineteenth century showed him to be a radical reformer.[15]

Mayer convinced through earnestness and sincerity. He provided general communal leadership through his important role in German-American circles and their intellectual life. He was the first Jewish leader in Pittsburgh to concern himself with interfaith relations. Since he was a founder of the *Leserverein,* it was not strange for him to be invited in 1872 to preach in Smithfield Street German Church – something most unusual in this period. He was even asked to participate in the dedication of several churches in Allegheny and so played a role totally distinct from that of any rabbi in continental Europe.[16]

We do not know whether his broad communal involvement was reflected in his sermons.[17] He was concerned about the plight of the new Russian Jewish immigrants and involved the congregation in these efforts as well as in the establishment of a school for these immigrants in 1882.[18] In contrast to Isaac Mayer Wise, who insisted that in America only the English language should be used whenever possible, Mayer continued to preach in German.[19] This became a problem in the last decade of the nineteenth century, and the congregation in 1893 engaged Rabbi Samuel Greenfield as assistant, to preach in English.[20] When Greenfield left in 1896, the board requested that Rabbi Mayer preach in English and German on alternate Sabbaths. No sermons of Lippman Mayer have survived. He retired in 1901 and continued as rabbi emeritus. He was modest, retiring, and well respected by his colleagues. A modest history of the congregation by him may be found in the Appendix.

Rabbi Lippman Mayer 1870s

Rabbi Lippman Mayer 1900

Lippman Mayer, with his highly educated background, was in a good position to determine the ideology of the congregation. His selection of the prayer book edited by Rabbi David Einhorn placed the congregation among the more radical reformers and their consistent ideology. The first edition of this prayer book was accompanied by a German translation congenial to the immigrant generation, even if not to their children. The English version was adopted later, as by the 1890s the community felt less at ease with German.

Lippman Mayer's involvement with the broader German immigrant community indicated an effort to improve interfaith relations beyond what had been possible in Germany. These efforts were thoroughly appreciated. As Rabbi Mayer's successor felt less connected to the German community, he changed his emphasis to build relationships with the broader American community.

As the first rabbi of Rodef Shalom, Lippman Mayer concerned himself with the ideology; he established a classical Reform pattern. His lectures and sermons provided solid adult education; the congregation grew, and he saw to the planning of a new synagogue. His concern for the new immigrants from Eastern Europe as well as orphans made him a communal force. Mayer's efforts in the Pittsburgh community brought recognition to the small Jewish community

(J. LEONARD LEVY (1865–1917)
(AT RODEF SHALOM 1901–1917)

"Religion means sociology as well as theology. The great prophets of Israel understood this .... They did not want justice dealt out in drops." With these words Rabbi Levy channeled the unspoken hopes of his congregants and gave them direction. The logic of his presentation, the self-assured manner, and the convincing voice provided hope and clear guidance. The colorful Englishman who assumed the pulpit of Rodef Shalom in 1901 immediately emphasized the English sermon. He insisted that his sermons be published,[21] and they were widely distributed.

Rabbi J. Leonard Levy

After an initial look at Pittsburgh and the "piles driven into the ground" for the new Eighth Street Temple, in 1901, he took a long summer journey to Palestine and the Near East. In 1905 he traveled to Japan in an effort to obtain Japanese support for the oppressed Russian Jews. These journeys, along with a good Jewish and university education, provided a broad understanding of the world.[22] He was interested in art and English literature, which brought a different perspective to the congregation.

Levy saw the potential for growth within the congregation, the possibilities for communal leadership, and the wider possibilities within the larger Pittsburgh community. Under his guidance the membership tripled, and a new building was erected in the most prominent neighborhood near the Catholic cathedral – neither one was particularly welcome by the Pittsburgh elite. His Sunday services and the published sermons were part of both congregation building and communal outreach. As editor of the *Jewish Criterion*,[23] he was the voice of the Jewish community that influenced the new immigrants.

His efforts extended far beyond the pulpit as he produced liturgies, religious school texts, and hymnals for the congregations. He also translated the first volume of the "Rodkinson" Talmud into English.[24]

Levy initiated a Sunday weekday service for a six-month season[25] so that those who were forced to work on shabbat could worship on a regular basis. It was not a substitute for shabbat services, which were held throughout the year. Engaged to preach alternate weeks on Saturday and Sunday, he preached on every Sunday and virtually on every shabbat. The titles of the shabbat sermons, announced in the weekly edition of the *Jewish Criterion*, indicated that he based those sermons on the Torah portion. No shabbat sermons have been preserved.

The pulpit was Levy's chief method of communicating his thoughts, and he saw it as the major vehicle for congregational guidance and education. He developed his skills in Sacramento and Philadelphia, where he followed the example of Rabbi Joseph Krauskopf.[26] Levy developed the Sunday pulpit to reach both the Jewish and the general public. Sundays with their brief weekday liturgy provided sufficient time to deal with themes thoroughly. These lectures of more than an hour in length were adult education as well as sermonic. Virtually every theme was well grounded in history and demonstrated wide reading.

SUNDAY THEMES – AN OVERVIEW

The Sunday lectures enabled Rabbi Levy to discuss a wide range of subjects during each season. These were divided into a few broad categories: 1. Religious topics seen from a Reform perspective, which included philosophical debates on the nature of God, the conflict between science and religion, evolution, new definitions of morality, and family life. 2. Internal Jewish issues such as cooperation across denominational lines, Zionism, the need for Settlement houses, the plight of the new Russian Jewish immigrants, and the attacks of the Orthodox on Reform. 3. General political and economic problems, such as the gold standard, war and peace, women's suffrage, child labor, unionization, crime and punishment, poverty, housing, as well as local political, educational, and social issues. 4. Books and plays including Ibsen and Shakespeare. These lectures were also the basis for the discussion of particular social problems during the latter years of his rabbinate.

THEOLOGY

When Levy dealt with the nature of God and other philosophical issues, he used a historical approach and moved from biblical times to contemporary Reform Judaism. The leading classical Jewish philosophers, such as Philo and Maimonides, along with Spinoza and Mendelssohn, were linked with Einhorn and Wise, but we should note that many nineteenth-century German Jewish thinkers were missing.

25

In Levy's rationalistic approach there was no conflict between science and religion. He often quoted Darwin and Spencer as he defended evolution.

Levy firmly believed that Judaism's mission was to bring about a universal religion in which all humanity would be united and all hatreds would cease. "Our sacrifice is meaningless, our self- devotion is senseless, our endurance of the world's injustice is absurd, unless we believe that our religion may greatly bless mankind as well as ourselves....Judaism shall yet cause the nations of the earth to dwell together in unity. Differences will harmonize; disagreements it will clear up; disputes it will settle, debates it will terminate; and over all the earth there shall be a simple faith in the One God and the One Family of Humanity, and in the One hope of elevation, here and hereafter."[27]

RITUALS AND OBLIGATIONS

Though Levy instituted the Sunday weekday service, he emphasized shabbat services as well as Friday evening home rituals. The congregation held shabbat services with a sermon each week. His colleague Rabbi Coffee stated "no Orthodox rabbi pleaded more earnestly for Sabbath attendance."[28] He stressed the need for concrete manifestation of religion, not only prophetic ideals.[29]

In an effort to make the holidays more significant to his congregants, he reinterpreted Pesah and reemphasized Purim by speaking on it every year on a Sunday.[30] He treated Hannukah similarly.

Levy stressed the need for Judaism in daily life. Although opposed to the details of the *Shulhan Arukh*, he wanted a modern rational approach to Judaism with a high sense of ethics to replace it.

ORTHODOX AND CONSERVATIVE JUDAISM

Levy dealt with Orthodox opposition both locally and nationally.[31] He felt that Orthodox Judaism could not appeal to his

Judge and Mrs. Josiah Cohen's 50th Wedding Anniversary Dinner

generation as it also no longer appealed to him. He had left its restrictions in England for the freedom of California. Yet he always had cordial relations with the Conservative Tree of Life Congregation. When Solomon Schechter arrived in the United States, he publicly welcomed him in an editorial.[32] He urged cooperation and sought methods to establish it. He saw the B'nai Brith as such a mediating organization.[33]

AMERICANIZATION

Levy had enormous faith in America[34] and democracy; it was the form of government that had provided rights for Jews and was responsible for "our modern exodus from Egypt."[35] Regular sermons on national holidays were part of the cycle. His efforts to Americanize were most clearly demonstrated through his liturgies, for example the *Pesah Haggadah*, which lauded American freedom, and asked that an American flag be spread on the table.[36]

ANTI-SEMITISM AND INTERFAITH RELATIONS

Concern about anti-Semitism loomed large although American Jews, in contrast to the Jews of Eastern Europe, suffered only discrimination, not persecution. Levy pointed to the Christian roots of anti-Semitism, the misuse of quotations from the New Testament, and the misunderstanding of the Jewish setting of the New Testament. The tone of these presentations showed that a fairly large number of Christians regularly attended the Sunday lectures, while others read them in pamphlet form. He treated such themes incidentally in other lectures, too. Levy was well acquainted with the New Testament and with the latest literature on it.

Levy succeeded in his interfaith efforts and was welcomed by liberal Christians who exchanged pulpits with him – something that had not been done before in Pittsburgh,[37] although his predecessor Lippmann Mayer had spoken in churches. He initiated an interfaith Thanksgiving service in 1908. Ministers from eleven different denominations participated. He spoke in a leading Presbyterian

28

Church, and its minister, Dr. Diffenbach spoke at the Eighth Street Temple. Levy's theme was "Cooperative Creed," which was printed and several thousand copies distributed.[38] In addition Levy spoke before numerous Christian fraternal groups.

The chief obstacle to such efforts seems to have been the dominant Presbyterian churches, which often did not welcome any other religious group, Protestant, Catholic, or Jewish.[39] He spoke of the "rock-ribbed, ironbound, conservative community. It seems to me that many Pittsburghers, like their ancestors, must have imagined that the Jews were like the coal in the surrounding hillsides, only fit to be burned." This statement appeared in a tenth anniversary lecture and was repeated five years later.[40]

Levy battled against the effort to include a Christian definition of God in the constitution of Pennsylvania. Efforts to provide Christian interpretations of Bible readings in the public schools needed his constant attention. He fought against teachers' insistence that Jewish children sing Christian hymns and attacked politicians and religious figures in these efforts. When he thought it necessary, he spoke out bluntly and used specific Christian fundamentalist pastors as his targets as with two ministers who told him to return to Russia in long detailed and often ironic sermons.[41]

He cited his own problem with a Russian official who would not permit his Jewish party to travel through Odessa when on a trip to Palestine in 1901. The consul suggested that he enter "Christian" on the application. Levy furiously objected and remained in Smyrna despite the danger of the plague.[42]

Levy also dealt with the economic accusations of anti-Semites and demonstrated that the power of Jews paled in comparison with the Christian captains of industry.[43]

Part of the effort of Sunday mornings was to enable Christians to attend a Jewish service and to learn about Judaism. In this Levy saw hope for the future. It would elevate the "religious aspirations of a large number of people, including Jews, Christians of every denomination, white and colored people, and men and women of orthodox and liberal tendencies and of every religious profession. If you are blessed with the slightest imagination, if you have but a modicum of faith, you might see, in the weekly meetings of this congregation, a harbinger of the good time that is yet to come."[44]

ZIONISM

Levy connected Zionism with the plight of poor Jews in Europe, particularly Eastern Europe.[45] His attitude toward Zionism was more complex than generally thought. He expressed himself both through the pulpit as well as editorials in the *Jewish Criterion*, which he edited and for which he wrote in virtually every issue. Aside from the personal opinion that he expressed in the *Jewish Criterion*, he influenced its general content. It reported regularly on the national and international Zionist meetings and carried long essays along with verbatim reports of speeches by such Zionists as Max Nordau.[46]

An early editorial expressed his attitude toward Zionism as "we respect, but do not provide unqualified approval..."[47] He also addressed Zionist groups from the very beginning of his rabbinate in Pittsburgh.[48] He did not favor political Zionism or a Jewish state, as he considered politics in conflict with prophetic religion. He, however, did strongly support a place of refuge in which the immigrants could peacefully settle and develop a new life. Levy had visited Palestine with his wife in 1901 and so was familiar with some of the issues first hand.

Levy addressed Zionist groups regularly and continued a friendly dialogue with them. Upon his sudden death, these groups joined the rest of the community in mourning and passed resolutions of gratitude for his help.

By 1916 he had become more open to Zionism and with reference to an earlier sermon stated: "But never has your Rabbi spoken against Zionism, nor will he ever unless he sees in the

30

movement what is not at present apparent." He found in Zionism much with which he was in complete sympathy. Furthermore, if the choice was between the materialistic Jew and the Zionist, he would opt for the Zionist. "Between the Jew who is lost to all Jewishness, who is dejudaized, whose ideals are of the earth, on the one hand, and the Zionist, who, whatever else he may be considered, is a dreamer, an idealist, an altruist, on the other hand, there can also be no choice."[49] He was close to Rabbi Stephen Wise in both his social and his political stance; Wise presided over his funeral in 1917.

THE NEW IMMIGRANTS

The hard beginnings for the new Jewish immigrant as well as the poverty of millions of Jews in Europe was treated regularly. He spoke with admiration of those who lived in the Hill District and struggled so bravely for a better life. He sought help for them through better housing as well as employment opportunities.[50] Levy prodded philanthropists to provide greater support. He supported the assistance that the B'nai Brith gave.[51] Levy spent a considerable amount of his time organizing help for the immigrants and saw to it that their plight was kept in front of the Jewish community through his lectures and the *Jewish Criterion.*

THE FAMILY AND JEWISH EDUCATION

Levy was particularly concerned with the Jewish education of children. He emphasized the responsibility of parents to introduce children to the basics of Judaism at home, to pray with them, to discuss morality, and to bring them to services together with the family. He especially stressed the role of the mother and sought to balance it with his efforts for women's equality. Family life, the rising divorce rate, and the double standard for men and women reappeared as themes. Levy followed these public discussions with private statements to parents.

Much of Levy's time was spent with the Religious School and its children. He encouraged the "Seekers" a group of young people whom he prodded toward social action. He took his role as a pastor seriously and mentioned it from the pulpit.

He felt that Jews needed to be responsible for the welfare needs of their own community and advocated a synagogue structure that would appeal to the working class Jew, something sought by the Union of American Hebrew Congregations and its creation of "People's Synagogues."[52]

WOMEN'S RIGHTS

On women's rights, Levy changed his attitude over the years. In a sermon of 1908, he could state: "When women refuse to become mothers of healthy children; when women despise motherhood, the nation is not safe; there is something 'rotten in the state,' somewhere."[53]

By 1915–16 Levy could indicate that women's role was not and could not be limited to the home.[54] He indicated that he had fought for women's rights for some time. "Can she, whose sphere is the home, be said to fulfill her function, if she is assigned the home, yet can directly exert no influence upon the legislators who frame the laws affecting so large a portion of that sphere?"[55]

SOCIAL AND ECONOMIC ISSUES

On many national economic and social issues he favored the position of Theodore Roosevelt whom he mentioned regularly in his lectures. He felt strongly about the disparity between the rich as well as the new middle class and the poor. He noted, for example, that there were only 400,000 people whose income was above $ 4,000 and who had to pay income tax, a fact he considered shameful. He spoke of the plight of the farmer who did not receive the same tariff support as the industrialists.

Levy's idealism matched that of many others. He felt that a period of internationalism was at hand. Karl Marx had sought to unite the workers of the world, David Lubin had pushed for an international institute of agriculture to eliminate speculation in food products, Lazarus Zamenhoff had created the international language of Esperanto. It was time for religions to move in this direction. Jews and Judaism could be leaders toward universal progress and peace.

Levy became a pacifist and spoke strongly against war. He supported universal service only as war approached in 1916 but felt that it should be used solely for peaceful ends.[56]   In each of his pacifist lectures, he stressed his patriotism by pointing to his offer as the first volunteer for military service in the Spanish American War – he volunteered on a visit to President McKinley before the war had broken out and was then selected as a chaplain by a battalion, but it did not see combat. As a step toward peace, he favored including Japan in the council of nations as they had made so much progress.

PITTSBURGH

Levy was happy in Pittsburgh and expressed this often; he complimented the city for its beautiful surroundings and for its culture Yet there were shortcomings. He felt that the city needed to change its reputation as a dirty, grimy difficult place. When he spoke outside Pittsburgh, he was often greeted by such remarks. He wanted to stimulate the citizenry to move in a positive direction, for Pittsburgh lacked parks, a mass transit system, and hillside plantings. There was too much dirt as well as corruption and neglect by the "best citizens"; while some sought to help, they were frustrated by an incompetent bureaucracy.[57]

Levy was concerned about cleaning up the corrupt politics; he took an active role in the reforms of city council and the school board. He considered the poverty shameful and fought for the rights of the workingman, better housing and transportation. He criticized the corruption in the public services offered – foul water, poor schools, poor sanitation, poor transportation. Everyone had a share in the blame, but "our 'best' citizens are too often the least interested in the moral issues that confront us, they too soon weary of well-

33

doing, too quickly lose heart, too early withdraw from a struggle which demands faith, self-sacrifice, persistence and courage."[58]

PULPIT GUESTS

Levy occasionally invited others, including rabbis from various cities to occupy the pulpit on Sunday. Their sermons were also published. One of the pulpit guests was Booker T. Washington, the Negro president of Tuskegee Institute.

AUTOBIOGRAPHICAL MATERIAL

More than his successors, Levy used details of his life for illustration. He fondly remembered his Orthodox childhood in Bristol, England, where his father was a minister. He was especially close to his mother. Israel Zangwill, the well-known author, playwright, and Zionist, was among his childhood friends.[59]   He spoke warmly of his years with Dr. Joseph Krauskopf in Philadelphia; only the determined invitation from Pittsburgh took him away from a city where he was happy and had a large following. Levy's wife, Henrietta Platenauer, was given a tribute in a sermon on "The Successful Wife."

STANDING IN THE CONGREGATION AND COMMUNITY

Levy's lectures aroused strong feelings. Many were inspired by him and followed his efforts. Others were violently opposed, and he mentioned an occasional threat on his life. More often he spoke about the aroused opposition with gratitude, for it led to discussion.

He regularly thanked the congregation for its support, for the complete freedom of the pulpit, for understanding that he was not interested nor had the time for ordinary sociability, and for his generous salary. Levy worked well with the leadership of the congregation; they were not mentioned by name, but his eulogy for Abraham Lippman makes it clear that the young rabbi and the aging president had a good relationship.[60]

President Taft visits 1909

The motorcade at Temple

On many occasions he demonstrated appreciation for past accomplishments within the congregation, as for example, a service commemorating the hundredth anniversary of the birth of Naumburg.

Following Levy's sudden death[61] in 1917, his funeral was attended by an estimated 12,000, who gathered in the street outside the Temple. This attested to his popularity and influence in the larger community. The publication of the Sunday lectures was a major part of this. Thousands of copies were made available each week. By 1910, 500,000 copies had been distributed.[62] He had a way of reaching out to children, so that he remained fondly remembered seven decades after his death, and his Yahrzeit remained noted in the Temple Bulletin through the 1980s.

SHABBAT SERMONS

We do not have the text of any holiday sermons or of those delivered on shabbat. The sermon titles that appeared in the *Jewish Criterion* indicate that they were formally prepared. Among the titles announced through the years were "Teach Me Thy Ways," "Worth Saying," "Family Quarrels," "What Mean Ye by This Service," "Ourselves and Others," "Forewarned is Forearmed."

STYLE

As Levy sought to educate his congregants in the Bible, he began his lectures with a biblical verse or preceded them with a biblical reading. Some were selected from the shabbat portion but more often from other books in order to illuminate the subject under discussion. He chose verses from Jeremiah, Isaiah, and others, but also used verses from Song of Songs, Ecclesiastes, Psalms, Proverbs, and the historical books. During Hannukah he read from Maccabees.

The internal construction of his sermons was clear and logical as may be seen by the subheadings in the margins of many printed texts. Although well worked out, they were not written in advance; each printed text indicated that it had been stenographically recorded,

The marriage of Edna Sophie Levy to Dr. Joseph Barach in September 1915. Dr. Levy, his wife, along with the groom's parents and the bridal party, then held a reception for 1,000 guests in the Assembly Rooms behind the Temple. Edna's uncle, David Lubin of Rome, Italy, led her into the Temple.

Rabbi Samuel Goldenson 1928

37

quite an undertaking for sermons sometimes thirty pages long. The corrections must have been minimal, as they were published during the following week, left on the seats the next Sunday, and distributed outside the synagogue. Reactions were sometimes mentioned the following week. The titles were enticing and well selected.

Usually the first third of the lecture, following a brief introduction, provided the background for the subsequent discussion. It was taken for granted that the auditors needed a good review or perhaps an introduction to a particular subject. Then came an analysis with arguments on both sides well presented. The last third of the lecture dealt with the action recommended.

For example, in a lecture entitled "Is there a Jewish Vote?" The first segments dealt with the biblical and rabbinic background of democracy, and then they turned to its influence on the Founding Fathers of America. The second portion dealt with the vote of various ethnic groups and with the injurious appeal to ethnic and religious prejudice. The final segment encouraged people to vote their conscience, to deal with the issues at hand, and not to be swayed by an appeal to specific group interests, real or perceived.

Levy's style was straightforward, with short, declarative sentences mixed with poetic language. On rare occasions he quoted poetry. His language was not ornate, nor overly sophisticated. His English accent must have made him popular with a congregation that still contained many German immigrants and that had conducted its services in German until his arrival. The delivery of the sermons required considerable energy in the large Temple, initially with poor acoustics and without the aid of a sound system.

J. Leonard Levy understood the possibilities which the new century and Pittsburgh offered. He Americanized the congregation and began to attract Eastern European Jewish immigrants through his communal activities, his sermons, and the *Jewish Criterion*. Energetic, aware of the possibilities, and able to lead forcefully, he

38

prompted the construction of a new synagogue, expanded the foundations of his predecessor and transformed the congregation.

SAMUEL GOLDENSON (1878–1962)
(AT RODEF SHALOM 1918–1934)

Pittsburgh was prosperous and adjusting to peace when Samuel Goldenson came to Pittsburgh.[63] The Jewish community had vastly expanded with several dozen small Orthodox and Conservative congregations and many social and charitable groups. Zionism, secular Judaism, and prosperity were competing for attention. The congregation selected a leader of opposite temperament from Levy as his first sermon, entitled "Character" demonstrated. It seems that they wanted someone more pastoral, meditative, and less combative. Goldenson led an introspective rabbinate. He came to Pittsburgh following a year of temporary leadership after Rabbi Levy's sudden death.[64] Goldenson was highly regarded by his colleagues, who eventually elected him as president of the Central Conference of American Rabbis. He was a major representative of classical prophetic Judaism with its idealism.

It is more difficult to write about Goldenson's pulpit as he published only a few of his sermons, and other records of those years are sparse. A primary source is the *Temple Bulletin* which began to appear regularly in 1919 and presented the titles of each lecture as well as some additional information from time to time. As radio was just becoming popular, Goldenson used this new tool to reach the broader public; sermons were broadcast on a schedule that varied from year to year. These along with other activities listed in the *Temple Bulletin* assured the prominence of Rodef Shalom in the broader community. Those who heard him during those years described him as philosophical and with a strong inward turn. He was given to introspection. His voice and method of delivery made him effective. Some Christians continued to attend his Sunday services. In contrast to Levy, he placed less emphasis on the shabbat service.[65]

OVERVIEW SUNDAY THEMES

An anthology of Goldenson's sermons was published in 1975; although published by the Rodef Shalom Congregation, half of its contents were delivered later or elsewhere. These Sunday sermons do provide us with some insight into his general message and their style. The titles announced in the *Temple Bulletin* show us other themes.

THEOLOGY

Goldenson's Reform Judaism was an inner religion with a strong emphasis on the spiritual, and he defined Judaism in this manner.[66] He was concerned with the problems of authority in Judaism and with the bond between the inner life and morality. He used the inner life of the prophets as a basis upon which to build.

The vast majority of the sermons were personal, with such titles as "The Educated Heart" 1924, "Can Human Nature Be Changed?" (1926), "Obstacles to Happiness" (1927), "Causes of Ingratitude" (1928).

During each season Goldenson also spoke on philosophical themes. The titles of these lectures were often abstract, such as "What Constitutes a Problem," "The Background of Heresy," "Life's Dimensions," "Spirituality and Spiritualism," "Morals and the Belief in God." The themes were worked out with emphasis on their inner logic and contemporary meaning, not in a historical or developmental fashion. Quotations from classical Jewish sources were rare.

Goldenson in the flapper age of the twenties wished to move his congregation to a more spiritual life.[67] The lectures that dealt with the inner religion often continued into personal responsibility that needed to grow from this. He sought to build the inner resources, conscience, and belief – a difficult task in any age.

WORLD PROBLEMS

As America struggled with its new role in the world, Goldenson began to deal with some of these issues through a series entitled "Americanization" and continued over the years to speak about the meaning of democracy as well as the direction that America was taking. He rarely addressed such major international issues as "The League of Nations and Public Opinion" (1933).[68]

Jewish problems or persecution in other countries appeared only with the rise of Nazism.[69] The assassination of Walter Rathenau, the highest Jewish government official in Germany, the plight of Polish Jewry, the problems of Russian Jews under the Soviets were not discussed, although occasionally something appeared in the Temple Bulletin.

SOCIAL JUSTICE

The other side of prophetic Judaism is social justice, and this became a theme at the end of the twenties with "Am I My Brother's Keeper – With Special Reference to the Coal Strike Situation" (1928), "An Interpretation of the Financial Crisis" (1929), "What Does the Coal and Iron Police Situation Mean" (1929). For the first of these lectures, he visited one of the small coal towns. "Breadline Prosperity" (1930) dealt with the Depression as did "Social and Moral Aspects of the Pittsburgh Employment Plan" (1931), and "The Social Significance of N.R.A." (1933). Aside from these practical lectures that dealt with the social problems of the times, he treated these issues in a more abstract and philosophical manner.[70]

ZIONISM

The twenties and early thirties were a period of rapid change in Palestine. The new settlements faced serious problems; there were Arab attacks, and the Hebrew University was established. All this was widely debated, but Goldenson almost totally ignored it.

His prophetic Judaism with its emphasis on the broader world also led him to be a principled anti-Zionist. He saw Zionism as a retreat to an earlier version of Judaism and repeated this major theme through the years.[71] Less flexible than Levy, yet he too favored Palestine as a place of refuge from oppression. He remained a strong opponent of Jewish nationalism. These feelings were expressed more forcefully after he left Pittsburgh at Temple Emanu-El in New York and as President of the Central Conference of American Rabbis, the national organization of Reform rabbis. He was defeated, however, by the Conference's passage of the Columbus Platform (1937), which favored Zionism.[72]

EDUCATION AND PITTSBURGH

Among the published sermons are several on schools and the profession of teaching. He was interested in elevating the status of the teachers as well as their pay. In one lecture he discussed the nature of the teaching profession and the high responsibilities that it entailed and the need for communal support for the teacher.[73] Goldenson also dealt specifically with Jewish education for both children and adults.[74] Other published sermons provided a critical view of the aesthetic and cultural life of Pittsburgh and urged a more thorough look at the political corruption.

ANTI-SEMITISM

In this period anti-Semitism did not loom as large as before, so Goldenson addressed it infrequently in full-length lectures or through references in other sermons. Strangely, he did not deal with the support given to anti-Semitism by Henry Ford, the publication of the *Protocols of the Elders of Zion*, the Klan, or Father Coughlin's vicious radio tirades; neither did he discuss foreign anti-Semitism.

INTERFAITH RELATIONS

From time to time he dealt with Christianity and with interfaith relations, but these were not major themes.[75] Goldenson annually

Rabbi Samuel Goldenson

SOLOMON BENNETT FREEHOF.

Born London, England, Aug. 8, 1892.
Baltimore City College.
A. B., University of Cincinnati, 1914.
Captain, University Debating Team,
 1911-12.
Phi Beta Kappa honors.
Student Assistant, 1913-14, 1914-15.
Kaufmann Kohler Prize for 1913-14.
Elected to the Faculty of the Hebrew
 Union College for 1915-16.
Oscar Berman Prize.
President of the Literary Society, 1913-
 1914.
Asso. Editor, H. U. C. Monthly, 1914-
 1915.
President of the Student Body, 1914-
 1915.
Thesis-subject for Rabbinical Degree:
 "The Institution of Ordination."

Solomon Freehof at ordination 1915

Rabbi Solomon B. Freehof 1925

43

invited leading ministers to occupy the pulpit, or they addressed one of the congregational groups.[76] He listed his appearances before church and civic groups regularly in the Temple Bulletin and thereby indicated his concern for good interfaith relations. He had a personal friendship with several ministers.

PULPIT GUESTS

Colleagues as well as an occasional professor from the Hebrew Union College were invited to the pulpit. There were relatively few guest preachers during these years.

STYLE

Although less academic than his successors, Samuel Goldenson sounded much more so. This was true both of the titles of his lectures and of their themes. The lectures were academic in tone rather than in content. He was earnest, spiritual, and demanding in style – tightly organized but with a less clearly identifiable pattern of construction. Samuel Goldenson's presentations were very direct. When he spoke on a subject, he introduced it in the opening sentence or dealt with the philosophical underpinnings. The arguments were logical and presented in rapid succession. It meant that he counted on his congregants to pay close attention. It seems that he used a manuscript in his delivery and so made more demands on his listeners, as this led to an essay format rather than an oratorical style that must have been difficult to follow.

Goldenson depended heavily on the Bible and particularly the prophetic books for his inspiration and citations. He rarely refers to rabbinic literature or for that matter to the classical or modern philosophers of Judaism. He took illustrations from the observations of personal lives as well as from the classics. When he spoke about the plight of the miners during a long strike in 1928, he visited a mining camp in order to learn about their working and living conditions first hand.

AUTOBIOGRAPHICAL MATERIAL

Goldenson virtually never referred to his own life, any personal experiences, or travels. He was an intensely private man. Even in his lecture on Pittsburgh, he focused on the more theoretical aspects of cultural and aesthetic rebuilding, with hardly a hint of the practical politics or the political corruption of Pittsburgh. It was given in 1924, a time of great prosperity in which he could have spoken quite boldly.

Samuel Goldenson was interested in the life of the spirit and a philosophical approach to Judaism. It was difficult to fit those thoughts into the high social life of that period. A small number of congregants were attracted by Goldenson's approach; a larger number admired his personal spirituality but felt it was for him and not for them. His opposition to Zionism did not change even in the threatening atmosphere of the thirties; within the Central Conference of American Rabbis, however, his views were rejected.

Under Samuel Goldenson's leadership the congregation continued to grow; he aided this effort by making it more democratic and eliminating assigned seats. Goldenson's efforts at social justice and an inner spirituality while less influential immediately, affected the lives of a fair number of congregants in the longer term

SOLOMON B. FREEHOF (1892–1990)
(AT RODEF SHALOM 1934–1966; EMERITUS 1966–1990)

Arriving in the depth of the Depression, the congregation as well as the nation needed hope, and Solomon B. Freehof's optimism was exactly right. The new rabbi of Rodef Shalom had been introduced to the congregation during the holidays of 1922; he had a reputation as a preacher and a scholar.[77] He came to Pittsburgh after a dozen years as professor at the Hebrew Union College and ten as rabbi of K. Anshe Maariv, a large Chicago congregation, as well as earlier service as a military chaplain in World War I. With a special interest in liturgy and his work on the Reform liturgy, it was clear that religious services and the sermon would be central to his rabbinate.

An apocryphal story has it that he told the board of trustees that there were two types of rabbis – those who served their congregation with their feet and those with their head. He was of the latter type and would leave pastoral efforts as well as work with communal boards largely to others. The pulpit dominated Freehof's rabbinate; he understood its potential and used it with grand effect.

Throughout his rabbinate, Freehof played a major national role in the Reform movement and later also internationally. He was one of the intellectual leaders of the movement and headed many special efforts and commissions. He served as President of the Central Conference of American Rabbis as well as of the World Union for Progressive Judaism. He wrote hundreds of responsa and extensively in the fields of Bible, Jewish law, homiletics, and education, with twenty-five books and hundreds of essays to his credit.[78] All this was balanced with family life and the hobbies of book-binding and woodwork. An interview on this may be found in the Appendix.

The Rodef Shalom congregation remained dominant in the broader Jewish community and provided leadership for virtually every Jewish organization. The board of the congregation had decided not to continue the temple as a community center with a gymnasium and swimming pool and instead to join the broader community in these areas.

Freehof led the congregation to build a new education wing (1937–38) and later large social facilities (1955–56). He supported the expansion of the Reform movement into a second congregation in the city (Temple Sinai) and into the suburbs (Temple Emanuel and Temple David).[79]

We possess a complete record of all Sunday lecture topics along with printed versions of many sermons and lectures. Portions of Sunday and Shabbat sermons appeared in the *Temple Bulletin* from the beginning of Freehof's rabbinate. By the 1940s outlines of shabbat sermons were published regularly. Complete holiday sermons were printed in the *Jewish Criterion*. For years a series of Sunday

46

sermons were radio broadcast. In addition there was the "Modern Literature Class," book-reviews conducted through the decades for a vast audience. They were another vehicle for reaching the congregation, but more important for ensuring its place in the broader community. Sermons and lectures were recorded for many years, and hearing them, when they become available on disks, will undoubtedly provide a fuller impression of these presentations.

OVERVIEW – SUNDAY LECTURES

Freehof inherited the Sunday pulpit and decided to use it as had his predecessors to reach a broad congregational audience. By this time the number of non-Jewish attendees was minimal in contrast to the days of J. Leonard Levy. Freehof's printed Sunday lectures were mainly intended for a Jewish audience, though those on literature were widely read by the general public. He reached out to the community through radio broadcasts of one lecture each month, his book-review, and with popular books and tracts.[80]

Freehof used the Sunday pulpit to educate the congregation and to present solid Jewish themes. Often the lectures were constructed so as to introduce a topic with the hope that the congregants would delve further into it on their own. The Bible, viewed in many different ways, biblical figures, Jewish history, and basic Jewish ideas were the most common topics. These were not academic lectures.

The Sunday schedule was arranged to appeal to the many segments of the congregation.[81] In the initial years Freehof stressed general world problems seen from a Jewish vantage point. His first Sunday lecture, which was broadcast, had the title "Is Hitler Doomed?" The inner self and broader Jewish themes, however, were not neglected. Generally a balance between broad political and social issues with specific Jewish themes, personal goals, and an occasional literary work was maintained.

The personal life of the congregant remained important. In

1935 there was the series entitled "The Road to Personal Victory," with the three subtitles, I. The Conquest of Fear, II. The Conquest of Inferiority, III. The Conquest of Hate. Slowly his technique was modified into series such as "The Best of the Bible," "The Heart of Shakespeare," and "Cities in our Life," which were continuous from year to year. This provided stability and attractiveness to the Sunday morning lectures.

The large audiences were attracted to the Temple partially through a desire to worship each Sunday morning, and in part through the title of the lecture. The choice of title, therefore, became important. The brief titles, that were eye-catching, were followed by a descriptive box that indicated the precise subject.

INTERNATIONAL ISSUES

Nazis, Communists, and the approaching war worried the congregation, and Freehof addressed these issues regularly. He spoke often on other national and international problems, far more than his predecessors; the titles of the sermons which have survived, are "Three Crucial Hours" (1939), "What will Keep us Out of War?" (1940), "England's Hour and Winston Churchill" (1941), "Partner and Problem – Our Russian Ally" (1942).[82] During most of 1942–44 the topics dealt with the war in one form or another. Freehof saw it as his task to provide insight as well as hope, especially for those whose family members were serving in the military.

ANTI-SEMITISM

American anti-Semitism was less of a problem than the events in Germany; these were treated on a regular basis both directly and in many sermons that dealt with the broader issues of war and peace, as for example "Jews in the European Caldron," "Goebbels and the German Mob" (November 20, 1938, immediately following Kristallnacht). By 1943 there was some inkling of the destruction of European Jews reflected in "Your Message to Hitler's Victims"

General Eisenhower with
the Jewish Welfare Board
including Dr. Freehof 1945

Senator Scott, President
Lyndon Johnson, Dr. Freehof

Dr. Freehof and Lillian 1976

Western Pennsylvania rabbis honor Dr.
Freehof's 80th birthday

49

(January 24, 1943) and "Savage Atrocities – How Will We Repay ?" (March 5, 1944, a broadcast sermon). "Modern Anti-Semitism – A New Disease" dealt with the underpinnings of twentieth-century anti-Semitism. American anti-Semitism, however, was also a concern as shown in the address, "How Strong is Prejudice in America?"

ZIONISM

In his first year, Freehof addressed Zionism through two lectures on "Palestine or Siberia," which dealt with the Soviet effort to establish a "Jewish" republic in central Asia, in January of 1935 and on Judaism as a race, religion, or nation in three lectures in February. He, as his predecessors, favored Palestine as a place of refuge, but never became a political Zionist. In the congregation and the Central Conference, he worked for compromise and a peaceful solution between the two extremes, despite personal ties with the Zionist movement.[83] The title of a lectures in 1936-37, however, demonstrated more than sympathy; "The Arab Revolt – Will It Blast Our Hopes" and "Is the World Already at War – Palestine, the Pawn."

A more open approach was shown in 1943 with two lectures entitled "Second Thoughts – Zionism and Americanism" and "Zionism and Reform Judaism." Again, in 1945, Freehof provided two lectures – "Advice to Zionists," and "Advice to Anti-Zionists."

With the founding of Israel in 1948 there were five lectures on that theme during that winter and spring,[84] and two the next autumn. The lecture, "Loyalty to America and Enthusiasm for Israel," in November of 1949 dealt with this issue, perceived as a problem by some.[85] On many occasions Freehof sought to bring about peace between the extreme anti-Zionists and Zionists. He pointed to the pride in the new land, its progress, and its ability to resettle millions of Jews, as well as the strong philanthropic bent of American Jews which would be our principal form of involvement.

AMERICA

Some Sunday lectures were displays of patriotism especially during the war years as well as reflections on the uncertainty that some Jews felt about their status as "How Strong is Prejudice in America?" (1936, 1938), "What Jews Must Fight for in America" (1938), "How to Behave as Jews Today" (1939), "My Right as an American" (1941), "The Jewish Gentleman" (a series of three, 1942), "The Religion of Our National Anthem" (a series of three, 1943). These concerns disappeared in the 1950s.

Freehof dealt with other current issues as they appeared.[86] He expressed no concern about Americanization, but about American Jewish unity.[87]

PERSONAL RELIGION

Each season contained at least one series that dealt with personal religion. This began in 1935 with a series entitled "The Road to Personal Victory." Often such thoughts were dominant in a Bible or Shakespeare lecture, but also in series as "What Takes the Joy Out of Modern Life ?" (1940). They became more important after World War II in the atomic age and with the failures of popular culture. Although these were the main subject for the shabbat sermons, Freehof seemed to feel a need to add more of them on Sundays, and these were more direct, not part of a Bible or Shakespeare series. In them he analyzed the problems and provided hope for their solution. For example the series: "What It Takes–To Face Life Today" (1947), "Everybody's Daydream" (1950), "People Have Changed" (1952), "The New World Needs More...." (1954).[88]

LITERATURE AND SHAKESPEARE

The "Heart of Shakespeare" series stemmed from a deep interest in literature. These lectures attracted the regular congregation and a large number of college students from nearby campuses for nine years. The main ideas of each play and its moral value was discussed.

At the conclusion of each calendar year, there was a lecture entitled "The Four Great Books." This presented a summary of four book reviews given earlier and brought the most notable literary themes of these books to the congregation. Freehof usually gave this lecture in other cities also.

BIBLE

A series concerned with biblical themes was given every year. These lectures provided a religious, not a critical, approach to the Bible. Freehof realized that most congregants rarely read beyond the weekly Torah portion, so he used these series to introduce the various books of the Bible as well as their greatest ideas. They were an enticement to read the books and to understand their meaning in contemporary terms.

JEWISH LITERATURE

Despite decades of preoccupation with rabbinic literature, a discussion of these writings rarely appeared. There were three lectures on the Talmud in 1940 and three on the prayer book, which Freehof had edited in 1941; Jewish law appeared only once. In informal presentations to groups of the congregational constituencies, Freehof often referred to specific questions for which he was composing responsa, but he did not expand this theme into fuller lectures.

HISTORY

In the early years Freehof rarely dealt with Jewish history, except during special anniversary years. Later, he created the series "Cities in our Life" (1960–1964), succeeded by "Strangers in Our History" (1965–1966).

HIGH HOLIDAYS

The High Holidays were a time for personal reflection, perhaps tied to a contemporary broader issue, but that was not its focus, with titles as "The Chosen Road," "Through the Dark Valley" (1942), "Our Fondest Wish" and "Our Deepest Faith" (1946), "All Our

52

Rabbi Mark Staitman, Albert I. Raizman, M. Lester Aaron, Rabbi Solomon B. Freehof, Lillian Freehof, Allen H. Berkman, Irving M. J. Kaplan, Rabbi Walter Jacob at the Freehof's 50th Wedding Anniversary in 1984

Rabbi Freehof in his study 1980s

53

Yesterdays" and "All Our Tomorrows" (1953), "Life and its Time," "Life and its Trouble" (1954), "Live by the Day," "Watch the Balance" (1959).

The themes for Rosh Hashonah, Yom Kippur, and Memorial Service were generally tightly linked through biblical verses or figures. Unfortunately, the texts of the memorial address have been preserved, but not transcribed.

STYLE

Freehof occasionally discussed his sermons casually with me as a young colleague, but nothing was written down before delivery, and printed texts came from stenographic or a tape recording. The themes were usually capable of summary in a single phrase.

Freehof often began obliquely with an introduction that led from ordinary life or from something that had nothing to do with his theme. Then he proceeded carefully to the theme, which was developed logically and was easy to follow. Each section had a similar introduction. The technique may have been challenging for the preacher but was rewarding for the listener, as it constituted a series of surprises.

Each section concluded with a brief summation. Often it reviewed not only the points just made, but the previous one as well. Finally, to cap the entire structure, there was a conclusion that summarized but also added something new to the sermon and thus retained the interest of the congregant. Any listener could repeat the ideas from the introduction to the conclusion with ease.

The sermons possessed imagination and poetry. The strong structure meant that less depended upon the delivery of the moment, which, after all, may be affected by the general well being of the speaker.

Emotional color was given through the clever use of

quotations. This was highly successful because Freehof had an extraordinary memory. He remained capable of long quotations in different languages to the end of his life. He used biblical quotations to good effect. He utilized the great poetry of Shakespeare and English classics frequently, but also of obscure poets. Often he inserted a bit of their life to give the quotation more meaning. The combination of poetry with little-known incidents from the life of a poet was effective; he rarely used personal incidents in his sermons.[89]

Freehof's fine diction and superb memory led to a literary style. Early in life he had made it a practice to read a newspaper article or essay and substitute his own words as a way of enriching his ready vocabulary. I knew immigrants who arrived at the end of the 1930s and regularly attended the Sunday lectures not only to listen to the theme, but also to improve their English and their vocabulary.

His published sermons were taken from tape-recordings with only the most minor corrections. When he dictated a lecture (if it had to be sent to the printer before delivery), he quickly reread it and made virtually no changes. I once watched Cardinal Wright dictate a short speech; gifted as he was, it was much more of a struggle for him to attain the right mood and words than for Freehof.

Freehof's manner of speaking was free of notes or a text. The sermon had been very carefully thought out, sometimes with notes for use at home, but no sentences were fixed, with the exception of a few opening and closing phrases. The sequence within a given portion remained fairly loose-knit until the sermon was delivered. Examples were sometimes changed, as could be seen from holiday sermons that were usually given twice to different segments of the congregation. This method enabled the speaker to adjust to the audience and their reaction. Furthermore, it led to a freshness of delivery accomplished with such ease and grace that the listener was unaware of the carefully achieved technique.[90]

SHABBAT

The shabbat sermon was important throughout Freehof's rabbinate and he gave it as much thought as the Sunday lectures; the sermons were published regularly in outline form. The sermons dealt with the Torah portion of the week and placed it into a personal framework. He also discussed social issues, but less so than in the Sunday lectures. These sermons have not been included in this analysis.

BOOK REVIEWS

Although Freehof spoke frequently before various Jewish and non-Jewish groups, he decided in his first year that it was preferable for non-Jews to come to the synagogue because it would also provide a passive introduction to Judaism. His vehicle was the book review,[91] as he had a major interest in contemporary literature. He selected a mixture of best-sellers and significant works and entitled the venture "The Modern Literature Class." The official sponsor was the Sisterhood, which provided an intellectual program and achieved a close bond to its rabbi. Twelve lectures, later reduced to eight, were given on Wednesday mornings in autumn. They frequently filled the 1500-seat Temple with a primarily non-Jewish audience. The publicity for the reviews consisted only of a postcard sent to those interested. These reviews were a phenomenon in Western Pennsylvania. They helped create an atmosphere of understanding among the Christian population. A selection from the series appeared in the Sunday cycle under the heading "Four Great Books." This was a summary of the best of the book reviews, which was often then given as a separate lecture in other cities where they were very popular. For fourteen years, a number of reviews were published by *The Carnegie Magazine* in an abbreviated form. Through them and those published in book form, one may capture the literary spirit of an age.[92]

STYLE

The method used by Dr. Freehof represented an interesting innovation in the field of the book review. The hour-long lectures were divided into three segments. A lengthy, oblique introduction often beginning with something totally unrelated eventually acquainted the auditor with the essential message of the book. In clear, original, and logical terms he developed the basic theme of the author. Numerous illustrations achieved clarity and maintained a high degree of interest. Then the central part of the review summarized the contents of the book as he briefly told the story. Finally, he drew some permanent lessons. This and the ethical meaning of the theme constituted the third and concluding section. The reviews provided Freehof an opportunity to express his thoughts on a large variety of topics. They were a dialogue with the absent author in which Freehof was the dominant figure.

BIBLE CLASS

Each spring from the late 1940s onward, Freehof gave a four-week Bible class intended for a mixed audience of three or four hundred Jews and Gentiles. This was both adult education and outreach to the general community. They were less formally prepared and permitted Freehof to express himself on specific themes or portions of biblical books. Despite their more informal nature, Freehof's method of logical organization prevailed. Even if he allowed himself to wander, he carefully summarized his thoughts at the conclusion. These classes provided an additional introduction to the Bible.

AUTOBIOGRAPHICAL MATERIAL

Freehof permitted himself autobiographical moments on an occasional shabbat and regularly on the shabbat of his bar mitzvah.

Although willing to speak of his earlier years in private conversation, he did not make this a theme in his sermons.

Solomon B. Freehof continued to build the congregation and establish its preeminence in the community principally through his oratory. Both in the congregational and in his personal life, Classical Reform appealed to him; he was concerned intellectually with liturgy and halakhah. He expanded the facilities of the synagogue with a new religious school and social wing. A new Junior Congregation looked after the needs of the younger generation. He led the congregation through the difficult Depression and World War II years with his optimistic views; in the prosperous 1950s membership reached more than 2000 families. At the same time he provided national and international leadership and devoted considerable time to scholarly and popular writing.

WALTER JACOB (1930–　)
(AT RODEF SHALOM 1955-1997; SENIOR SCHOLAR 1998–)

I assumed the leadership of the congregation in 1966 after eleven years with the congregation.[93] My tenure began in 1955 and was followed by two years in the military chaplaincy at Clark Air Base in the Philippines. Through the late 1960s and 1970s the metropolitan Pittsburgh economy continued its postwar decline, although it appeared more robust than it was. Many young people moved to cities that offered greater opportunities. Civil Rights issues and Vietnam dominated. Later, the milltowns and their economies collapsed with the rapid decline of the steel industry. It was to be a time of economic and civic turmoil.

By 1966 the congregation had again changed. Still large, it was destined to diminish as other economic regions grew at the expense of Pittsburgh and attracted the next generation. It would grow again during the 1980s. All programming was affected by the

58

Chaplain Jacob, U.S. Airforce,
Clark Air Base, Philippines 1955

Irene Loewenthal and Walter Jacob
at their wedding in London 1958

Three generations of rabbis
Benno Jacob, Ernest I. Jacob
Walter Jacob 1932

Irene and Walter Jacob 1998

59

weekend escapes of some congregants to country homes, Fallingwater being the most famous of them, and long winters spent in Florida.

Changes in ritual and the prayer book had to be made; I chose to proceed slowly with limited divisive discussion and thus avoided internal divisions. The congregation remained in the city and restored its historic building (1990–91). An endowment was created in 1985. The governance of the congregation became more democratic.

The broader Jewish community had also changed, with the focus now on centralizing funding and agencies. This meant that both nominal and real leadership had shifted. The Reform movement expanded which I encouraged; Rodef Shalom assisted the new congregations and maintained helpful relationships with all.

Interfaith dialogue needed to be shifted to include not only the leading clergy, but also the broader leadership. This led me, under the auspices of the Brotherhood, to establish the Milton Harris interfaith lectures, which provided an intellectual program. The lectures bring outstanding Jewish thinkers[94] to an audience of four hundred Christian clergy anually. Much had to be done with ethnic groups, particularly during the Civil Rights debates. This included the creation of Horizon Homes, the first group home for handicapped children, on which Irene and I worked for several years, as well as the leadership of Project Equality, an interfaith effort to promote Afro-American businesses.

The congregation was looking for more than preaching, with a greater emphasis on education and pastoral efforts. This needed to be balanced with general communal efforts as in earlier times. The new Friday evening service and experimental services needed attention. I emphasized adult education and taught classes every week, more during the summer months, which had often been left without activities, and scheduled other classes and lectures.[95] All of this meant rebalancing the rabbinate.

Rabbi Jacob in his study 1966

The installation blessing of Rabbi Jacob as Senior
Rabbi by his father, Rabbi Ernest I. Jacob 1966

Rabbi and Lillian Freehof with Irene and Annette Jacob before the
installation service

61

Involvement in civic and cultural organizations interested me more than my predecessor. Serious study and writing was on my agenda, and I continued this with articles, essays, thirty-two books, and five hundred plus responsa. Activities with the Central Conference of American Rabbis, its responsa committee and eventually its presidency, then the presidencies and associated efforts for the Freehof Institute for Progressive Halakhah and the Associated American Jewish Museum, as well as translating and publicizing the works of my grandfather, Benno Jacob. Helping Irene with different aspects of the Biblical Botanical Garden was also high on my agenda. Later the development of Liberal Judaism in Germany and the Abraham Geiger College were important to me. Some details may be found in the Appendix. These activities were balanced with time set aside for family life with Irene and our children, Claire, Kenney, and Daniel, which included games, hobbies, sports, skiing, and long cross-country camping trips as well as international travel, music and art.

It is difficult to analyze one's own sermons, especially as my general approach to life has been not to look back, but to the future. Until this paper I have not reread old sermons, as each decade demanded its own approach and the preacher also, I hope, matured.

OVERVIEW – SUNDAY THEMES

By 1966 the Sunday service had changed and was addressed to an entirely Jewish congregation. The tradition of this service was so strongly established at Rodef Shalom that efforts to experiment with a late Friday evening service failed, but I expanded the early Friday evening service. The older generation liked this format, so I continued to use it for adult education till the late 1980s, but after almost ninety years, this service had run its course. Sunday morning had the advantage of a congregation that was fully awake and ready for a lecture; in order to provide a full morning, the service was preceded by a breakfast with a speaker from the community.[96]

Three hundred sixty clergy attend the first Harris Interfaith Lecture in 1971 presenting Dr. Samuel Sandmel, with Bishop John McDowell presiding. Seated, Dr. Sandmel, Ruth Harris, Dr. Jacob, Rev. Hicks. Standing Dean Shannon, Harold Dubinsky, Bishop McDowell, Richard Adelsheim, Rabbi Staitman

Claire and Walter Jacob
1962

Daniel Jacob, Speaker of the House of Representatives, O'Neill, Rabbi Jacob, 1978

Kenney, Walter, Irene and Daniel at the retirement dinner 1997

Daniel, Eslyn, Irene, Walter 2003

In this configuration I saw the Sunday lecture as a Jewish response to the issues of the times, a way of dealing with the personal problems faced by congregants, and as adult education. The congregation with its 1800 families was large and varied and contained an entire range of ages. I presented a mixture of lectures on historical and ethical themes along with discussions of contemporary issues. Current problems, history, Bible, liturgy, philosophy – usually grouped in series of three – were my pattern. Adult education courses sometimes paralleled the lectures and provided an opportunity for discussion. Selections of these sermons along with a holiday and shabbat sermon were published each year in pamphlet form and distributed to the congregation and to the general public. Some sermons were also published in national anthologies.

INTERNATIONAL ISSUES

The war in Vietnam along with the arms race were frequent themes.[97] This war and other issues raised serious moral issues and also had major ramifications within the United States.[98] The gap between the conservative older generation and the demonstrating college students needed to be bridged.[99] During my rabbinate there were times of grave international tension as well as a long period during which America was uncertain about its international position. These issues were discussed both on Sunday and on shabbat.

ISRAEL

Israel faced many problems and needed the support of the American Jewish community. It was necessary to rally that support during various crises[100] and to stimulate interest generally. The land needed to be celebrated, but with an eye toward the future more than the past.[101] The points of view of the Palestinians also had to be treated, although this was not always welcome.[102] When Israel took

Rabbi Jacob with President
Carter at the White House

Senator John and Teresa Heinz, President
Ford,
Irene and Walter Jacob

With the German Ambassador,
Dr. Issinger, upon receiving the
Knight Commander Order of the
Federal Republic of Germany
1999

With John Cardinal Wright at his
invitation in Rome upon his elevation
to Cardinal 1968

the wrong turn, criticism was in order. Opposition to the Reform movement in Israel needed to be kept before the congregation.[103]

CIVIL RIGHTS

My involvement with civil rights and dialogue groups led to topics that needed a pulpit response, especially as the decades long alliance between Jews and Negroes collapsed. Negro anti-Semitism had to be regretted and denounced.[104] School busing was an issue for all the parents in the congregations some of whom threatened withdrawal of support for the public schools. The slaying of Martin Luther King Jr. brought violence; it meant that the issues of integration had to be reviewed and placed in a very long-term perspective. Unfortunately, the enthusiasm for civil rights waned and was replaced by impatience.[105]

RABBINIC LAW AND CUSTOM

Although Solomon B. Freehof had published a series of volumes on responsa and readily discussed halakhah and responsa in private conversation, he virtually never made them the topic of Sunday lectures. This generation of congregants wished to know how Judaism responded to contemporary issues and what the tradition had to say about them. These were often issues of national policy as well as personal interest. The death penalty, abortion, drugs, pollution, medical problems among other issues became themes.[106] Questions asked by colleagues as well as lay individuals for which I prepared responsa told me what was on people's minds. The Jewish tradition provided relevant answers or guidance from which it was possible to create responses to totally new questions raised through scientific advances.

The rites of passage in Jewish life needed to be seen from a Reform perspective; they were frequently not well understood.[107]

66

Rededication of the Augsburg synagogue
1985

Restored synagogue, Augsburg, Germany

Dedication of the Geiger College 1999

Assimilation and intermarriages were major issues and needed regular and forceful discussion.

The Reform movement adopted a series of new liturgies with different theologies that also were not clearly understood.[108] At the same time, customs and ceremonies were changing, and the older generation did not grasp the reasons for such changes; they saw them as a movement in the direction of an Orthodoxy that they had sought to leave behind. They did not understand that their rationalistic Judaism lacked an emotional appeal that customs and symbols provided. Concrete manifestations of Judaism, not necessary for their generation, were needed for their grandchildren.

JEWISH PHILOSOPHY

Although formal philosophy had never been my special interest; it could not be neglected through the pulpit as it had been for decades, so a series on the great Jewish thinkers both past and present were presented over the years; some of this was basic education in modern Jewish philosophy.[109] Another series demonstrated that the classical thinkers were relevant to our time[110] and dealt with theological questions.[111]

Congregants held a wide spectrum of personal theologies; they needed to be given a more solid foundation and occasionally challenged.[112] Reform Jewish thought had also changed through the decades as was apparent through the new practices, but the underpinnings were not sufficiently understood.[113]

YOUTH PROBLEMS

The generation of the 1960s and 1970s was opposed to many things - religious, political and cultural. Their restlessness and uncertainty about goals needed to be confronted and also explained to the older generation.[114] Cults of various kinds as well as Jews for Jesus were attracting some young people. Drugs were widely used by young Jews and brought a new range of problems.[115]

WOMEN'S ISSUES

The rights of women and their place in modern society had not been an issue for a long time but needed to be seen in a new light.[116] Furthermore, women as rabbis remained a foreign notion, especially to the older women of the congregation. I spoke on the topic and perhaps more important, brought a female colleague in 1978 and two colleagues as pulpit guests in 1981;[117] they were followed by others whom I thought more effective than lectures. I also decided to engage Ruth Langer, the daughter of a leading Temple family, as a student rabbi as a practical introduction to women rabbis. Feminist issues were discussed on shabbat and Friday evenings.

CHRISTIANITY AND OTHER RELIGIONS

The religious world had broadened and so I discussed some of the religions of the Far East.[118] Fundamentalism in Judaism and Christianity became topics in the 1980s. As our understanding of Christianity had to be deepened, I turned both to the basic literature of the New Testament, to some outstanding Christian thinkers, and to the different ways in which Jewish thinkers had viewed Christianity.[119]

Various churches, including the Roman Catholic Church, issued statements about Judaism that radically changed their views.[120] My personal friendship especially with Cardinal Wright,[121] Bishop Wuerl, Protestant professors, such as Mauser and Von Waldow, among others, at the Pittsburgh Theological Seminary, as well as many neighboring ministers, made such discussions possible. The mood and atmosphere had changed, which made cooperation on social problems much easier.[122]

ANTI-SEMITISM

Anti-Semitism which had loomed so large for each of my predecessors had receded. I mainly discussed it as happening in other lands - Argentina, Syria, Ethiopia, and Russia.[123] There were the Soviet show trials and decades of problems with the oppression of Soviet Jews.[124] It was also now possible to turn to the historical roots of anti-Semitism in a more dispassionate way.[125]

THE AMERICAN AND PITTSBURGH JEWISH COMMUNITY

American Jewish life was being interpreted in the Jewish and popular press more and more through surveys and the collection of data. The interpretations were not always accurate and needed to be challenged.[126] In addition, there was an undue emphasis on the funding agencies, which have been and continue to be important but should not dominate Jewish life.[127]

HISTORY AND JEWS IN OTHER LANDS

Jewish history has been of lifelong interest to me, so such themes appeared in series of lectures; as history has rarely been emphasized in the current American education system, it was not easy to use these themes.[128] My background made me especially interested in the European Jewish past and the Holocaust, so I treated them from time to time, also through reviews.[129] A large number of congregants traveled regularly to foreign lands and asked about their Jewish population, so I introduced a series to deal with various lands and their past and present.[130] American Jewish history had also been neglected, and various anniversaries provided opportunities for special discussions.[131] Although I had traveled to most of the places discussed, these were not personal travelogues, but an attempt to introduce different Jewish civilizations and to understand how we had adjusted.

BIBLE

The relevance of the Bible was constantly challenged by many who had never read more than a few chapters on any biblical book. A basic familiarity, outside the normal shabbat readings, had to be established. I began with this task in 1967 and continued it through the years.[132] Some were introductory lectures, others dealt with specific themes that were relevant to current problems.

JEWISH LITERATURE AND ARTS

Art and music have been important in Jewish life, but have usually been treated as a background for other things. My own interest in both led me to speak about them and to introduce special services that concentrated on our music and its history as well as performances of jazz and modern dance.[133] I preferred to deal with the visual arts through the creation of a Temple Gallery in which a regular series of displays were held and later, the Associated American Jewish Museums, but I also spoke regularly about Jewish art and leading Jewish artists.[134]

Reviews of important books have traditionally been a part of the Sunday series, which I continued, but with emphasis on Jewish books, as many congregants rarely read Jewish matter.[135]

PULPIT GUESTS

From the beginning I thought it important to introduce leading Jewish figures to the congregation, so a series of scholars and colleagues appeared in the Sunday schedule regularly. Experts in their field, they were selected for their ability to reach a nonacademic lay audience. My associates had an opportunity to preach at this service. As occasions for interfaith activities were numerous both in the congregational programming and in the broader community, I invited only a limited number of non-Jewish clergy to the pulpit.

It was important to me to bring the Reform community together on a regular basis, so joint services with my colleagues were held to celebrate special occasions

STYLE

I emphasized an expository teaching style. The aim of each lecture was both to summarize the subject under discussion and to entice the congregant to further reading. This meant a delicate balance between providing and interpreting information as well as leaving matters sufficiently open to encourage exploration. As these lectures were part of a formal service and were part sermon, they usually contained a hortatory element.

I preferred tight logical organization with introductions somewhat similar to Freehof's style and that of my father. The logic enabled the auditor to follow and made it unnecessary for me to have any notes. I preferred constant eye contact with the congregation which enabled me to react quickly.

As during most weeks of the season I had three or four lectures and sermons in addition to class instruction, funerals, weddings, and civic presentations, many of the lectures were prepared in a brief outline form during the summer when there was enough time for the necessary background reading. The outline was then sufficient to recall the facts and the framework into which I had placed them. After a brief review and some alterations, the speech was ready and could be left at home.

I have always found it useful to be entirely free of any manuscript or outline. This has relieved me of the need to carry anything to any occasion – lecture, sermon, wedding, or funeral. Furthermore it has made it possible to react to the congregation. If the point was not clear or the reaction unexpected, it has been possible to restate matters in a different way. The chief problem with this type of delivery is dependence on a steady flow of synonyms that come readily when wide awake and less so when tired. This also proved to be a bit of a problem initially when I began to lecture often in Germany in German, as my range of synonyms is more limited, but a bit of courage and the willingness to struggle made it possible to continue the same pattern in that language.

A balance between being relaxed enough to sense what is happening to the audience, but tense enough to be able to convey some excitement was not easy to achieve initially, but over the years it became second nature.

SHABBAT AND EREV SHABBAT

Shabbat services have been continuous since the beginning of the congregation; I felt that they should be emphasized and encouraged shabbat attendance. The sermons continued to be formal with an emphasis on ethical questions, religious practice, family life, the education of children, the spiritual life, and current social concerns. After the Sunday services ended I incorporated a broader range of such themes into the shabbat service. This was also the time to challenge the congregation and to get them to think about a different point of view. The Torah portion of the week was usually in some way related to my themes. I generally dictated the sermon outlines for publication after the weekend; they continued to be published in each issue of the *Temple Bulletin* and present a fairly complete record through the decades. I have not included them in this analysis as we have them for only Freehof and me. Leadership kallahs provided a setting for experimentation with different liturgies.

The briefer *erev shabbat* service with an attendance of about one hundred congregants lent itself to a sermonette connected with the Torah portion of the week. I used it primarily to deal with current issues and especially to motivate younger congregants to action.[136]

CHILDREN'S SERVICES

J. Leonard Levy prepared a formally printed children's liturgy and conducted such services regularly. Dr. Goldenson brought the older children into the synagogue for some of the Sunday morning services and sermons. Dr. Freehof instituted regular shabbat family services for the older children with the large children's choirs providing the music and a class leading each month's service for the congregation. He rarely spoke to the younger children. I felt that children's services were important, prepared a series of service pamphlets for various age groups over the years, and conducted the services whenever the Religious School met throughout the years. For those services I invented stories or prepared short sermonettes. The family services on shabbat were augmented by children's holiday services for *Pesah* and *Sukkot* in addition to the High Holidays.

The teenage youth groups often held services in outdoor settings or at over night institutes. I worked with the leadership in preparing those services and attended whenever possible.

HOLIDAYS

Holidays were a time for exploring the inner life. *Rosh Hashanah* and *Yom Kippur* were also times to refocus the congregation and to ask questions about prevailing opinion on social as well as personal issues. Some holiday sermons were published each year. I generally avoided timely topics.

Rabbis Staitman and
Jacob 1997

Rabbis Jacob and Bisno 2004

Rabbi Jacob, President and
Rabbi Homolka, Provost of
the Abraham Geiger
College, Berlin/Potsdam
1998

Rabbi Zemer, Director of the
Freehof Institute for Progressive
Halakhah, Pittsburgh and Tel
Aviv, Rabbi Jacob, President
1995

75

Book Reviews

The book reviews of the "Modern Literature Class" had become a major institution in the broader community and the congregation.[137] After a year's hiatus, I continued them in a modified form. As contemporary writing interested me less than it did my predecessor, Dr. Freehof, I gave only the opening review and invited my colleagues to give the others. This added a different tone to the reviews but also made them less attractive over the years. They continued to bring an audience of five to seven hundred each Wednesday morning and remained a unique Pittsburgh phenomenon.

A Retrospective

The half century of my rabbinate saw America expand and prosper while metropolitan Pittsburgh declined; I tried to minimize the effect of this on the congregation. The numerous older members of the congregation required a slower pace of change than Reform Judaism nationally. I insisted that my younger colleagues had the freedom to experiment with different service formats and innovative youth programs. The prosperous times made the restoration of the main synagogue possible. My goal was to emphasize worship, the reintroduction of rituals and *halakhah* along with regular, serious, adult learning and social action.

The Rodef Shalom pulpit has been absolutely free and without the slightest interference by the board of the congregation. As the congregation has been broadly based and not dependent on a small group for its financial support, divergent opinions were accepted and welcomed. Those who held different points of view on social and political questions were encouraged to discuss them with the rabbis, but the right to differ from the pulpit was never questioned. The pulpit was to teach, challenge, comfort, and stimulate the congregation.

The long tenure of each rabbi permitted the rabbi to become well acquainted with the congregation and the broader community. It also allowed for growth and maturation.

The nature of the sermon has changed along with the congregation, which has long been native born and largely college educated although often Jewishly illiterate, something that is slowly changing. The world of the media and the culture of instant brief unreflective response has taken its toll. Yet the sermon and pulpit lecture have remained resilient and have responded to the times even if in unfashionable ways.

A century and a half has built a pulpit tradition not only at Rodef Shalom, but in the broader American Jewish community. The five of us who have led Rodef Shalom as its senior rabbis for most of these hundred fifty years can consider ourselves fortunate. We, and my successors, Dr. Mark Staitman and Rabbi Aaron Bisno, have sought to continue a fine tradition and have been supported by the congregation for which each of us can be everlastingly grateful. Since Rabbi Goldenson, we have been helped enormously by a fine group of associate rabbis as well as excellent Temple administrators.[138] God has blessed us with opportunities and we have tried to use them wisely.

A rabbi sometimes can sense the immediate influence of a sermon, but often it is the occasional remark of a congregant years later that shows that the spoken word has had an effect. Each in our own way have made the appropriate effort.[139]

"We are standing at the foot of the mountain of great and new aspirations... And the challenge comes to us, the Children of Israel, to recapitulate in our own day, the consecrating experience of our forbearers..." (Samuel Goldenson).

"My religion is based upon the acceptance of the Eternal God as my Father and upon my treatment of my fellow-man as my brother. To work in hope; to accept the past in gratefulness and to strive to add to the good for the future; to be honest in all my dealings and expressions; to worship the truth; to be loyal to my country and to my ideals to seek salvation through character; to treasure the truth of Scripture and to labor to advance Israel's purpose; to do justice, to love mercy and to walk humbly before God; to live that I may die regretted and to die in the faith that I may live after death; – that is my religion." (J. Leonard Levy).

"As our work is blessed, we will have seen many grow up under our guidance. A generation or two will have lived by our light. In those days of realization the uncertainty of youth is transmuted into the confidence of age, and restlessness merges into peace.... In deep understanding and in glad acknowledgment we will offer to our Master the heave offering of faith." (Solomon B. Freehof).

"All of us are working together in a garden. This is the garden of God, of Judaism, our religion. In any garden there are times of harvest...; now we must begin again. A garden cannot be neglected. We must plant and till it again so that we will have other harvests in the future. In a garden there is work for everyone. All of us may be engaged in useful tasks – to plan, to plant, to mend fences, to look toward the future. There is enough for our lifetime in this garden of God and if we labor with diligence, we will make this our Garden of Eden." (Walter Jacob).

Notes

1. In the nineteenth century there was no consistency in the spelling of the name of the congregation both when used by members in private communications and in the official records of the congregation. This essay will generally use the current spelling (Rodef Shalom) even for the earliest period, but not always.

78

2. Leopold Zunz, *Die gottesdienstlichen Vortraege der Juden* (Frankfurt, 1892: J. Kauffmann); S. Maybaum, *Juedische Homiletik*, Berlin, 1890; Israel Bettan, *Studies in Jewish Preaching*, Cincinnati, 1939; Solomon B. Freehof, *Modern Jewish Preaching*, New York, 1941; Nachum Glatzer and Marc E. Saperstein have also written on this topic.

3. Charles I. Cooper, "The Story of the Jews of Pittsburgh, " *Jewish Criterion*, Twenty Fifth Anniversary Number, May 31, 1918, 49: 41, pp. 19-112; Jacob Feldman, *The Jewish Experience in Western Pennsylvania 1755-1945* (Pittsburgh, 1986: The Historical Society of Western Pennsylavania). After the founding years, Feldman showed little interest in the development of the religious communities. The other historical studies of Pittsburgh Jewish life have thus far been limited to biographies of communal leaders, published oral histories, a few specialized works such as unpublished theses and papers. Several films have also been made.

4. Troy Hill Cemetery was established in 1847 by the Bes Almon Society; and it subsequently became the cemetery of Rodef Shalom.

5. M . L. Aaron, *One Hundred Twenty Years- Rodef Shalom, Pittsburgh* (Pittsburgh, 1976). Mr. Mannheim was engaged by Schaarai Schemaim in 1848; the congregation had been formed in 1847. In 1850 Mr. Sulzbacher was engaged by Beth Israel which had broken off from Schaarai Schemaim. When the two groups reunited in 1853 Mr. Marcussohn was engaged.

6. Jacob Feldman, *The Jewish Experience in Western Pennsylvania*, Pittsburgh, 1986, p. 21.

7. Was it due to the conservative religious climate or was Pittsburgh considered mainly as a point of transit for travel farther West or were the economic opportunities too limited?

8. The congregational school existed in a more formal way from 1861 to 1869. Josiah Cohen, born in Plymouth, England, came to the United States as a teenager. *Jewish Criterion*, May 12, 1905.

9. *Centenary Pamphlet*, April 1913.

9. We know nothing about ideological discussions that may have taken place; the *American Israelite* is silent on this; contemporary Pittsburgh newspapers may provide some clues.

11. Naumburg, who died March 4, 1902, was born in Treuchlingen, Bavaria, in 1813; he emigrated to the United States in 1848 and settled in Philadelphia, where he served Kennesset Israel as reader, teacher, and cantor from 1850-1860. He remained in

Pittsburgh till the 1890s.

Naumburg came from a long line of cantors who could trace their lineage to 1680. He had a fine cantorial voice and also played the violin. He prepared a rhymed metrical version of the Book of Proverbs in German. His family consisted of three daughters and two sons. One of his daughters married Josiah Cohen, who played a prominent role in the life of Rodef Shalom virtually from its beginning. In 1913 the congregation held a commemorative service on the occasion of the hundredth anniversary of Naumburg's birth. *American Hebrew*, March 1902; *Jewish Criterion*, 14:13, March 7, 1902.

12. Born in Müllheim, Baden, educated in Karlsruhe and at the Universities of Würzburg, Berlin, and Heidelberg, where he received his Ph.D; he simultaneously studied at the Yeshivah of Rabbi Bamberger. He returned to Karlsruhe to continue his rabbinic studies under Dr. Plato and received his *semihah* from Consistory of the Jews of Baden from Rabbis Geismar, Schott, and Fuerst. He began by teaching at the seminary, then became rabbi of Gälingen, Baden; dissatisfied with the conservative religious atmosphere, he left for America and was briefly rabbi of the French Congregation in New York. In 1869 he accepted the pulpit of Selma, Alabama, and then came to Pittsburgh in 1870. Earlier, he had married Elise Hecht. One of their sons, Harry Mayer, became Rabbi of B'nai Jehudah in Kansas City in 1899. Another son, Dr. Edward Mayer, was very active at Rodef Shalom and served as Religious School Chairman when the new school building was built and dedicated in 1938. At the memorial service for Rabbi Mayer, Rabbis David Philipson, Henry Berkowitz, Emil G. Hirsch, Felix Adler, and A. Harrison from other cities along with Dr. E. Donehoo (Presbyterian), Rabbi Michael Fried, Tree of Life; Judge Josiah Cohen presided. He was remembered as a good friend by colleagues whom he helped.

13. Michael A. Meyer, "German-Jewish Identity in Nineteenth-Century America," in Jonathan D. Sarna (ed.), *The American Jewish Experience*, New York, 1986.

14. Mayer's interest in the broad principles of Judaism was reflected in the design of the dome of the new Eighth Street Temple, completed in 1902. In the cupola the following names were inscribed: Abraham, Moses, Hannah, Samuel, Elijah, Amos, Hosea, Isaiah, Micah, Hulda, Jeremiah, Ezekiel, Judah Maccabee, Hillel, Johanan b. Zakkai, Akiba, Saadiah, Rashi, Ibn Ezra, Maimonides, Moses Mendelssohn, David Einhorn, Samuel Hirsch, I.M. Wise. The inclusion of two women is noteworthy.

15. In 1869 he was elected as secretary of the Philadelphia Conference, but participated only marginally in the discussions. He induced Rodef Shalom to be the first "eastern" congregation to support of the Hebrew Union College and was responsible for its largest bequest. He issued the invitations for the Pittsburgh Conference of 1885 which set the course of Reform Judaism for half a century. He was one of the founders of the Central Conference of American Rabbis. He preached

in many other cities which brought him a national reputation.

16. *Rabbi Dr. Mayer 1841-1904*, (Dora Mayer Felsenthal and Louis Mayer Felsenthal, eds.), 1986, unpublished booklet of clippings.

17. Mayer was a Trustee of the Western University of Pennsylvania as was also later J. Leonard Levy, and helped the University obtain the Kaufmann Clinic. He founded the first public kindergarten in Allegheny County and was for years director of the German Home for the Aged. In 1880 he helped to establish a branch of YMHA. He was a trustee of the Gusky Orphanage, vice-president of the United Hebrew Charities of which he was a founder.

18. Felsenthal and Mayer, *Rabbi Dr. Mayer 1841-1904.*

19. Jacob Rader Marcus, *United States Jewry, 1776-1985*, Detroit, 1993, Vol. 2, pp. 82 ff.

20. M. L. Aaron, *Op. Cit.*, p. 5. Rabbi Samuel Greenfield, a Pittsburgher, was the first editor of the *Pittsburgh Jewish Criterion*, established in 1895. (*Jewish Criterion*, July 16, 1937, where his death was noted in an editorial). He was a graduate of the Hebrew Union College and had briefly served a congregation in Peoria, Il. On the holidays he and Rabbi Mayer alternated with German and English sermons.

21. Dr. Joseph Krauskopf, the brilliant Philadelphia rabbi with whom Levy served, had initiated this custom for his Sunday lectures and published them for thirty-six years.

22. Levy was educated at Jews College, University College, and Bristol University. He became an Orthodox rabbi at the age of 20 in 1885 and soon was dissatisfied with the Orthodox establishment. His brother, Meyer, served as rabbi of a California congregation and recommended him to Sacramento, where he settled in 1889 (*Jewish Criterion*, 21:2, p. 19). He married Henrietta Platenauer in 1888 and the family had two daughters. His wife reached the age of 102 and was a strong personality in her own right to the very end.

23. Jacob Feldman, *Op. Cit.*, p. 106. Founded in 1895 by Rabbi Samuel Greenfield; with Charles Joseph was appointed as second editor in 1899. He shared this task with J. Leonard Levy from 1901.

24. For a discussion of his liturgical works see the essay by Ruth Langer in this volume.

25. This innovation was vigorously attacked by the Orthodox, and Levy defended them both in the *Jewish Criterion* and at the beginning and conclusion of each year's Sunday service season. (October 20, 1901; April 9, 1906; April 20, 1907, etc.). They were well attended and often filled the synagogue. Several hundred also attended shabbat services at which family groups were more likely to be present. When the congregation moved to the Carnegie Hall in 1905 after the Eighth Street Temple had been sold, some concern about the attendance of Allegheny members was expressed, but they and those settled in the newer East End continued to come in large numbers. *Jewish Criterion*, 20:9, Feb. 10.

26. Joseph Krauskopf (1858-1923) was vice-president of the Pittsburgh Conference of 1885 and elected as rabbi of Keneseth Israel in 1887 where he established a Sunday service. He regularly published his sermons. He was remembered especially for his establishment of the National Farm School in 1896. Levy served as associate at Keneseth Israel in Philadelphia from 1893-1901. Some of Levy's sermons given in Philadelphia were published, including a booklets of the sermons from 1893-1901. He noted that Keneset Israel had been the first congregation to publish sermons regularly and Rodef Shalom the second.

27. "Founders of Faith," March 15, 1908.

28. Rudolph I. Coffee, "Joseph Leonard Levy," *Yearbook of the Central Conference of American Rabbis* (New York, 1917:CCAR Press) Vol. 27, p. 238. Rabbi Coffee gave a eulogy for Levy at the Central Conference annual meeting.

29. "Say unto Israel, Go Forward," April 16, 1911, pp. 12 ff.

30. "No Surrender," March 19, 1916.

31. Several sermons were devoted to this topic over the years. He also dealt with this issue in editorials in *Jewish Criterion*.

32. *Jewish Criterion*, 14:19, April 18, 1902.

33. "The B'nai Brith Opportunity," November 29, 1914, pp. 10 ff.

34. See the essay by Susan Kalson in this volume for more details.

35. "Wanted - A Mother," December 17, 1916, p. 18.

36. For a fuller discussion see the essays in this volume by Ruth Langer, Susan Friedberg Kalson, and Eileen Lane.

37. There was a problem with one of these exchanges, but it was eventually worked out as Dr. Diffenbach was much in favor of it. December 6, 1908.

38. "Brother Against Brother," December 6, 1908, p. 19.

39. See various essays in Samuel P. Hays (ed.), *City at the Point* (Pittsburgh, 1989: University of Pittsburgh Press).

40. "A Review, A Criticism, a Forecast," April 4, 1909, p. 13   "Minister and Congregation," April 2, 1916, p. 4.

41. "God in the Constitution," January 1, 1911, pp. 12 ff.

42. "America and Russia," March 26, 1911, pp. 12 ff.

43. "The Taming of the Shrew," December 29, 1912, pp. 2 ff.

44. "The Trend of the Future," March 9, 1913, pp. 176 f.

45. For another analysis see the essay by Barbara Burstin in this volume.

46. Max Nordau's address at the Fifth Zionist Congress in Basel (*Jewish Criterion*, 14:5), as well as constant reports of the proceedings of the various congresses. There were long reports about the "Territorialist Question." Local Zionist activities were regularly reported under the heading "Zionist Notes" and "Zionist Bulletin." He praised Israel Zangwill, a childhood friend who had grown up in Bristol and now was a staunch Zionist. "Plays with a Purpose III: The Next Religion," January 28, 1917.

47. *Jewish Criterion*, 14:4; 1902.

48. "The Zionism of the Prophets," given on January 9, 1902, *Jewish Criterion*, 14:5, 1902.

49. "The Next Step in Judaism," October 29, 1916, pp. 14 ff.

50. "War Against War," December 6, 1914, pp. 8 ff.

51. "Am I My Brother's Keeper?" November 28, 1915, pp. 14 ff.

52. "America and Russia," March 26, 1911, pp. 4 ff.

53. "The President and His Policies," April 19, 1908, p. 16.

54. "Wanted - A Mother," December 17, 1916, p. 21.

55. "The Desirable Woman," November 21, 1915, p. 20 f.

56. "The Peace of Justice," December 25, 1904, "The Fruits of War," December 5, 1915, "The Making of Munitions," December 24, 1916, " February 4, 1917. "A Time for War and A Time for Peace," April 8, 1917. Also a sermon by Rabbi Horace J Wolf as pulpit guest "The Military Obligations of Citizenship," February, 4, 1917.

57. "Let Us Alone," December 10, 1916, p. 22; "Everybody's Business," November 12, 1916.

58. "Innocent or Guilty?" December 27, 1908, p. 21.

59. "Plays with a Purpose III: The Next Religion," January 28, 1917, pp 65 f.

60. When Levy was selected as rabbi, the new Temple on Eighth Street was under construction. It soon proved to be too small and the site too constricted for expansion to accomodaste the congregation which had grown far beyond the 130 families that belonged when he arrived. The religious school had expanded from 60 students to more than 600 pupils. This meant that a new synagogue had to be built. As the congregation began to think about it, a Presbyterian church became interested in purchasing the Eighth Street building, and it was sold to them. At that time the congregation had not purchased another site or even begun with any architectural specifications. Levy was willing to take the chance and to endure the aggravation entailed in temporary quarters for all activities, including the Religious School housed in two locations, as well as the construction and financing. By 1907 a much larger main synagogue and adequate quarters for the Religious School had been completed. All this occurred early in Levy's rabbinate. Although the efforts in that direction were not mentioned in the lectures, they must have been considerable and time consuming. For a full discussion see the essay by Richard Rosenzweig.

61. Folklore has it that he caught a cold, which led to pneumonia, while speaking at a Liberty Bond rally. Whether correct or not, it demonstrates his reputation for patriotism and communal involvement.

62. "A Review, a Criticism, a Forecast," April 4, 1909. In 1902 he mentioned that 3000 copies of each week's lecture were distributed with 1000 to the congregation, 1000 to those in the community who had requested it, and 1000 for general distribution. "The Spirit of Modern Judaism," April 6, 1902.

63. Goldenson's parents had moved to Rochester, N.Y. upon arrival in the United States and he grew up there. He was ordained at the Hebrew Union College in 1904 and served Temple Adath Jeshurun, Lexington, Ky. which he had organized from 1904-1907; then he served as rabbi at Beth Emet in Albany, N. Y. from 1907-1918. At the same time he studied at Columbia University for a Ph..D. He was forty when

he came to Rodef Shalom. In 1934 he became rabbi of Temple Emanu-El in New York. He was active in the leadership of the Central Conference of American Rabbis and led the anti-Zionist faction. He was president of the Conference from 1934 to 1936. Married to Claudia Mayer in 1905, they had three children. His wife died in 1938. After his retirement he often preached in small congregations in the South.

64. Rabbi Meyerovitz, who graduated in 1917, served till Goldenson's arrival in August 1918; Peter Glick led the Religious School ,and Rabbi Philo of Youngstown, the Confirmation class. Rabbi Zepin led the High Holiday services, and various other rabbis preached during the year.

65. The Confirmation class of the Religious School was asked each week to abstract the sermon or to compose a reaction to it. Occasional comments upon the quality of their work appeared in the *Temple Bulletin*.

66. "American Judaism," 1918; "Does Judaism Have a Future?" 1920; "Jewish Imperatives," 1921; "Judaism as a Religion," 1922; "The Roots of Reform Judaism," November 25, December 7, 16, 1923; "Empty-Handed Religion," March 2, 1923; "Can Human Nature Change?" March 14, 1926.

67. "What Ails Youth?" April 24, 1926; "Wealth and Well-being," February 19, 1928.

68. "The League of Nations," 1918; "What is Right with the World," 1921; "America First - In What Sense," 1922; "Woodrow Wilson and the Eternal Tragedy," February 10, 1925; "Whither America?" December 15, 1928.

69. "Haman, Hitler, and Minorities," March 19, 1933; "Hitlerism and Civilization," November 19, 1933.

70. "Morals and Politics ," 1920, 1928, 1931; "What is Practical?" 1921; "Liberty and Responsibility," April 20, 1924; "Some Counterfeits of Liberalism," November 8, 1925; "Judaism and Social Justice," January 30, 1927; "Liberty and Society - Do They Conflict?" April 8, 1928; "Are Your Assets a Liability?" December 30, 1928; "Breadline Prosperity," March 30, 1930; "Is Charity Enough?" March 6, 1932.

71. "Jewish Nationalism," 1920; "What is a Jew," 1921; "Loyalties" 1922; "Religion and Nationalism - How Far Are They Compatible?" April 16, 1933; "Nationalism and Religion," December 3, 1933.

72. Goldenson became one of the founders of the American Council for Judaism and remained active in it throughout his life.

73. "The Community's Obligation to the School Teacher," April 27, 1919.

74. "Religion and Education," 1924; "What Parents Owe Their Children,"
1918, 1933; "The Modern Mind," 1926.

75. "The Jewish Problem,"1920; "The Jew - The International Scapegoat," 1921,
"Judaism and the Interchurch World Movement" 1920; "Shylock - Jews and
Gentiles," 1923; Judaism and Christianity," 1932.

76. "Jesus of Nazareth - In the Light of Jewish and Christian History," January 10,
1926; "Judaism and Christianity - How Do They Differ?" February 1, 1931.

77. Biographical data, essays on Freehof's contribution in the realm of Jewish
education and liturgy as well as to the Central Conference of American Rabbis, and
a bibliography may be found in Walter Jacob, Frederick C. Schwartz, Vigdor W.
Kavaler eds., *Essays in Honor of Solomon B. Freehof* (Pittsburgh: Rodef Shalom
Press, 1964).

78. Theodore Wiener and Lillian Freehof, "The Writings of Solomon B. Freehof," in
Jacob, Schwartz, Kavaler, *Essays in Honor of Solomon B. Freehof*, Vigdor Kavaler
ed., *The Sermon Continues*, (Pittsburgh: Rodef Shalom Press, 1983).

79. Some initial financial support was provided for each of these congregations.
When Temple Sinai was founded Rodef Shalom closed its membership to aid it and
provided several trustees.

80. During the years as rabbi of the congregation, Freehof wrote a number of popular
adult volumes on the Bible among them *Preface to Scripture* (1950) in which every
book of the Bible as well as its major themes were discussed. In a similar vein he
wrote commentaries on Psalms (1938), Job (1958), Isaiah (1972), Jeremiah (1977),
and Ezekiel (1978). None of these books played a major role in the selection of
Sunday morning topics. The same was true of his popular studies of the liturgy.
(1942). He often spoke about historical aspects of the liturgy during the High Holiday
services but did not devote lectures to this topic.

Beginning in the 1940s Freehof developed a major interest in Jewish law and
wrote *Reform Jewish Practice* (1944, 1952), followed by eight volumes of responsa
as well as *The Responsa Literature* (1955) and *A Treasury of Responsa* (1963) which
were introductions to this literature, but none of this material appears in his Sunday
lectures.

81. A complete list of titles will be provided in the future.

82. Many of the early sermons were wire recorded, and although some of the wires
have survived, the machine for transcribing them has not. Later sermons have been
tape-recorded and are now undergoing conservation.

83. One brother, who lived in Washington, was a fervent Zionist. His father was a personal friend of Yitzhak Ben Zevi, the second president of Israel, who introduced him to his second wife. One of Freehof's best friends among colleagues was Abba Hillel Silver, a fervent Zionist. Others such as Barnet Brickner were also close.

84. "The Jewish State - Can It Survive?" "The Jewish State - and American Jewry," "The Holy City, Past and Future," "What England Wants - In Palestine," "The Palestine Reversal - What Will It Mean?"

85. Freehof chose to ignore a small splinter faction, members of the anti-Zionist American Council for Judaism. When they left the congregation, he made no fuss and saw them quietly drift back over the years.

86. "What Jews Must fight for in America," December 18, 1938; "Jewish Citizens in Public Office," January 15, 1939; "The Great American - A Composite," February 12, 1939; "The Small American - A Comedown," February 19, 1939.

87. "American Jewish Unity - A Fact, a Plan, or a Mirage ?" December 3, 1944.

88. Three lectures each: "It Takes Courage to Live," "Cheap Phrases of a Vulgar Age," "I Wish I Could Believe."

89. Humorous poetry from his youth or from his days as a student at the Hebrew Union College could regale an audience of friends and younger colleagues. Long forgotten whimsical verses or anecdotes of half a century ago were presented with unusual freshness.

90. Although Freehof appeared to be looking directly at his audience, he was actually concentrating on his topic. When he began to speak he often removed his glasses and without them he could not see clearly . This enabled him to concentrate and not be distracted. As he always used two pairs of glasses, never bi-focals, he often after a lecture selected the wrong pair and appeared to have difficulty walking; this led to the misimpression that his eye sight was bad, it was excellent and he had no difficulty with the small print of talmudic commentaries.

91. A list of the titles may be found in *Books of Fifty Years*, Walter Jacob, ed., (Pittsburgh: 1984, Rodef Shalom Press), pp. 177-197. Each season Freehof spent a portion of the summer reading books presented by the publishers and organized those selected under a general theme such as 1935-1936 - The World Today - the Past Recaptured; 1936-37 Landscapes - Leaders, etc.

92. *Books of Twenty Years* (1954), *Books of Thirty Years* (1963), *Books of Fifty Years* (1984).

93. Interestingly enough, I continued the pattern of foreign born rabbis as I was born in Augsburg, Germany and arrived in the United States in 1940. For biographical data and a bibliography see Peter S. Knobel and Mark N. Staitman, eds., *An American Rabbinate, A Festschrift for Walter Jacob* (Pittsburgh,. Rodef Shalom Press, 2000).

93. The following scholars lectured: Dr. Lewis M. Barth, Dr. Herman Berlinski, Dr. Michael J. Cook, Dr. Stanley Dreyfus, Rabbi Dov Edelstein, Dr. Emil Fackenheim, Professor Joseph Glass, Dr. Hugo Gryn, Dr. Joseph Gutmann, Dr. Joshua O. Haberman, Dr.Susannah Heschel, Dr. Walter Homolka, Dr. Peter S. Knobel, Dr. Jacob R. Marcus, Dr. Kerry M. Olitzky, Dr. Jakob J. Petuchowski, Dr. W. Gunther Plaut, Dr. Richard Rosenthal, Dr. Samuel Sandmel, Dr. Ronald B. Sobel, Dr. Jack D. Spiro, Dr. Samuel M. Stahl, Dr. Elsie R. Stern, Dr. Trude Weiss-Rosmarin, Dr. Bernard Zlotowitz.

95. Adult education classes were regularly taught by my associate, Vigdor Kavaler, as well as myself. We tried to provide as wide an array of classes as possible from introductions to subjects to highly specialized themes. My emphasis was to schedule them morning, afternoon, early and late evening, so that they would be as convenient as possible. For several years I coor - dinated our classes with those of other congregations, so that cross-registration was possible. In addition I organized kallot weekends in the countryside for various boards.

For more than a decade, my associate and I conducted the classes for prospective converts for all area Reform congregations.

96. In 1973 a survey of the congregation was taken to assay the interest in the Sunday service. As it was inconclusive and as the attendance remained good, I continued it *(Temple Bulletin*, March 26, 1973).

97. "Pangs of Pacifism," February 6, 1966.

98. "Passover and Vietnam," April 30, 1967; "Midsummer Nights Dream or Nightmare," March 17, 1968; "Vietnam - War or Peace - How Long?" April 20, 1969.

99. "Restless Campus - Anxious Nation," November 1, 1970; "Terrorism - What Do They Want?" February 26, 1978.

100. "Middle East Aflame," December 25, 1966; "From Crisis to Crisis," December 22, 1968; "Israel, the Permanent War," April 18, 1971; "Israel Today - Peace When?" December 26, 1982.

101. "Israel at Twenty-Five: I - Toward a New Zionist Ideology, II - Its Intellectual Achievements," April 1 and 22, 1973; "O Jerusalem!" December 4, 1977.

102. "Jews and Arabs I - Our Common Cause, II Explosive Nationalism," December 2 and 9, 1973; "The Arab Mind and the Future of Israel," January 14, 1979.

103. "Religious Freedom in Israel 168 B.C.E.. - 1968 C.E.," December 31, 1967.

104. "Impatient Negroes," January 15, 1967; "Jews and Negroes," January 22, 1967; "Negro Anti-Semitism," March 16, 1969.

105. "Busing," January 30, 1972; "Violence," February 6, 1972; "Our New National Holiday - Martin Luther King Jr. Day - Black Progress - Where Has It Gone?" January 12, 1986.

106. "Judaism and Modern Science I - Who Shall Live and Who Shall Die? II - Psychedelic Drugs," November 24, December 1, 1968; "Our Times - Our Problems II - Judaism on Abortion, II - Judaism on Pollution, III - Judaism on Drugs," November 22, 29, December 6, 1970; "Questions My Colleagues Have Asked" March 25, April 8, 15, 1984.

107. "Rites of Passage I - Bar Mitzvah, II - Death, III - Marriage," April 6, 13, 20, 1980.

108. "Poets of the Prayer book," February 16, 1975, "The New Union Haggadah," March 30, 1975; "Theology of Our New Prayerbook," March 21, 1982.

109. "The Search for Jewish Philosophy, I - Abraham Heschel, II - Mordecai Kaplan, III - Franz Rosenzweig," March 7, 14, 21, 1971; "Modern Philosophies of Judaism I - Abraham Geiger, II Zacharias Frankel, III Samson Raphael Hirsch," November 2, 16, 23, 1986.

110. "Modern Questions - Classic Response I - How to Believe the Bible - Rashi, II - Why Believe in God - Maimonides, III - What to Believe About History - Graetz," March 12, 19, 26, 1972.

111. "What Can We Still Believe I - About the Bible, II - About God," December 4, 11, 1966.

112. "Jewish 'Teenage' Surveys - What Do They Mean?" January 21, 1968; "Jewish Identity," February 13, 1973.

113. "Changing Reform Judaism I - Our Principles, II-Our Practices," January 9, 16, 1977.

114. "College Children - A Restless Generation," February 19, 1967.

115. "New Religious Experiences - Jewish Jesus Freaks," December 17, 1972; "New Religious Experiences - Meditation Groups," December 24, 1972; "Jews for Jesus - Is This Group Dangerous?" February 5, 1978.

116. "Our Times - Our Problems - Women's Liberation," November 15, 1970.

117. Rabbi Julie Wolkoff and Rabbi Melanie Aron.

118. "The Religious Condition in the Orient," November 7, 1971.

119. Earlier I published *Christianity through Jewish Eyes - A Quest for Common Ground*, Cincinnati, Hebrew Union College Press, 1974 (in subsequent printings, New York, KTAV Publishing), which became a widely used college and adult education text.

120. "The New Ecumenism - How Far?" April 13, 1969; "The New Vatican Declaration," February 2, 1975.

121. The Cardinal's invitation to me and Irene to be present at his elevation in Rome provided an opportunity to speak with many leading Catholic figures.

122. I saw to it that the Temple became the site for the regular meetings of the Pittsburgh Area Race and Religion Council, ably led by my friend Rev. Donald Mc Ilvane. I invited many other groups to use the facilities and several interfaith and inter-religious groups were founded at the Temple.

123. "Where It Is Bad - Russia and Argentina," March 19, 1967; "Syrian Jews - What Can We Do?" January 16, 1972; "A New Wave of Anti-Semitism," November 29, 1981.

124. "Soviet Show Trials," January 10, 1971.

125. "The Foundations of Modern Anti-Semitism I - Martin Luther, II Richard Wagner, III Russian Hatred," December 11, 18, 25, 1983.

126. "Where Are We Going I - As American Jews, I I- As Pittsburgh Jews," January 7, 14, 1968; "Jewish Demography - Jewish Population Problems," January 28, 1979.

127. "The United Jewish Federation - An Evaluation," January 8, 1978.

128. "They Changed Our History I - Caesar and Tolerance, II - Martin Luther, III - Napoleon," February 26, March 5, 12, 1967, and continued in 1968 and 1969; "Turning Points," December 20, 27, 1970, January 3, 1971.

129. "While Six Million Died" (A Review), December 3, 1967; "The Holocaust and Skokie," April 23, 1978; "Kristallnach - A Fortieth Anniversary," November 12, 1978; "When Memory Comes" (A Review), January 27, 1980.

130. "Come Travel with Me," November 23, 30, December 14, 1980, January 9, 16, 1983, January 8, 22, 1984.

131. "The American Jew I - July 4, 1776, II - May 26, 1865, III - World War I," November 23, 30, December 14, 1975; "Looking Forward with America," November 21, 1976.

132. "Our Old Bible in Our New World: I - The Twenty-Third Psalm - What About Faith and Personal Religion? II - A Kingdom of Priests - Israel and Nationalism, III - Swords into Plowshares - Pacifism or Folly?" December 10, 17, 24, 1967; "Our Bible for Adults," February 15, 22, 1970.

133. "A Sermon through Song," March 9, 1969; "A Folk Rock Service," December 28, 1969; "Milhaud's Sacred Service," January 18, 1970; "The Avodah Dance Company," April 2, 1978; "Music of Janowski," January 25, 1981, "Avodah Dance Company," November 8, 1981.

134. "Lost Jewish Art," February 12, 1967. I used the Associated American Jewish Museums to create a small gallery around the Levy Auditorium and in this way to educate the congregation and Religious School on aspects of Jewish art.. The five major traveling exhibits that I curated, began here as did a series of local exhibits. In the reconstruction of the building in 1999, a permanent gallery space was included, but without provisions for displays of photographs and paintings.

135. "Jewish Books You May Have Missed," January 13, 20, 27, 1980.

136. As I never had a problem with sermon ideas and as I had a long drive to the outskirts of Pittsburgh each Friday afternoon in order to bring our daughter home, this was a good time to work out the sermonette and it always proved more than adequate (Claire was in the D.T. Watson Home for many years, which helped her with cerebral palsy and other problems).

137. My way of reaching out to the non-Jewish community was the Milton Harris Interfaith Institute, which brought four hundred ministers to the synagogue each year to listen to an outstanding Jewish scholar who provided an intellectually stimulating lecture. The following lectuers appeared: Dr. Lewis M. Barth, Dr. Herman Berlinski,

Dr. Norman V. Cohen, Dr. Michael J. Cook, Dr. Stanley Dreyfus, Rabbi Dov B. Edelstein,Dr. Emil Fackenheim, Dr. Joseph Gutmann, Rabbi Hugo Gryn, Dr. Joshua O. Haberman, Dr. Susannah Heschel, Dr. Walter Homolka, Dr. Peter S. Knobel, Dr. Admiel Kosman, Dr. Jacob R. Marcus, Dr. Kerry M. Olitzky, Dr Jakob J. Petuchowski, Dr. W. Gunther Plaut, Dr. Richard Rosenthal, Dr. Samuel Sandmel, Dr. Ronald B. Sobel, Dr. Jack D. Spiro, Dr. Samuel M. Stahl, Dr. Elsie R. Stern, Dr. Trude Weiss-Rosmarin, Dr. Bernard Zlotowitz. This effort plus numerous sermons and lectures in churches and before civic groups reached out to the non-Jewish population and improved interfaith relations.

136. The following served as assistant and associate rabbis from 1923 onward: B. Benedict Glazer, Henry Kagan, Jacob Rothschild, Charles Lesser, Floyd S. Fierman, Murray Rothman, Harold Silver, Philip Gershon, Walter Jacob, Frederick C. Schwartz, Sherman Stein, Frederic Pomerantz, Kenneth Segel, Charles Levi, Howard Kaplansky, Mark Staitman, Debra Pine, Andrew Busch, Jessica Locketz, Peter Stein, Sharon Henry, and Daniel Young. The following served as administrators from 1904 onward: Bernard Callomon, Louis N. Broudy, Chester G. Bandman, Vigdor W. Kavaler, Susan Trivers, and Jeffrey S. Herzog.

139. Samuel Goldenson, "The Present Status and Future Outlook of Reform Judaism," *Yearbook of the Central Conference of American Rabbis* (Cincinnati: 1925), vol. 34, p. 298.
J. Leonard Levy, "My Religion," *My Religion* - A Sermon give on November 19, 1905, Sermon Series 5:3, p. 19.
Solomon B. Freehof, "First Fruit," A Sermon delivered at the Hebrew Union College, February 23, 1924, *Hebrew Union College Monthly*, Vol. 10, p. 9.
Walter Jacob, *Installation Sermon*, November 6, 1966, Service of Installation, p. 20.

RODEF SHALOM—PHYSICAL SPACE
1860–1996

Richard L. Rosenzweig

The physical spaces occupied and used by the Rodef Shalom Congregation were conceived and built to fit the needs and aspirations of its members and, in turn, have influenced the tone and nature of its congregational functions and activities. As homes are physical spaces that shelter relations, the congregational home provides the physical spaces that shelter and nurture the relations of the congregants to their leadership, to each other, and to their inner selves and beliefs.[1]

The Congregational leadership defined the philosophy and set the objectives for the physical spaces and setting according to changing needs and times. The spaces then in turn set a tone for the activities and relationships that occurred within them. The dedications of the newly created or restored spaces provided both culmination and beginning. Interior spaces for worship were for half the life of the Congregation organized by an aristocracy of wealth that gave way to the democratization of the space by the abolition of assigned pews.

The history of the Rodef Shalom Congregation is bound up in the physical spaces it has occupied, its institutional homes, its buildings, and the ambiance of the surrounding neighborhoods. The collective leadership of the congregation chose the locations and created the buildings with deliberation and foresight. The dedications of newly completed facilities traced the evolution of the congregation, marked the culminating achievement of new and beautiful buildings, and focused the aspirations of the congregation on its future. At these dedications the congregational leaders spoke, linking the congregation's past to a future filled with the advantages that the new or restored building would provide in inspiring spaces for worship and friendly spaces for learning and congregational activities.

The congregation had to react and adapt to waves of immigration, the Great Depression, two world wars, the Baby Boom, and more recently the changing demographics and economic base of the Pittsburgh region. The stature and greatness of the congregation through the past 150 years derives from the wise and fortunate choices of its lay and spiritual leaders and from the well-considered decisions regarding the location and construction of its buildings— the creation of its institutional homes.

The Rodef Shalom Congregation was chartered on November 9, 1856, and rented its first spacious location for its thirty-five members and fifty pupils on St. Clair Street in the City of Allegheny in 1859.[2] The first location that Rodef Shalom could call its own, a physical space to which to tie its identity by ownership, came with the purchase of property on August 30, 1860, in downtown Pittsburgh on Hancock Street (soon to be renamed 8th Street), between Penn Avenue and Duquesne Way. John Herron and his wife, Clarissa, conveyed to "The Corporation Styled Rodef Scholem" in what was then the Fourth Ward of the City of Pittsburgh, a lot 187 feet from the corner of Penn Avenue on the eastern side of Hancock Street with dimensions of 60 feet by 89 feet. The purchase price was $4,000, with a purchase money mortgage of $3,000. The Herrons conveyed a second adjoining parcel directly to "Rodef Scholem" on May 22, 1862, 20 feet by 89 feet for $975.[3]

The Hancock Street Temple, a three-storied structure with an imposing facade, was built on the Herron parcel in 1861 and dedicated on March 20, 1862. Rev. William Armhold presided. Rev. Morris Raphael of New York was the featured speaker. Twenty-one-year-old Josiah Cohen, who four years before had emigrated from England and had been engaged by the congregation to teach English in both the day school and the Sunday school (while studying law), also spoke eloquently.[4]

Isaac Mayer Wise wrote about this 1862 dedication ceremony in *The Israelite* of December 14, 1863. According to Dr. Wise, the Polish and German factions that had formed the predecessor congregation ten years before had united in peace and harmony, with 50 members and 53 seat holders representing 150 families living in this city and vicinity.[5] The congregation had a day school and a Sunday school. The day school taught Hebrew, German, and all the English

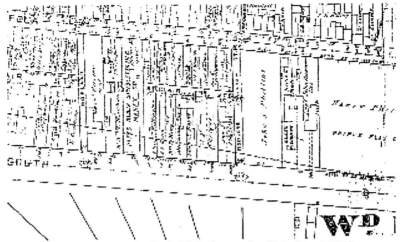

Rented quarters for Rodef Scholem at St. Clair Street 1859

Site for the first building of Rodef Scholem, Hancock Street, later
Eighth Street, purchase in 1860

95

branches of a primary education.[6] The Sunday school was for religious instruction exclusively. Dr. Wise quoted from the text of "Professor" Cohen's speech, which placed the dedication of the new Temple in the grim context of the national catastrophe of the Civil War:

> It is not my desire to mar the pleasure of this banquet by calling up all the gloomy scenes which have surrounded this nation during the past three years, and which still hover round it, threatening—threatening to obliterate that government which is the grand center from which is drawn all of life's privileges, and from which the politically oppressed draw consolation.... These joyful surroundings seem to be in strange contrast with the cause which brings us here.... Let us prove, by our liberality here this evening, that the Jewish heart beats as strongly in favor of the restoration of the Union as any of America's other sons. Let us prove that, in spite of the rumored lethargy on the part of the Israelites, we are invoking every means in our power to advance the cause of our country, and when the veil of prejudice which hides our true character shall be torn from the eyes of those who would malign us, they will find that Israelites...are serious and earnest...on behalf of the Union.[7]

Hancock Street, between Penn Avenue and the Allegheny River, contained the massive Christ Methodist Church at the corner of Penn, next to which was the Pittsburgh Female College.[8] Across Hancock from the Christ Methodist Church and the Pittsburgh Female College, directly in the middle of the block on the east side of Hancock, stood the Rodef Shalom building designated on the plat as the "Hebrew Church." Just north of it stood the Second Presbyterian Church. This block, which now has only parking lots behind the modern but small Integra Bank building, formerly the Commercial Bank and Trust building, leaves no trace that it was once a vibrant area of churches and a women's college, in the middle of which, for 44 years, was the site of the Rodef Shalom Congregation. In 1888 the Rodef Shalom building on what was now 8th Street underwent extensive remodeling. On September 2, 1888, according to the program of the event, the "Remodelled Temple" building on 8th Street was rededicated. Samuel Wertheimer, the chairman of the Building Committee, introduced the program, and the main address

Rodef Scholem near two Presbyterian churches 1862

Rodef Scholem 1862

97

was by Josiah Cohen, Esquire, now a prominent lawyer and leader of the congregation. The sermon was given by Dr. Lippman Mayer (spelled Dr. L. Maier in the program), who had been appointed rabbi of the congregation on May 1, 1870, and was to serve until the appointment of Dr. J. Leonard Levy in 1901.[9]

The congregation's numbers remained static between 1860 and 1900 at fewer than 150 families. By 1900 the wave of immigrants from Eastern Europe that had occurred in the 1890s, and their quick assimilation and economic progress, provided a fertile source for growth in congregational membership. It appeared that the Hancock Street Temple, built during the Civil War, was no longer adequate.[10] Dr. Mayer planned to retire in 1901, and a search began for a new rabbi. The congregation was at the brink of unprecedented growth that would occur within the next five years. The decisions to build a new temple on the 8th Street site and to appoint Dr. J. Leonard Levy of Philadelphia as successor to Dr. Mayer occurred almost simultaneously.

In 1901 a beautiful new building was to replace the Civil War era structure on the same 8th Street site. According to *The Pittsburg Leader:*

> The new edifice in elegance of design and costliness of structure will rival some of the most important church buildings of the city. It is to be built of Philadelphia pressed brick with stone trimmings and will occupy the entire ground space, covering a frontage of 80 feet and extending back 90 feet with a 20-foot annex in the rear for the use of the congregation societies. While the cost of the building cannot be estimated as yet it is expected it will exceed $100,000, as this amount has been placed at the disposal of the building committee. Mr. S. Wertheimer is chairman of the building committee and states that no expense will be spared to make the new temple one of the finest houses of worship in the two cities. The congregation is made up of some of the wealthiest representatives of the Hebrew race in this section of the country.[11]

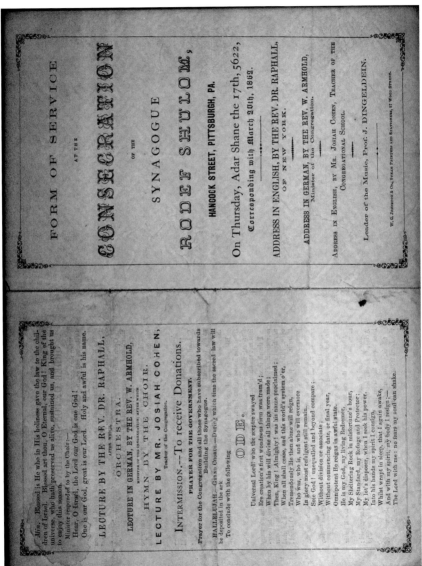

FORM OF SERVICE

AT THE

CONSECRATION

OF THE

SYNAGOGUE

OF THE

RODEF SHOLOM,

HANCOCK STREET, PITTSBURGH, PA.

On Thursday, Adar Shane the 17th, 5622,

Corresponding with March 20th, 1862.

ADDRESS IN ENGLISH, BY THE REV. DR. RAPHALL,
OF NEW YORK.

ADDRESS IN GERMAN, BY THE REV. W. ARMHOLD,
Minister of the Congregation.

ADDRESS IN ENGLISH, BY MR. JOSIAH COHEN, TEACHER OF THE
CONGREGATIONAL SCHOOL.

Leader of the Music, Prof. J. DINGELDEIN.

W. G. JOHNSTON & CO., STEAM PRINTERS AND STATIONERS, 57 WOOD STREET.

Min. Blessed is He who in His holiness gave the law to the children of Israel. Blessed art thou, O Eternal, our God! King of the universe, who hath preserved us alive, sustained us, and brought us to enjoy this season.

Minister responded to by the Choir:—
Hear, O Israel, the Lord our God is one God!
One is our God, great is our Lord. Holy and awful is his name.

LECTURE BY THE REV. DR. RAPHALL,
AFTER WHICH

ORCHESTRA.

MINISTER OF THE CONGREGATION AFTER WHICH

HYMN BY THE CHOIR.

LECTURE IN GERMAN, BY THE REV. W. ARMHOLD,
Teacher of the Congregation.

LECTURE BY MR. JOSIAH COHEN,

INTERMISSION.—To receive Donations.

PRAYER FOR THE GOVERNMENT.

Prayer for the Congregation and all those who have subscribed towards
Building the Synagogue.

HALLELUJAH.—Given Chorus.—During which time the sacred law will
be deposited in the ark.
To conclude with the following

ODE.

Universal Lord! who the sceptre swayed
Ere creation's first wondrous form was fram'd;
When by his will divine all things were made;
Then, King ! Almighty! was his name proclaimed;
When all shall cease, and this world's system o'er,
Tremendously He then alone will reign.
Who was, who is, and who will evermore
In glory most refulgent still remain.
Sole God ! unequalled and beyond compare;
Without division or associate;
Without commencing date, or final year,
Omnipotent He reigns in awful state.
He is my God, my living Redeemer,
My Sheltering Rock in misfortune's hour,
My Standard, my Refuge and Protector;
My lot's disposer, when I seek his power.
Into his hands my spirit I consign,
While wrapt in sleep, that I again awake,
And with my spirit, my body I resign ;—
The Lord with me: no fears my soul can shake.

Dedication Program of 1862

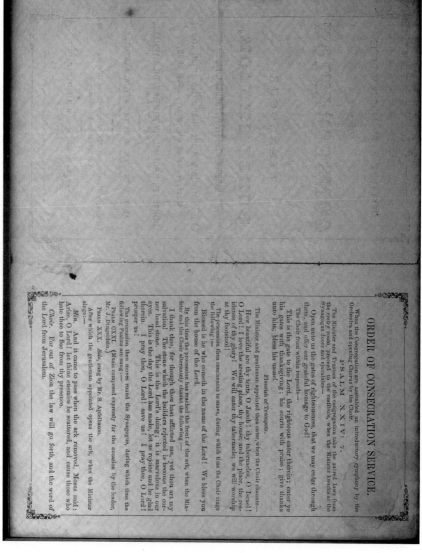

Dedication Program of 1862

Rededication Program of 1888

The new building had 800 seats on the ground floor and 200 seats in the balcony. According to the history of the congregation written by Marcus L. Aaron on the occasion of the 120th anniversary in 1976:

> The new structure at the old location was a compromise to meet the needs of the Congregation at a time when most of the members lived in Allegheny and would have preferred to have the Temple on the north side of the river—a solution which would have been wholly unacceptable to those who saw the East End as the future center of the Jewish Community.[12]

The new 8th Street sanctuary and school cost $100,000. At the dedication ceremony pews were auctioned off, raising $122,000, that cleared all debt.[13] President Abraham Lippman and Secretary Charles Zeugschmidt signed beautifully engraved certificates of ownership. The organization of the congregation's physical spaces of worship based on an aristocracy of wealth was to last another 21 years before it was abolished.

The dedication of the new sanctuary, on the evening of September 6, 1901, was the subject of the "Souvenir Dedicatory Number" of the *Jewish Criterion* of September 6–7, 1901. According to this publication, membership at Rodef Shalom had doubled in the five months since Dr. Levy had been appointed rabbi in April 1901, growing from 128 families to over 300. The "Intellectual Colossus" of the American pulpit, Dr. Emil G. Hirsch of Chicago, delivered the sermon at the dedication. Abraham Lippman, the president, and Samuel Wertheimer, long-time chairman of the Building Committee, received special honors from Dr. Levy as the "Grand Stalwarts of the Congregation." The *Criterion* published the full text of the remarks of each speaker, including those of Samuel Wertheimer, chairman of the Building Committee; Abraham Lippman, president; Rev. Dr. Lippman Mayer, rabbi emeritus of the Congregation; J. Leonard Levy, rabbi; Josiah Cohen, vice president of the congregation; Dr. W. J. Holland, Presbyterian minister; and Rev. Dr. Henry Berkowitz from the Rodef Shalom Congregation of Philadelphia. William Armhold, who had led the congregation from

THE LAST SERVICE

Held This Morning in the Eighth St. Jewish Temple.

OLD BUILDING TO BE RAZED.

Costly Church Edifice to Be Erected on its Place at Once.

TOUCHING FAREWELL SERMON.

Last Day in the Old Building.

Pittsburg Leader
Oct. 30, 19

The *Pittsburgh Leader* reports
on the closing of the Eighth Street
Temple 1900

103

1861 to 1865, and now 87 years of age, was present and recognized at the ceremony.[14]

The speakers celebrated the achievement of the new building as an embodiment of the congregation's aspirations for the future. Dr. Berkowitz stated that:

> God's blessing has indeed permitted the Rabbis, officers and members of this congregation to advance from strength to strength to the happy consummation of this hour.... [W]e dedicate it as a Temple of Morality, whence the inspirations of right living shall pass into the hearts and homes of the people, to ennoble and purify...a Temple of Humanity, where its lofty precept of human brotherhood shall...be translated into the practical lessons that make for equality and justice...a Temple of Learning, where the hallowing of education may be like a continual offering on the Altar of Truth.[15]

Samuel Wertheimer thanked Charles Bickel, the architect; Otto Benkart of the firm of James Wherry & Co., the contractors; and William Willet, the artist who furnished all the glass work, including the Memorial Windows.[16] Abraham Lippman reflected that the congregation had grown in 40 years from 35 members and a temple unsatisfactory in its equipment to a congregation of nearly 300 families and a temple magnificent in proportions and complete in appointments. Like Josiah Cohen at the 1862 dedication of the first synagogue on the site, Mr. Lippman placed the event in the context of the welfare of the entire nation. Josiah Cohen had noted the horrors of the Civil War in stark contrast to the joyful occasion on March 20, 1862:

> Beneath this general joy, beneath the rose-like tint which catches our eye at every corner, a thorn which though hidden by the occasion, I deem it my duty to bring to light...the thunder tones of Sumter gave birth to one of the bloodiest pictures on the page of time....[17]

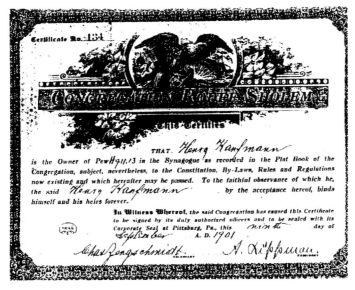

Pew Certificate of Rodef Sholem 1901

Temple on Eighth Street, 1901

105

Mr. Lippman spoke of the peace and tranquility of 1901:

> Upon the occasion of the dedication of the first Temple, sadness filled this broad land of ours, and war clouds were lowering on the horizon of our country's welfare. Today we see on all sides, however, only peace, contentment, prosperity and the horoscope of the future shadows forth for us only the choicest blessings of life. What a wondrous change in national affairs have these intervening years wrought, and what a corresponding and proportionate improvement in our congregational life have these years brought about. And for all these bettered conditions, for this magnificent house of worship we have to thank the munificence of a generous Jewish community, and the labors and energy of our best citizens.[18]

The Congregation was outgrowing its new building as it was being built, reaching 300 families at the time of the 1901 dedication and 450 by 1905. Many credited this increase to the new rabbi, J. Leonard Levy, an outgoing and articulate Englishman who made a great impression on the entire Pittsburgh community and beyond.[19]

In December 1904 the congregation agreed to sell the 8th Street property and new building to its neighbor, the Second Presbyterian Church, whose facilities it had used while the new building was being built.[20] The congregation continued to use its former 8th Street building as guests of the church on Saturdays and holy days, with Sunday services held at the Carnegie Hall on the North Side (now the Pittsburgh Public Theater)[21] while it constructed a new facility on Fifth Avenue in the Oakland section of Pittsburgh.[22] The 8th Street building continued in use as a church until the dissolution of the Second Presbyterian Church on December 31, 1959. The building was photographed in 1960 before its demolition, and a large print of this photograph hangs in the Temple hallway.[23]

The congregation saw the Oakland and Shadyside of 1904 as the most desirable cultural and residential area of Pittsburgh.[24] The neighborhood surrounding the future temple site was one of large

PROGRAMME of a Competition for the Selection of an Architect for the Synagogue of the Rodef Shalom Congregation, Pittsburgh, Pennsylvania

PART I

General Statement

Program for the architect
selection for the Fifth
Avenue Temple

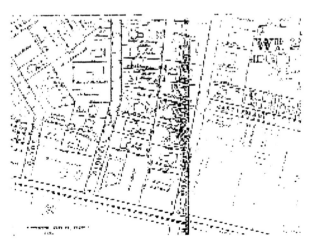

Fifth Avenue site plan 1904

homes on large lots.[25] The street names for Morewood, Fifth, Castleman, and Clyde remain the same. Bidwell became Devonshire between 1904 and 1911. In 1904, according to the Plat, an Electric Road (trolley) ran along Fifth Avenue.[26] Families on Fifth included Ferguson, Guffey, Collard, and W.B. Negley between Morewood and Amberson, and L. J. Herron between Bidwell and Clyde.

Bernard Rafferty owned the vacant lot in the middle of the Fifth Avenue block between Morewood and Bidwell. This lot was the first Fifth Avenue property acquired for the congregation in 1905. The lot measured 127 feet along Fifth Avenue, with a depth of 238 feet, almost a perfect rectangle. Bernard Rafferty had purchased the property from Samuel Keys on November 7, 1883, but died on July 6, 1891, without ever building on the lot. The lot remained in his estate until his executors, Gilbert T. Rafferty of New York and Charles Donnelly of Pittsburgh, deeded the parcel to Abraham Lippman, "Trustee for The Rodef Sholem Congregation," on April 22, 1905, for the sum of $60,000, with a purchase money mortgage to the executors of the Bernard Rafferty estate of $30,000.[27] Abraham Lippman held the Rafferty property as Trustee until December 18, 1905, when he deeded it to "The Rodef Sholem Congregation" in consideration of $5 and the assumption of the $30,000 mortgage.[28]

The congregation wasted no time in preparing for construction on the Fifth Avenue property. By June 12, 1905, the Building Committee, chaired by Marcus Aaron, presented a "Programme of a Competition for the Selection of an Architect for the Synagogue of the Rodef Sholem Congregation, Pittsburgh, Pennsylvania."[29] The "Programme" listed in numbered paragraphs the requirements for the new "institutional church." The primary emphasis was on provisions for public worship, but the structure was also to be "suitable for other functions in the fields of educational, charitable, and social work." Among the mandatory features were the repository for the Torah, 3 feet wide, 5 feet high, and placed 3 feet 6 inches above the step from the pulpit platform; a full pipe organ with choir gallery 10 feet deep and 20 feet "broad," and an auditorium seating 1,450 with no more

Architectural renderings by Henry Hornbostel 1906

than 350 in a rear gallery. The seat widths were to be 20 inches on the main floor and 19 inches in the gallery; the central aisle was to be no less than 5 feet wide, the space from the front seats to the pulpit platform was to be no less than 8 feet, and no other aisle was to be less than 3 feet wide.

The "Programme" specified the nature and size of the Sunday School classrooms, the "minister's study" of 250 square feet, and a Sunday School auditorium to seat 250, expanding to 500 by opening partitions. It further called for an architectural style that was to be neither Gothic nor Moorish, but was to "have a character of simplicity, depending for effect upon excellence of line and general proportion."[30] The four Memorial Windows from the 1901 8th Street Temple were to be preserved, to be viewed from the sanctuary in a setting suitable for the display of stained glass. The building was to be designed for the contingency that the adjoining lots would be ultimately occupied by buildings, such as apartment houses—perhaps one of the reasons for the lighted inner dome. Construction and finish were to be inexpensive, but sound and in good taste, with external walls of brick and terra cotta, hardwood trim, tinted plaster surfaces, windows filled with leaded glass of simple pattern, and heating by steam and forced ventilation.[31]

The cost was not to exceed $150,000, and the design could not exceed 1 million cubic feet. Lastly, the "Programme" contained a Plan of Site and schematic of the 8th Street Temple's Memorial Windows to be incorporated into the structure.

The project was awarded to Palmer & Hornbostel of New York. Henry Hornbostel had designed Carnegie Institute of Technology for Andrew Carnegie and, later, the Soldiers and Sailors Memorial, the City-County Building, Grant Building, and Smithfield Street Congregational Church. Of all these Pittsburgh landmarks, the Rodef Shalom Temple may well be his most beautiful and unique creation. He proposed for the new temple bricks of local clay, handmade tiles, and a double dome 90 feet in diameter, the first of its size to be built without structural steel. The stained glass window in the dome, later called the "Eye of God," would filter light dramatically into the sanctuary. The 1907 Kimball organ is the only one of its kind still in use.[32] Sheet 1 of the Hornbostel drawings shows the overall plan. The 1906 Hornbostel architectural rendering is remarkably close to the finished building.

The American Architect of March 18, 1908, discussed the Palmer & Hornbostel design. According to the article, the dome was patterned upon Santa Sophia of Constantinople, a Christian church turned Turkish mosque, but with the spherical dome changed to a square type, said to be the largest of its kind in existence:

> The dome consists of two intersecting barrel vaults joined at the corners by groins which meet at the apex. The main arches of the dome are broken at the top to allow for a central skylight. The expansive white walls are finished in cream colored Kittanning brick, with terra cotta trim. This trim, which is in the form of a band, below the parapet, about the cheneau at the base of the dome and in the decorations at the main entrance doorways is straw-colored, picked out with blue, yellow and white decorations. The building consists of an auditorium 92 feet square, with an adjoining wing, which is used for the Sunday School and other purposes. The dome which surmounts the auditorium is built of Guastavino structural tile, and is made up of a double shell. The height from the floor of the auditorium to the inner dome is 79 feet. The roof is covered with Greek Pan tile, the greenish shade of which give an effective color contrast.
>
> The interior of the auditorium is interesting on account of the dark-stained oak paneling which surrounds the room. The decoration is in gold leaf. Above the paneling the interior is plastered in untinted sand finish. It is intended at some time to finish this in stucco. The chandeliers are of gilded wood, with decoration picked out in blue enamel. Their spread is about nine feet. The seating capacity of the room, inclusive of the gallery, is about 1,400. The organ, which is said to be the third largest in the country, has 72 stops.[33]

Two contemporary assessments of Hornbostel's Rodef Shalom Temple are offered by Franklin Toker and Walter C. Kidney. Franklin Toker, an associate professor of architecture at Carnegie Mellon University in 1980, was instrumental in obtaining the designation of

111

the Temple Sanctuary in the National Register of Historic Places. Professor Toker is quoted in "Historic Landmark," which appeared in *The Pittsburgh Press* of May 25, 1980:

> The Temple Sanctuary is one of the two or three first products of the Beaux Art movement in Pittsburgh, which was popular in the United States between 1900 and 1935. Such monumental structures took as a starting point the expression of an institution's purpose, and was *[sic]* designed to be impressive to the public and add status and respect to the institutions which would occupy them such as religious buildings, colleges, and banks. The Temple has curved walls taken from Roman architecture, two vestibules and two sets of impressive doors opening to the unique jewel-box sanctuary. The outside dome creates a monument for the city, the other, inside, is for the congregation, like St. Peter's in Rome.
>
> The inside dome is framed in theatrical looking electric lights which derive from the influence of architect Louis Sullivan, mentor of Frank Lloyd Wright. Hornbostel was one of the first architects to use industrial yellow brick, but wrapped it in bands of color through the use of terra cotta trim. The building suggests a diadem or tiara because of the jewel-like lights around the skylight.
>
> Hornbostel had great leeway, since designers of synagogues are not bound by a recognizable style of Jewish architecture as are designers of churches and mosques. Hornbostel created a unique building by focusing on the congregation itself. He is saying what is important are the worshipers, whom he puts under the dome and encloses in the bands.[34]

In his 1985 survey of Pittsburgh architecture, Walter C. Kidney described Hornbostel's work on the Rodef Shalom Temple:

> Using his favorite material, cream-colored brick and terra cotta, he created a compact, massive structure that appears as a simple enclosure of the inner spaces. To dramatize the skyline of the building, yet emphasize the space within, he covered the temple itself with a great Louvre dome of cream-colored terra cotta ribs and green roof tiles. To enliven the brick wall surfaces, he inserted bands of terra cotta that serve as well to tie together details that might otherwise have seemed to drift in such large plain areas.

Rodef Shalom Temple with the school building 1908

Levy Hall construction
1938

Levy Hall 1939

113

At the entrance he made very early use of polychrome terra cotta—the glazing technique had just been developed — In frames with mingled geometrical and leaf ornament, and over the central doorway he put a pediment with a menorah against a stained-glass window of leaping flames.

Inside, beneath a Guastavino tile vault with a large central skylight, Hornbostel designed a quietly sumptuous interior of mahogany and gilt, focused on an ark in the Ionic order. Lit from above by the skylight, which is framed by lightbulbs, the temple is also lit by six stained-glass windows and blue-and-gold chandeliers.

Rodef Shalom has served two purposes well: as a dignified place of worship and as an ornament to an elegant neighborhood.[35]

The cost to complete the structure was $250,000, substantially more than the mandated $150,000. Even with the sale of the debt-free 8th Street Temple, this expenditure placed the congregation in debt. Construction was completed in 1907, dramatically changing the character of the Fifth Avenue block between Devonshire and Morewood.

In the 1911 Plat Book the footprint of the new Rodef Shalom buildings appeared in the center of the block of Fifth Avenue between Morewood and the recently renamed Devonshire.[36] Roxanna Pinkerton had sold her mansion with the wraparound driveway at the corner of Fifth and Devonshire to E. F. Jackman. Holmes, Beggs, and Stewart still retained their properties. The William Scott property was now held by Fidelity Title and Trust Company. Directly across Fifth Avenue were the properties of L. Dilworth, Forse, R. Miller, Hostetter, and a very large estate of E. T. Edwards. Although the new temple was completed in 1907, at Dr. Levy's request it was not dedicated until 1917, when it had been cleared of debt. Tragically, Dr. Levy died only three days after the final payment had been made.[37] The headline in *The Pittsburgh Dispatch* of April 30, 1917, declared "Rodeph Shalom Edifice Formally Dedicated During Funeral Service of Rabbi." The accompanying article stressed Dr. Levy's determination and described the simple service in his memory. Fifteen thousand people attended the funeral and burial at West View Cemetery. Dr.

Stephen S. Wise of the Free Synagogue of New York conducted the service. Recognizing Dr. Levy's wish that there be no eulogy, he instead spoke of this "Temple which was his shrine of shrines." According to *The Dispatch,* Dr. Wise "gave a sermon which though brief was a most notable utterance by reason of its significance." His concluding remarks linked the dedication ceremony and the memory of Dr. Levy:

> Almost the last earthly tidings to gladden your rabbi's heart was the report of the generosity of the membership of the Congregation at its annual meeting—on Monday night in cancelling the last item of indebtedness, and thus setting the Temple free. The officers and members of the Congregation have empowered me, by this word, formally to dedicate this Temple Rodeph Shalom to the loving worship of Almighty God, the God of Israel, and to the loving service of man, and, in the earthly presence of their teacher and leader, to dedicate this Temple as in his spirit and to his memory, so that for all time it shall be known to you and to your children that the dedication of the House of God is bound up with the life, the service, the memory of Rabbi J. Leonard Levy.

The peace and tranquility of 1901 gave way in 1914 to world war. The congregation, which dedicated its first sanctuary amid the horrors of the Civil War and enjoyed peace at the 1901 dedication of its second sanctuary, now dedicated its third building as the nation entered the First World War. On April 6, 1917, President Wilson, with the concurrence of Congress, declared war on Germany.

Many remember the temple building behind the sanctuary. It was modified in conjunction with the 1938 building program and, except for the chapel, was completely demolished during the 1955 construction. It had served not only as a school but as a community center for the Jewish community in the East End before the construction of the Y.M. & W.H.A. in Oakland. There was a swimming pool and gym with regular swimming and dance classes during the week. The swimming pool was filled in to make a social hall, used for activities such as the Purim Carnival, the meetings of Boy Scout Troop 14, and other temple functions. The half-court basketball court in the old school building remained but was unused.

The elegant, dimly lit, original Falk Library that served as the meeting room for the Board of Trustees could not be preserved.

The assigned pew system that raised the funds for the construction of the new 1901 8th Street Temple came into conflict with the wishes of the great majority of the members as the congregation grew and became more diverse. When the 8th Street Temple was sold in 1905, the pew assigments were transferred to the new temple. The pew certificates were called in, and new and presumably comparable seats were assigned to the certificate holders, as the letter of Henry Kaufmann regarding the return of his certificate illustrates. A bid procedure was issued by the Pew Committee by Order of the Board of Trustees on September 7, 1907.

By 1922 the majority of the congregation found that the organization of worship space by reason of ability to pay reflected an outmoded and discredited concept of aristocracy by financial position. The Board of Trustees had formed a committee in 1921 to study the issue of assigned pews and to make a recommendation. On March 16, 1922, the *Third Report of the Committee on the Unassigned Pew System* was adopted by the Board of Trustees of the congregation. This report, issued in printed booklet form, made a fundamental change in the manner in which the physical spaces of the temple sanctuary would be allotted during worship. Josiah Cohen, now 82, a distinguished judge and president of the congregation, served as ex-officio member of the committee, which was chaired by Louis J. Affelder. The report, in the eloquent style of Judge Cohen, states, in part:

> [We] must unselfishly strike off the shackles of prejudice of habit, however gripping they may have been, and, instead of pew property rights, adopt permanently the free and unassigned pew system....

> In past ages, when the Jew was an outcast, persecuted and despised, there was still an aristocracy among his people, an aristocracy of learning and of faith. This was his only title of nobility. Shall we now, notwithstanding this glorious heritage, substitute that other aristocracy, which among all peoples in all

Temple 1907 skylight and two of four windows taken from 1902 building

ages has been the source of evil and not of good? Shall we in this Congregation adopt this discredited aristocracy, or shall we remain true to that other, which has enabled every Jew in every land to hold up his head, unabashed and unashamed, among the best?

Our Congregation stands at the cross-roads. There are two paths, the one backward, the other forward, backward to old traditions, old prejudices, and old habits, reasonable at the time because of the restricted conditions of the Jew's existence; the other forward, with broad vision, great liberty, and absolute freedom in which to cultivate new ideals for the inculcation and dissemination of a religion knowing no distinctions except those based upon righteousness and justice. This Congregation will not now, on this momentous question, be untrue to itself.

> Judge Josiah Cohen, Ex-Officio
> Dr. Samuel H. Goldenson
> Marcus Aaron
> A. Leo Weil
> Peter Glick
> Louis J. Affelder, Chairman

With the congregation well established and still growing in the 1920s, the Board of Trustees began the slow and difficult project of acquiring the adjoining properties. The fear of apartment house development on adjoining Fifth Avenue lots, as recognized in the 1905 "Programme" of specifications for the sanctuary, as well as the need for an expanded school, school auditorium, social hall, and off-street parking, made the land acquisitions a continuing process. The 1904 Plat shows the surrounding lots that would eventually constitute the present congregational site.

The Beggs family owned the property extending 75 feet along Bidwell, adjoining the Pinkerton property, and extending behind the Rafferty property 205 feet to the Holmes property. Beggs had sold the property to H. W. DuPuy on July 12, 1919.[38] The Union Trust Company, Trustee under the will of Harry Wilfred DuPuy, on June 16, 1922, conveyed the property to William Gardner for $57,500, with a $37,500 mortgage.[39] William Gardner, an intermediary, immediately conveyed the property to the Rodef Shalom Congregation, which

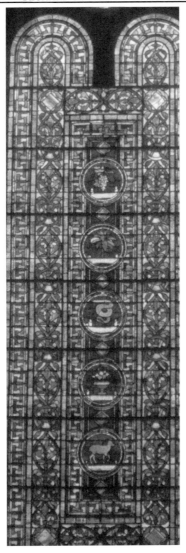

Wndow depicting the symbols of the twelve tribes, added in the 1930s

assumed the mortgage.[40] The 1923 Plat Book reflects this acquisition.[41]

The large house of S. S. and Roxanna Pinkerton loomed with its stone turret to the left of the Rafferty property. The turret is visible in the 1908 photograph of the then recently completed Temple Sanctuary. The Pinkerton property, part of which is now the Biblical Garden, extended 109 feet on Fifth Avenue and 241 feet along Devonshire. The Pinkertons sold their house and lot to Edward F. Jackman on May 3, 1904.[42] On October 29, 1928, the Executors of Edward F. Jackman sold the property to Marcus Aaron for $60,000.[43] He and his wife, Stella, immediately conveyed the property to Rodef Shalom Congregation on November 1, 1928, for $1. The witnesses to the deed were C. G. Bandman and Carrie N. Cohen.[44] The fact that the Rafferty, Beggs, and Jackman properties were acquired through intermediaries suggests that these property owners may have been reluctant to sell to the congregation. The neighborhood was composed of wealthy gentile families, and even the Reform Rodef Shalom Congregation might have been viewed as an intrusion on *their* space.

All property acquisition or thoughts of expansion were shelved with the advent of the Great Depression, which had a serious effect on the congregation, and for a brief time even seemed to threaten its very survival. S. Leo Ruslander, president of the congregation, wrote to the membership on April 3, 1933, requesting back dues: "It may be necessary to close our doors. At the present moment we do not have enough funds on hand to meet our payroll, and the banks will not loan us any more money." According to Mr. Ruslander's autobiography, the members heeded his plea, paid up, and the doors were never closed.[45]

By late 1937 the Great Depression was winding down and the congregation's economic situation had apparently vastly improved. On October 3, 1937, the Board of Trustees set up a special campaign committee to raise funds for a new auditorium to be named the J. Leonard Levy Hall, a small chapel to be made from the present school

Temple and Freehof Hall 1956

Levy Hall with complete stage, seating 550

Cohen Chapel, seating 125

121

auditorium and to be known as the Josiah Cohen Chapel, and a social or community center to be known as the Sisterhood Hall. By October 31, 1937, the committee had raised $325,000, $285,000 of which was pledged in a single evening during which Dr. Goldenson, Dr. Freehof, and Mr. Aaron spoke.[46]

The Board of Trustees rejected the first set of bids totaling $372,000 and placed a cap on the building project of $338,000. Messrs. Ingham and Boyd were the architects with Alfred Marks as associate.[47] On May 1, 1938, the Board approved a contract with Siesel Construction Company. The final cost as reported at the Board meeting of October 9, 1938, was $336,716, which made the new building the first to be erected in the Pittsburgh Jewish community within the budgeted limit. The 1939 Plat Book shows the configuration of the new buildings.[48]

As reported on the front page of *The Pittsburgh Sun-Telegraph,* the construction of the new school building was the subject of a celebration at the Concordia Club on May 24, 1938, a father and son dinner sponsored by the Men's Society (later the Brotherhood) of Rodef Shalom. Football star Marshall Goldberg talked about good sportsmanship and the thrill of big football games. Rabbi Solomon B. Freehof announced that the school building would be finished in time for the opening of school in the fall, and wished the boys and girls of Rodef Shalom well: "May they be happy in a new school building and in its splendid classrooms learn to be good Jews and good citizens." [49] But once again the prospect of a congregational achievement was clouded by world events as German advances on Czechoslovakia coincided with the completion of the new buildings. According to a *Sun-Telegraph* report on the same date as the father and son dinner, new German troop movements occurred on the German side of Czechoslovakia's southern border, and Germany demanded the withdrawal of Czech troops from the Sudeten districts.

It was not until 1949 that the congregation succeeded in acquiring the key corner property at Fifth and Morewood owned by William R. and Nathaniel Holmes. The vacant corner lot measured

Rodef Shalom interior 1966

Sukkot and the harvest of the years

123

187 feet on Fifth and 190 feet along Morewood. The second Holmes lot with house extended 111 feet on Morewood with a depth of 200 feet. These lots were essential to protect the Morewood and Fifth corner from apartment development. On August 15, 1947, the Sterling Land Company, a developer of apartment buildings owned by Arthur McSorley, purchased both Holmes parcels.[50] The long-feared apartment building on the Morewood and Fifth corner seemed imminent. Sterling held the property for more than two years. Through the efforts of Board member David Glick, the congregation succeeded in purchasing the corner property from the Sterling Land Company on December 28, 1949, for $65,000.[51]

The Stewart family owned the property next to the Holmes residence, extending 115 feet north along Morewood and 195 feet west toward Devonshire. Stewart sold to Grant and Carolyn Curry, as shown on the 1939 Plat, who in turn sold the property on May 4, 1954, to Harmain Inc., owned by Louis H. Harvey and Charles W. Mains.[52] On June 30, 1954, Harmain Inc., again an intermediary, conveyed the property to the Rodef Shalom Congregation for $25,050.[53]

By 1954, the general prosperity and the first effects of the Baby Boom brought another major building project. The congregation began raising funds for an additional building on the Holmes property. According to the Minutes of the Board meeting of June 1, 1954, $708,325 had been raised, and the Board authorized the architects to complete the plans for the entire building program. On February 27, 1955, M. L. Aaron, president of the congregation, requested that the Board increase the fund-raising goal to $900,000 "so that we may complete the new building and equip it in a manner worthy of a great Congregation and the high purpose which we seek." The request was approved and contracts were awarded totaling $751,228, exclusive of architects' fees, painting, landscaping, furniture, and kitchen equipment, which would bring the total cost to $900,000.[54] The architects were Alexander Sharove and Harry Lefkowitz.[55]

Falk Library and Board Room 1960s

Rabbi Jacob's study 1970s

At the annual meeting of the congregation on January 22, 1956, President Aaron marked the 100th Anniversary of the congregation. He cited the two central objectives of the congregation, the furtherance of the cause of religion, and the maintenance of a good school:

> We have built a great sanctuary. Now we are engaged in another great undertaking, designed to test the sincerity of our religious purpose. We have added classrooms where young and old may be instructed, libraries where they may come to read and to seek the guidance of the written word, and a great meeting room where the members of this Congregation and their families may gather in rededication to the ancient heritage of our faith.

The dedication services for the new building were held on Friday, May 11, and Saturday, May 12, 1956. As reported at the Board of Trustees meeting of December 16, 1956, even with the new buildings with additional classrooms, registration for the Religious School had to be closed at 1230 students. The enrollment was 534 on Saturday and 692 on Sunday, with 55 regular teachers and 3 teaching specialized courses.

The final property acquisition for the Temple site was completed on May 2, 1961. The Scott family owned the Devonshire lot next to Beggs, which had 82 feet of frontage on Devonshire and a depth of 199 feet, extending to the rear of the Stewart property. William E. and Ruth McCoy acquired this property, which had changed hands several times, from Thomas M. O'Donnell on August 15, 1956.[56] The McCoys sold the property directly to the congregation on May 2, 1961, for $41,600.[57] By 1961, Rodef Shalom had acquired all its present site, which comprised a near square averaging 400 feet on each side: 423 feet along Fifth Avenue, 397 feet along Devonshire, 399 feet between Devonshire and Morewood, and 421 feet from Fifth north along Morewood.[58]

The congregation added an entry vestibule in 1979 and the Biblical Garden in 1986. The June 13, 1979, application for the vestibule showed a 12-by-18-foot enclosure, which was approved by

Restoration of the Temple exterior
1989-1990

the Pittsburgh Zoning Administrator. The vestibule provided a suitable entry from the parking lot.[59] The application of July 29, 1986, for the congregation's Biblical Garden on the Pinkerton/ Jackman parcel on Devonshire included a 6-foot open iron fence and an 18-by-25-foot garden pavilion. The Pittsburgh Zoning Board approved a variance for the fence, and the Zoning Administrator approved the pavilion as an accessory use to a synagogue.[60]

By 1987, the 1907 building as well as the newer school buildings were much in need of repair. Outer and inner walls were cracked, terra cotta tiles were missing, and leaks in the dome-shaped roof of the sanctuary had caused water damage to the interior walls. The structure, however, remained sound. The Building Committee faced the choice of piecemeal repairs to the roof and interior, or a complete restoration, both inside and out. After much debate, the congregation chose restoration. Many of the original drawings for the building were located in the Guastavino archives at Columbia University. Over 150 members of the congregation participated in planning and fundraising. Eight million dollars were raised for the restoration and an additional million for a maintenance fund. The plans for the restoration were drawn by the New York architectural firm of Ehrendrantz, Eckstut & Whitelaw, with UDA Architects of Pittsburgh as consulting architects. Eighty-four drawings on microfilm covering every aspect of the restoration are on file with the Pittsburgh Department of Building Inspection. The general contractor was Jendoco Construction; various subcontractors were also involved.[61]

The project included five phases: roof restoration, sanctuary exterior, windows and marble, exterior of school and Freehof Hall, and the sanctuary interior. The first phase began in June 1989.[62]

The scope of the restoration was all-encompassing and even provided for improvements undreamed of by Henry Hornbostel. Ten new "acoustical clouds," circles of steel and clear glass in a contemporary design, were suspended from the ceiling in the front. With 388 small speakers on the backs of the seats, the original acoustical problems were solved. The original ivory plaster of the

Restoration of the Temple interior
1989-1990

dome interior had been covered with canvas and horsehair faux stone to improve the sound. The new technique permitted the restoration of the ivory plaster. The stained glass dome was removed, cleaned, repaired, and reinstalled, protected by a new skylight.[63]

The restoration plan called for removing and restoring the colored and glazed terra cotta and replacing much of the facing brick. The gold leaf work on the wood paneling and chandeliers was restored with a Dutch metal process. The stained glass windows were cleaned, the seats were reupholstered and padded, and new special handcut carpet was installed. As Rabbi Walter Jacob observed shortly before the rededication, the intent was to restore the temple to its original condition in 1907, but with modern improvements: "In order to preserve the Temple's majestic past, painstaking efforts were made to replicate the building exactly as before."[64]

As part of the restoration project, new stained glass windows by Barney Zeitz were installed in the rear entry vestibule. Zeitz had crafted the windows in the building's interior foyer a few years before. Rabbi Jacob also noted that "the windows take us from the more concrete world (the parking lot) to the abstract." Zeitz used a technique of fused and bonded glass that offers the optical quality of seeing outside the glass while giving the effect of stained glass.[65]

The restoration project was marred by the death on August 16, 1990 of Paul Shumaker, a carpenter who was crushed when a load of wooden planks weighing 1000 pounds fell from a crane. The planks were to be used to repair the fire damage from an electrical fire of July 3, 1990, that caused $250,000 in damage to the foyer, women's rest room, and balcony. The fire began in an enclosure between the first and second floor; because that area was destroyed, it was impossible to determine whether the restoration work caused the fire.[66] During the first use of the restored sanctuary on Rosh Hashana eve, September 20, 1990, Rabbi Jacob paid tribute to Paul Shumaker, asked the congregation to bow their heads in silent tribute, and declared "may his memory continue as a blessing."[67]

Restoration of the Temple chandeliers
1989-1990

The fire at the end of the restoration project 1990

The formal rededication occurred at the Sukkot Service on the evening of October 3, 1990. President Marvin Josephs recognized those who had made the restoration possible. Dr. Walter Jacob addressed the congregation on this dedicatory occasion, and, like Josiah Cohen in 1862 and Abraham Lippman in 1901, placed the occasion in the context of the times:

> This of course is a time of harvests, of a very rich harvest, and we not only thank God, but every one of you, the leaders who are on the pulpit today and hundreds of others who in so many ways have contributed to this wonderful sanctuary. It is a dream realized, an ideal attained, and in our life we realize very few dreams, but this is one of them, and we should feel proud as did our ancestors in 1907 when this sanctuary was completed.

> It is difficult for us to recapture that spirit. 1907 is so long ago, but it was a time of marvelous optimism. It was a time when we and the nation around us felt that the Messianic Age was around the corner. When it became necessary to fight a war a few years later, it was to be a war to end all wars. When that was over, the League of Nations was founded out of complete idealism. So it was a time of marvelous idealism, and that idealism of course did not last through the whole century. This has been a century filled with terror and war and destruction, but now at the end of the century perhaps we can recapture some of that spirit.

Rabbi Mark Staitman spoke of the building as a source of identity for the congregants:

> When the fire broke out at Temple, and many of us stood across the street, I listened to the comments that people made. Not just you members of the Congregation, but people in the community, neighbors, people passing by, people who had heard of the fire on the radio and came.

> There was a sense of loss in the community because, as people said, this building represents the history of our community. It is one of those historical landmarks that gives us a sense of rootedness. It represents the kind of hard work that has always been a part of our community. It was important for us to restore this sanctuary because this building represents that kind of history which defines who and what we are. Restoring and maintaining this

The Temple 1991

133

building is a part of that which defines who we are, and has added to the aesthetic quality of the community. To do it in a way such that as people walk in they are truly inspired. This sanctuary is in a sense a way of talking about beauty which inspires us to know our potential.

The Rodef Shalom Congregation has defined itself by its physical spaces, the choice of its locations, and the design of its buildings. In turn, this has created an ambience of place, a dignity of structure, and a beauty of design and execution that has permeated and inspired every aspect of its congregational life. The congregational leaders commemorated the creation of new buildings with dedication ceremonies. They celebrated the new or restored edifices as embodiments of the purpose of the institution in the context of the greater community.

The "joyful surroundings" of the 1862 dedication contrasted with "the gloomy scenes of war" (Josiah Cohen). The beautiful new building of 1901 harmonized with the "peace, prosperity, and contentment" in the country and the world (Abraham Lippman). The 1901 building was to be a "Temple of Morality and Learning, an inspiration for right living" (Dr. Henry Berkowitz). The 1907 sanctuary was designed to "express the institution's purpose, to engender respect, yet to focus on the Congregation itself, under the dome and enclosed in bands, a simple enclosure of inner space" (Franklin Toker). The sanctuary was identified in 1917 with the life and work of J. Leonard Levy as "his shrine of shrines, dedicated to his loving service and his earthly presence as leader and teacher" (Dr. Stephen S. Wise). Every congregant gained an equal share of the inspiring inner space of the sanctuary with the abolition of the assigned pew system in 1922. "The only aristocracy was one of learning and of faith" (Josiah Cohen). The 1938 building program provided "splendid classrooms where the children would learn to be good Jews and good citizens" (Dr. Solomon B. Freehof). The 1956 expansion of the school to accommodate over 1200 students prompted President M. L. Aaron to note that "we have added classrooms where young and old may be instructed, libraries where they may come to read and seek guidance."

The comprehensive restoration of the sanctuary occasioned a return to the themes of place in the context of history. "The Temple was built in 1907 in a time of marvelous idealism, followed through most of the century by terror, war, and destruction. Now at the end of that century perhaps we can recapture some of that spirit" (Dr. Walter Jacob). "It was important to restore the 1907 sanctuary since it represents the history that defines who and what we are, which inspires us to know our potential" (Rabbi Mark Staitman).

By 1999 it became clear that the education and social activity spaces of the congregation needed to be reworked in order to meet the demands of the next century. Much of the interior layout of the building was changed. A new entrance from the parking area was designed to include an adult learning center; on the first floor it led to several large, informal gathering sites.The Levy Hall was reconfigured into a medium size synagogue which could also be used for lectures and concerts. A new and much larger library as well as a reference library was created. A gallery to display our growing collection of Judaica was added along with a series of multi-purpose and meeting rooms. For the first time an archive area was incorporated. Proper accomodations for our growing pre-school along with a renovated playground were created. The Sisterhood rooms were expanded as was the Gift Corner along with office space. A new kitchen was installed and the building's mechanical, heating and cooling system were overhauled. A series of elevators and sloped walkways made the entire building handicapped accessible. (This paragraph along with the pictures on the next pages have been added by the editor.)

The physical spaces of the Rodef Shalom Congregation in 2005, the Fifth Avenue land and buildings in the Shadyside neighborhood of Pittsburgh, Pennsylvania, are primed and ready to shelter, nurture, and inspire its members in all their congregational pursuits throughout the 21st century.

Adult Education Center
and Entrance
2004

Welcome Center and Commons Area
2004

Lippman Library
2004

Archives
2004

Wechsler Gallery
2004

Levy Hall and Synagogue
2004

Notes

1. Jo Blatt, "Use of Material Culture to Understand Ideas about Women," paper presented at Pennsylvania Humanities Council, Harrisburg, Pennsylvania, October 1995. Recent social historical studies of domestic architecture suggest that the design and organization of interior space in a home can influence the behavior of its inhabitants significantly. This concept has intriguing implications for the study of institutional space as well. See, for example, Dolores Hayden, *Redesigning The American Dream, The Future of Housing, Work and Family Life*, New York, 1984; Dolores Hayden, *The Grand Domestic Revolution: A History of Feminist Designs for American Homes, Neighborhoods, and Cities*, Cambridge, 1981.

2. Marcus L. Aaron, *Rodef Shalom Congregation, One Hundred and Twenty Years*, Pittsburgh, 1976, pp. 1–3. The City of Allegheny, later incorporated into the City of Pittsburgh as the North Side, is set out in maps of the era in *Allegheny Plat Book, Volume 1, Wards 1–8, 12–13, 21–24*, 1907, Plate 7, which shows St. Clair Street in proximity to the baseball field that became Exposition Park, as illustrated.

3. The handwritten copies of the deeds are found in Deed Book Volume (hereinafter DBV) 147, p. 206, and DBV 153, p. 349. The *Atlas of Pittsburgh Plat Book, 1872, Fourth Ward*, pp. 22 and 23, show these parcels with the designation "Hebrew Church," as illustrated. The 1914 Plat Book for Wards 1–6, 9, Plate 4, shows the parcels in greater detail and dimension, but by now the building is designated "2nd Presbyterian Church" to which Rodef Shalom conveyed the property on February 1, 1905, for $150,000, DBV 1378, p. 281. Deed Book Volumes are located on the second floor of the Allegheny County Office Building on Ross Street. The Plat books are on the mezzanine floor of the same building.

4. Aaron, p. 3.

5. Aaron, p. 4, taken from *The Israelite 10*:26, p. 212.

6. The Columbian Council begun by 50 women who met at Rodef Shalom in 1894 (later the National Council of Jewish Women) began a Russian school to teach English, which later merged with the day school at the suggestion of Rabbi Mayer. The combined school peaked at 1400 students and 58 volunteer teachers, *Unsigned History*, p. 2 which has been reproduced in the Appendix.

7. *Israelite 10*:25, p. 204, December 14, 1863.

8. The Pittsburgh Female College was founded in 1854 under the management of the Methodist Episcopal Church. It was not a predecessor to the Presbyterian-established Pennsylvania Female College, which is now Chatham College. Laberta Dysart, *Chatham College, The First Ninety Years*, Pittsburgh, 1959, p. 16.

9. A copy of the program of the event as illustrated. Aaron, p. 5.

10. *The Pittsburg Leader* of October 20, 1900, reports on "The Last Service." The article reported the following: "Dr. L. Mayer concluded the last service with a sermon. He reviewed the history of the congregation, a record of peace and prosperity, and expressed the hope that the same good fortune would attend the church's progress in its new undertaking. During construction of the new building, the Presbyterian church next door was placed at the congregation's disposal by the pastor, Rev. S. Edward Young. The plans for the new temple are being prepared by Architect Bickel. The present Temple, erected 40 years ago, was first presided over by William Armhold, who celebrates his 87th birthday and is said to be a man yet well preserved physically and mentally."

11. *Pittsburg Leader*, October 20, 1900, "The Last Service."

12. Aaron, p. 6.

13. *Unsigned History*, p. 2. According to the a notice of the Pew Committee of September 30, 1907, a pew comprised four seats and ranged in price from $500 to $1000.

14. *Jewish Criterion 13:*14, September 13, 1901, published in Pittsburg and Philadelphia, single copies 5 cents.

15. Ibid., *Jewish Criterion*.

16. The Memorial Windows were moved into the Fifth Avenue Sanctuary. No. 25 of the specifications for the Fifth Avenue Temple states "Four memorial windows, now in the old Temple, are to be preserved in the new."

17. *Israelite 10:*25, p. 204.

18. *Jewish Criterion 13:*14.

19. *Unsigned History*, p. 2.

20. The sale closed on February 1, 1905, by deed from Rodef Scholem Congregation of Pittsburgh to Trustees of the Second Presbyterian Church, DBV 1378, p. 281, for the consideration of $150,000. The Second Presbyterian Church sold its next door building to the Reformed Presbyterian Church. By 1914 both the Christ Methodist Church and the Pittsburgh Female College were gone, replaced by an industrial building and a fire station. The wide promenade of Duquesne Way along the Allegheny River was by 1914 bisected by a railroad.

21. At the time of this writing, 1996; it is now (2002) the Hazlett Theater.

22. Aaron, p. 7.

23. The records of the Pittsburgh Presbytery, 801 Union Avenue on the North Side, reveal that the Second Presbyterian Church voted to dissolve on October 10, 1959, effective December 31, 1959. Jay Budde, Finance Director, provided this information. A 1960 photo shows a much deteriorated structure. One hundred years saw the transformation of this vibrant block of churches and schools to parking lots and a few deteriorated buildings, whereas the Oakland and Shadyside area fulfilled the expectations of the congregational leaders of 1904 who made the decision to move.

24. *Unsigned History,*, p. 2.

25. *Pittsburgh Plat Book,* 1904, Vol. 2, Plate 1, 20th Ward.

26. Note 20.

27. DBV 1414, p. 1.

28. DBV 1420, p. 396.

29. Those who accepted the Committee's invitation to take part were Pittsburgh architects Allison & Allison and Charles Bickel, Albert Kahn of Detroit, and New York architects Palmer & Hornbostel, Pilcher & Tachau, and George B. Post & Sons. Charles Bickel had been the architect for the 8th Street Temple dedicated in 1901.

30. This reflected the principles of Augustus Welby Northmore Pugin (1812–1852), the designer of the British Houses of Parliament and hundreds of cathedrals and churches, that there should be no features about a building that are not necessary for convenience, construction or propriety, and that ornament should be limited to the essential structure of the building. Patrick Nutgens, *The Story of Architecture,* London, 1983, 1995, p. 238. The Hornbostel design, although not Gothic or Moorish, did not strictly comply with this criterion since it contained what Hornbostel termed "completely useless curved walls taken from Roman architecture" as well as bands of color by means of terra cotta trim, double dome, and jewel box lights around the inner dome. Sylvia Sachs, "Historic Landmark," *Pittsburgh Press,* "Sunday Roto", May 25, 1980.

31. The advances in technology of the last twenty years of the 19th century provided perfected central steam mechanical forced-air heat, full electrification of lighting, modern sanitation, and the use of prefabricated standardized materials, including the mechanized manufacture of bricks and tiles. Site operations were mechanized as well, requiring the organization of a building contractor. Structural steel was perfected and

the advances in glass making made large expanses of glass possible. The Crystal Palace built in London in 1851 brought these innovations together to permit classical designs to be adapted to the latest technology. Nutgens, pp. 240–41. The Rodef Shalom buildings of 1907 combined the most modern technology and building techniques with classical design and handcrafted finishing. Hornbostel combined industrial yellow brick with handmade terra cotta trim, theatrical use of electric light bulbs with stained glass and Roman style curved walls, all to create a powerful emotional experience for those entering the Temple.

32. *Unsigned History,* p. 2.

33. "Rodef Sholem Synagogue, Pittsburg, PA., Palmer & Hornbostel, Architects," *American Architect 93:*1682, March 18, 1908, p. 499. The notes to the article supply additional details. The dome was built without steel, but of the Guastavino construction of interlocking tiles. The wing behind the main auditorium contains the Sunday school, assembly room, class room, club room, a library and the minister's study. The main auditorium a wainscot twenty feet high constructed of oak runs entirely around the walls. The seating is individual theater type. "The entrance feature and the frieze that encircles the building, executed by the Atlantic Terra Cotta Co., may be regarded as one of the most successful attempts in this direction that has been accomplished in this country."

34. Sylvia Sachs, "Historic Landmark," *Pittsburgh Press* "Sunday Roto", May 25, 1980, pictorial feature, mounted on a board and under protective plastic in the Temple archives.

35. Walter C. Kidney, *Landmark Architecture, Pittsburgh And Allegheny County,* Pittsburgh, 1985, p. 245. Hornbostel, who was half-Jewish himself, according to Kidney, designed two synagogues in Pittsburgh, Rodef Shalom being the earlier and better known. The other is B'nai Israel, on Negley Avenue. Kidney notes that there is no specifically Hebraic architectural tradition, and most architects of the early twentieth century faced with the problem of a synagogue would have either adapted Islamic motifs or have treated it as a Classical public hall. Hornbostel was more original.

36. The Pittsburgh Plat Book, Vol. 4, 1911, Wards 7, 14, and 15, Plate 5.

37. Aaron, p. 7.

38. DBV 1965, Page 536.

39. DBV 2127, Page 470.

40. DBV 2127, Page 471.

41. Pittsburgh Plat Book, Wards 7, 14, & 15, 1923, Plate 5. The Jackman and Holmes properties remain unchanged since 1911. Across Fifth Avenue, L. Dilworth sold to P.S. Mudge, who substantially enlarged the house.

42. DBV 1329, p. 306.

43. DBV 2358, p. 652.

44. DBV 2367, p. 710.

45. S. Leo Ruslander, *The Life and Times of S. Leo Ruslander (A Quasi-Autobiography)*, Pittsburgh, 1964, pp. 147–48.

46. Minutes of the Board of Trustees Meetings of October 3 and 31, 1937.

47. Unsigned, *Rodef Shalom Restoration Project History*, p. 1.

48. Pittsburgh Plat Book, Wards 7, 14, & 15, Plate 5, 1939. By 1939 the Jackman and Beggs residences were demolished, and the northern portion of the Jackman lot and the Beggs lot contained the J. Leonard Levy Hall and new school building. Across Fifth Avenue, P. S. Mudge had acquired the adjoining property of E. H. Housleman, demolished their house, and built a walled garden. Next to the Mudge walled garden, W. McK. Reed had sold the large property for the Devonshire Road subdivision.

49. *Pittsburgh Sun-Telegraph 22:*112, May 24, 1938, p. 1.

50. DBV 2961, p. 472.

51. The Minutes of a Special Meeting of the Board of Trustees of November 3, 1949, reflect that David Glick, acting for the congregation, obtained an agreement of sale for the Holmes property from Sterling Land for $65,000. The membership approved the purchase at a special meeting of December 18, 1949. The deal closed and the deed was recorded on December 28, 1949, DBV 3086, p. 30.

52. DBV 3342, p. 92.

53. Ibid.

54. At about the same time Rabbi Freehof had become impressed with a young rabbinic student at the Hebrew Union College. At the Board Meeting of March 8, 1955, President M. L. Aaron reported that Dr. Freehof had engaged, subject to Board approval, a young man by the name of Walter Jacob to serve as assistant rabbi from March 15 to July 31 at an annual salary of $7000. Mr. Jacob was a senior at Hebrew Union College in Cincinnati and would be ordained the first week in June. He was to

serve in the military as a chaplain beginning in August. The Board gave its sanction to Dr. Freehof's action and Rabbi Jacob was elected as assistant rabbi. Meanwhile, pledges to the building fund had reached $815,000.

55. Unsigned, *Rodef Shalom Restoration Project History,* p. 1.

56. DBV 3529, p. 285.

57. DBV 3903, p. 496.

58. Dr. Jack N. Ochs, Professor of Economics at The University of Pittsburgh, has made the following rough estimates of the current cost for land and buildings by use of historical records on construction costs and the increase in the Consumer Price Index.

Herron property, 1860—$4000	$250,000
Herron property, 1862—$975	61,000
Sale of 8th Street Temple, 1905—$150,000	5,300,000
Rafferty property, 1905—$60,000	2,400,000
Temple construction, 1905–07—$250,000	8,800,000
Beggs property, 1922—$57,500	860,000
Building construction, 1938—$336,716	4,100,000
Holmes property, 1949—$65,000	400,000
Stewart property, 1954—$25,050	138,000
Building construction, 1955—$900,000	4,700,000
McCoy property, 1961—$41,600	205,000

The 1990 restoration at a cost of $8 million with a $1 million maintenance fund is equivalent in translated dollars to the original 1905 cost. According to Dr. Ochs, the investment is fully justified from an economic standpoint, assuming the restored building is as good as new with no restoration needed for another 85 years. Jack N. Ochs, Ph.D., Letter of March 28, 1996.

59. The Pittsburgh Zoning office on the Third Floor of 200 Ross Street, downtown, has records on the Temple going back only to 1968. Mayor Pete Flaherty ordered all earlier records destroyed as an economy measure. Only ledger books of building permit applications exist for the years 1873 through 1916. These are on microfilm in the Special Collections of Hillman Library of the University of Pittsburgh, third floor.

60. The plans are in the office of Building Inspection on the same floor of 200 Ross Street, on microfilm. These go back with regard to the Rodef Shalom property only to 1979.

61. Unsigned, *Rodef Shalom Restoration Project,* p. 2.

62. The first 28 drawings were filed with the Department of Building Inspection on June 20, 1989. Sixty-five more drawings were filed on January 9, 1990, four more on August 20, 1990, and the final fifteen on January 31, 1991.

63. Patricia Lowry, *The Pittsburgh Press,* September 20, 1990.

64. Iris M. Samson, *Jewish Chronicle,* "Modern Techniques Help Restore Beautiful Past," September 27, 1990.

65. Ibid.

66. *Pittsburgh Post-Gazette,* July 4, 1990, and August 10, 1990.

67. *Pittsburgh Post-Gazette,* September 21, 1990.

JEWISH IMMIGRANTS TO PITTSBURGH

Eileen Lane

In 1956 on the occasion of Rodef Shalom's centennial, the President of the congregation, Marcus Lester Aaron, compiled a wonderfully informative history[1] that although basically chronological, concentrated on our rabbinic leadership. Aaron's history, the only complete narrative we have, was later reproduced and extended as the basis for a commemorative publication[2] in the year we rededicated our restored sanctuary. Now, through the various events and presentations of this year's celebration, we will have woven a rich tapestry of historical perspectives on the congregation. My topic will offer another thread of our congregational history. It will speak not only to the ethnicity and ethnic diversity of this congregation, but how as individuals and an institution we responded to various waves of Jewish immigration to this country and this city and how that affected our development as a congregation.*

This is an immigrant congregation, an essential though probably not a very startling revelation. Beginning with Dr. Levy, all our rabbis have preached on the subject of all Americans being immigrants. Writing of Dr. Levy, Dr. Jacob said that it was Leonard Levy who made a congregation of Americans from a congregation of immigrants.[3] We need to begin farther back and acknowledge that this was a congregation of immigrants long before Dr. Levy arrived in 1901. We should explore the early immigrant tradition and the origins of this congregation more fully.

As present-oriented Americans, we are selective about our history and think of immigrants in terms of starving Irishmen, boat people, or illegal Hispanics. We know about Ellis Island and the Statue of Liberty, and we concentrate our studies of immigration on the mass migration from Europe that was in full flood from the 1890s until 1924, as the vast majority of American Jews descended from that wave of immigration; they are our immigrant ancestors. That is true for the majority of Rodef Shalom's present-day congregants. Yet Jews also came earlier as immigrants to these shores.

* Some personal comments on writing this essay appear at its end

It was a handful of Sephardic Jews that in 1654 got permission from Peter Stuyvesant to settle in New Amsterdam and became the first Jewish immigrants in America.[4] Up to 1720, it was in the port cities of the eastern seaboard that other Jews, the majority of whom were of Spanish-Portuguese origin, settled, some 300–400 of them.[5] By the time of the Revolutionary War, twenty-five hundred Jews were in America.[6] The majority of these were actually from Central and Eastern Europe, but they accepted the prevailing Sephardic *minhag*. The next wave of immigration was predominantly, but not exclusively, Jews from Germany. It started in the 1820s, when the Jewish population in the United States was about 6,000, and peaked in the 1850s,[7] when economic depression and the repressive aftermath of the continental revolutions of 1848 impelled movement to the prospering American republic. By 1860 the Jewish population in the United States was 150,000.[8] We refer to those Germans as "early settlers," according them a status akin to that of the Mayflower Pilgrims. These were our founders and a generation of immigrants: not one of our congregational founders was native-born. Dr. Freehof said it so well: "Every group is an immigrant group, the difference is only one of date of arrival."[9]

It was really quite late in that wave of German immigration that any established Jewish community was formed in Pittsburgh on a permanent basis. We all learned about Pittsburgh being "The Gateway to the West," and we tend not to put that into any context or time frame. By the 1820s, with the opening of the Erie Canal and, later, the National Road (now Route 40), the gateway to the west for Jewish and other immigrants was to the north and south, actually bypassing Pittsburgh. As a result, other inland cities such as Albany, Cincinnati, Louisville, and Milwaukee had larger and earlier organized Jewish communities than Pittsburgh.[10] Nor was Pittsburgh the original place of settlement for many of Temple's earliest families.[11] They tended to transmigrate to Pittsburgh from their original points of entry, largely for economic reasons and, later, because they had family connections here. The massive fire in Pittsburgh in 1845 further retarded the progress of the city.[12] It was not until the time of the Mexican War, the expansion of the railroad, and the Civil War that

148

Immigrants 1870

Success in the next generation

Pittsburgh's economy, making a transition from a trading to a manufacturing center, really boomed and made the city more hospitable and attractive to immigrants. That transition was reflected in the occupations of the city's Jewish citizens, who moved from trading and peddling into retail shopkeeping and later light manufacturing businesses.

By 1850 the city census showed thirty-five adult Jewish men. The city directory, which listed birthplaces as well as occupation, indicates that Jews were not only of German, but of Prussian-Polish and Russian origin as well.[13] By 1860, four years after Rodef Shalom had been officially chartered, the city had at least 300 Jewish inhabitants.[14]

Given the size of this relatively small Jewish community, the ethnic origins of the earliest immigrant congregants were far more diverse than is generally assumed. Although Jews from Bavaria and southwestern Germany predominated, the pioneer Jews of Pittsburgh were actually from a variety of regions, and some had spent time in other areas of America.[15] Jews emigrated here from the eastern provinces of Germany; they were Prussian and Polish natives who arrived in the mid-1840s, many to escape conscription into the Russian army. There were Dutch and other Sephardic Jews. There were English Jews, some originally from Russia and the continent, who moved here after other points of initial settlement in America. In the 1860s, in the wake of repression following the failure of the Polish insurrection, Jews also emigrated here from Poland and Lithuania.[16]

It is clear that Rodef Shalom's early founders were not *landsmen* from the same town or region, but from diverse places. We all know about the split in the first congregation organized in Pittsburgh, which precipitated Rodef Shalom's founding following the dispute over the hiring of Reverend Armhold. Perhaps less well known is the fact that by 1860 a Prussian-dominated congregation, Beth Israel, and the remaining members of the original bifurcated congregation all came together into the single Rodef Shalom

Immigrants 1890

Sweatshop 1890

DeRoy Brothers 1880s

congregation.[17] At that time there were just too few Jews to adequately support more than one religious body.

Another reason for the merger was to be able to properly finance the construction of a synagogue building on Eighth Street, which would truly establish a visible Jewish presence in the city. So there was unity and compromise, and early on it was evident that this was a congregation of heterogeneous origin. Nevertheless, the Teutonic nature of the congregation prevailed. Temple's 1856 articles of association stated that the founders associated because they were impressed with the necessity for a German religious society and declared that its proceedings should be according to German forms.[18]

What did this mean? This meant using the German language. This meant adopting the Ashkenazic *minhag,* and it implied, under the leadership of the early German-born individuals—Armhold, Naumburg, and Lippman Mayer—worship that was described as reform, having emanated from the reformist thinking that had taken hold in the 1830s in German-Jewish intellectual circles.

Was there an implied exclusivity in this? Certainly not at this point. Even more germane, it wasn't unique. It was the prevailing pattern of synagogues in other regional cities at the time with similar German origins. It was also the prevailing pattern in the contemporary ethnic churches of Pittsburgh, a city with a large German community and experiencing an influx of gentile German immigrants.

In fact, German gave rise to important early interfaith relations, not only informally among congregants and their non-Jewish business associates, but more formally through Dr. Mayer, who was associated with every German-American movement in the city.[19] He spoke on several occasions in German churches. He was a director of the German Home for the Aged, and he founded the first public kindergarten, a German innovation, in Allegheny County.

Social historians tell us that immigrant groups wish initially to be seen on their own terms, not through the eyes of the dominant host culture. Immigrant religion tends to be static, even an idealized holdover from the homeland, which does eventually fade away, but language is one of the longest enduring elements. Nor was Rodef Shalom unique in the Jewish community in this linguistic characteristic. Tree of Life split with Rodef Shalom over matters of religious practice, but its membership was also largely German or German-speaking, and it maintained German as its vernacular language until 1898. Its affiliated school was known as the Hebrew German School Society.[20]

Before Dr. Levy's arrival Rodef Shalom had a diverse immigrant membership, and we see emerging patterns of attitudes and activities relating to even those immigrants who did not affiliate with the congregation, a pattern that in part emanated from the background of our rabbis. It was not until the election of Dr. Staitman in 1997 that this congregation chose an American-born senior rabbi. As a result, it was our rabbis who were perhaps more conscious of and sensitive to immigrants and the congregation's immigrant roots than many of the congregants themselves. (It is curious, too, that Dr. Freehof, himself a native of London, referred to his predecessor, Dr. Levy, also an Englishman, as the last of the important immigrant rabbis in our Reform movement).[21]

The sensitivity to an immigrant experience may explain why all our rabbis have been exceptionally highly regarded and popular with nonmember immigrants. It began with Lippman Mayer and the Eastern European Jews, who came in increasing numbers after 1880. Even though more Orthodox in their orientation, these immigrants had great respect for Dr. Mayer. He raised funds for them, helped find them jobs, encouraged and supported them in setting up their own synagogues, sponsored lectures, and in 1890 founded the Russian school, which met in the Temple basement, where new immigrants were taught English.[22]

Dr. Mayer was concerned not only with the immigrants arriving in Pittsburgh, but with the welfare of Jews throughout the world. His charitable projects included the founding of a Pittsburgh

153

branch of the Alliance Israelite Universelle, which collected money largely from members of Rodef Shalom to be sent to poor Jews elsewhere and to refugees from Russia.[23] Rabbi Mayer was joined and supported in all these activities by members of his congregation. Rodef Shalom members founded and led for many years the first local and overseas philanthropic agencies, among them the Hebrew Benevolent Society and the Hebrew Ladies' Hospital Aid Society. Abraham Lippman was simultaneously president of this congregation and of the Benevolent Society. The funds collected at the High Holiday appeal after 1880 were regularly allocated by the Board to the Benevolent Society and other relief agencies.[24] So, from an early date, both individually and institutionally, this congregation helped those suffering persecution abroad and those who immigrated here to escape those persecutions. These sustained efforts have to speak of more than an elitist attitude or a means to avoid the embarrassment of an influx of unassimilated foreigners.

In 1880 the Jews of Central and Eastern Europe, of the empires of Germany, Austria-Hungary, and Russia, and of the Balkan countries numbered more than 6 million or about 80 percent of the world Jewish population.[25] At that point some 300,000 Jews were in America,[26] approximately 2000 of whom were in Pittsburgh[27] and of which 81 families are recorded as being members of Rodef Shalom.[28]

Over the course of the next 100 years, the Jewish world witnessed a massive shift in its population, resulting in the presence of almost 50 percent of world Jewry in the United States. The beginnings of that shift can be traced to the year 1881 in Russia, when the assassination of Tsar Alexander II was followed by a wave of anti-Jewish rioting. There had been a small emigration from the fringes of the Russian empire before this, but now the heartlands of Russia's Jewish population were struck with a passion to depart. Jewish immigration into the United States, the principal destination of the movement from the outset, suddenly leaped from an unprecedented 8,193 arrivals in 1881 to more than 17,000 the following year.[29] Between 1880 and the end of free immigration in 1925, 2.5 million Jews arrived in the United States.[30]

"The Seekers" - a young people's discussion group
across social lines, organized by Rabbi Levy1910

"The Elites" - a social club reported by
Jewish Criterion 1916

The pogroms following the Tsar's assassination were not the only stimulation for this movement. The situation was compounded by the expulsion of Jews from Moscow in 1890 and Russia's years of war, revolution, and pogroms between 1903 and 1907.

Other causes of the huge migration had less nefarious but equally compelling causes. Probably the most important was a Jewish population explosion in Eastern Europe, generating nearly insoluble questions of sheer physical survival. Economic development failed to provide a sufficient livelihood for Jews, and governmental policies excluded them from newly industrialized cities, kept them off the land, and burdened them with drastically restrictive decrees. The feeling among Jews was that emigration abroad or revolution at home were the only options open to them. The Jews of Rumania, themselves mostly nineteenth-century immigrants from Russia seeking a better economic position, suffered greatly from arbitrary and occasionally violent treatment as aliens without rights.[31] In Austrian Galicia the Jews enjoyed emancipation from 1867, but the economic backwardness of the area fostered the highest emigration rate in Eastern Europe.[32] Facilitating this inclination to leave was the well-developed transportation system, so that by railroad and steamship, the journey to America could take just two weeks. Entry into the United States was virtually free, with barely 1 percent of the arrivals turned away.

The pace of immigration increased with each decade, peaking from 1903–1914 with somewhere near 76,000 arrivals annually.[33] By the end of this period of "Great Immigration," 4.5 million Jews were in the United States. Similarly, the Jewish population of Pittsburgh had grown from 2000 in 1880 to well over 50,000 in 1925.[34] By that time Rodef Shalom's eighty-one families had also grown to close to twelve hundred.[35]

This growth occurred at precisely the time of massive immigrant influx and logically suggests that immigration directly affected this congregation. Why, then, is there seemingly so little direct evidence to support this assumption? On the one hand, I do not think

156

the absence of direct references implies anything negative, and it becomes even more understandable considering the sources I had available. Furthermore, I have the sense that, given the very massiveness of this immigration (not only Jewish; over 10 million immigrants came to the United States during this time),[36] it was more a commonplace than an extraordinary phenomenon. Immigrants were, so to speak, the perpetual background music of the day, and so it was for Jews as well. Moreover, Temple, as a religious institution, was not the primary point of contact for immigrant or resettlement activity; that role belonged to individuals and to a growing number of more secular and community-based social service agencies. That is not to say that members of this congregation were not involved. They were, not only as supporters, but as founders and leaders of those service and philanthropic agencies, but that was separate from the Temple context. Yet even Temple as an institution had its own direct involvement in supporting those activities, for all parts of the established community felt responsible.

We know that the relationship between these Eastern European Jewish immigrants and their German Jewish forerunners was frequently very complex and rather tense, perhaps less so in Pittsburgh than in a city like New York, because the numbers were less overwhelming. The divisive uptown-downtown mentality existed, but it found less overt expression in the context of a religious institution than it did in other social, educational, political, and organizational settings. Moreover, there is no evidence to suggest that Rodef Shalom did not welcome immigrant members. That there were periods in our congregational history when we had closed or restricted membership is a myth. In fact, during only one very limited period in the 1940s was membership purposely closed (though even then with some exceptions) in order to assist the establishment of Temple Sinai.[37] In the earlier period there were indeed factors, including the location of the Temple, some basic religious issues, and economic reasons why Rodef Shalom would not have been universally appealing to immigrants, but no barriers were imposed. In fact, changes at Temple, in its facilities, its rabbis, and its own administrative policies directly and indirectly fostered growth and integration.

Other intrinsic factors also argued for immigrant intake as a source of Rodef Shalom's congregational growth. Eastern Europeans eagerly sought self-improvement, made heroic efforts to be self-sustaining, were driven by a historically conditioned appetite for education, and were strongly attracted by American culture. For a great many immigrants who were rapidly self-supporting, economically and socially upwardly mobile, and anxious to be thoroughly Americanized, the model of Rodef Shalom – established, modern, and Americanized – was increasingly attractive.

This appeal dovetailed with the contemporary direction and philosophy of Reform Judaism and Rabbi Levy. Levy himself was concerned with speeding the process of Americanization and fostering unity within his congregation and the community. From his pulpit he addressed the newest immigrant members of his congregation, offering affirmation of their adoption of a new and vital American Judaism to replace what they had known and practiced in Eastern Europe. At the same time he challenged the perception, which was common at the time, that immigrants caused anti-Semitism, and so he gained acceptance for the new immigrants and helped to integrate them into the congregation.

But let us revisit briefly some of the archival material and assess the environment at Rodef Shalom, how Temple responded to this immigration, and how it was, in turn, influenced by it.

First, what were the issues of the day that the Trustees were addressing? They were, quite simply, conducting straightforward and essential institutional business. The Board was not a debating society discussing world or even local events; they generally met monthly to run a congregation, down to what we might consider the minutiae of reviewing and approving payment for every single bill. They hired rabbis and school teachers and choir members. They somewhat ineptly pensioned off employees. They conducted elections, organized special occasions, supported the work of the Union of American Hebrew Congregations (UAHC), and sent representatives to conferences. They responded to requests and dispensed charitable funds. They

Young immigrants 1890s

Koltin brothers - Louis,
Morris, and Izzie 1910

German immigrants 1930s

159

annually reviewed the membership rolls and the subscriptions of every member, many of whom during several periods of economic recession requested fee adjustments; some even resigning, though a good number rejoined later in more prosperous times. Contrary to popular belief, this congregation struggled financially, and the annual and capital gifts from more affluent members proved essential to the congregation's financial well-being. The point is that the Board wasn't preoccupied with immigrants, but with the internal affairs of Rodef Shalom.

Three significant issues did surface during this period: first, changes in the rabbinate; second, providing facilities as first the Temple was rebuilt downtown and then, within three years of its dedication, required a new building to be started at our present location; and, third, changing from a system of private pew ownership to unassigned pews. These three issues were somewhat interrelated and all have bearing at least indirectly on the subject of immigrants.

When, in 1890, the Board searched for its first associate rabbi (incidentally, it took three years to find and secure a suitable candidate), the preeminent requirement was that he be trained in the English language, a move necessitated by the now exclusively English-speaking children of the founding families.[38] This younger generation needed to be reunited with a synagogue that was becoming foreign to them. English was not Dr. Mayer's preferred language. During the three-year tenure of Rabbi Greenfield as associate rabbi, a Sunday service with English lectures was inaugurated (these Sunday services were revived under Dr. Levy. They were welcomed by a congregation that appreciated their educational and intellectual approach and were held at a time that better accommodated their working week schedule). When Rabbi Greenfield left, he was specifically commended for increasing membership.[39] At the same time, Dr. Mayer was asked to alternate delivery of his Sabbath sermons between the two languages.

When Dr. Mayer retired in 1901, the same year the new downtown Temple was under construction, J. Leonard Levy was hired. Born and educated in England, he obviously met the criteria for a "rabbi at home in the English language."[40] Not only Dr. Levy's language facility, but his exceptional intellect, broad-ranging interests, boundless energies, passion for social justice, and extraordinary oratorical skills brought new life into the congregation.

Within a year the size of Rodef Shalom had doubled, and within three years the congregation had outgrown the thousand-seat sanctuary and its religious school facilities downtown.[41] There was no room for the exponential increase in membership that Levy was attracting. The effort toward acculturation and integration of Judaism and American life promoted under Dr. Levy was in tune with congregational desires and resonated with the well-educated, Americanized, younger generation of future Temple leadership whom Levy cultivated through his "Seekers" group. His efforts must also have been appealing to the new, rapidly assimilating generation of immigrants.

The 1909 visit of President Taft was a stunning recognition of this successful acculturation of Judaism into the mainstream of American life representing, as the minutes record, "the first occasion on which a President of the United States ever occupied a Jewish pulpit and delivered within a Jewish House of Worship an address during Divine Worship."[42]

In 1911 a by-laws revision clearly stated that membership was open to any Israelite who wishes to become a member and goes on to detail the application and approval process.[43] No mention is made of German forms or American citizenship, the latter requirement appearing in a number of Jewish social clubs and organizations at the time. Also, from my reading of the minutes, no applicant was ever rejected. It wasn't until a 1926 by-laws revision that members were to be characterized as "any person of the Jewish faith believing in a liberal or Reform interpretation of Judaism."[44] That was the only test and may actually have been related to an earlier policy change regarding school enrollment by which the Board decided to cease admitting children of nonmembers. I would speculate that the equally phenomenal growth of the religious school must have been fueled by the children of immigrants. The increased membership following the adoption of both these policies confirms both the openness of the congregation to a diversified membership and the increased proclivity toward Reform practices of those immigrants now readily agreeing to join.

It was, finally, Rabbi Goldenson, whose inspiration led to the abolition of the old system of pew ownership. With this change, any sense of elitism gave way to membership on a fully equal, more economically accessible, and democratic basis. The open-pew system also enabled the greatly expanded and expanding membership to be accommodated within the same physical facility. By the time the changeover was accomplished, from 800 families in 1920 the congregation had grown to close to 1200.[45]

Increasing membership was not the only index of Rodef Shalom's relation to the "Great Immigration." Largely because of the involvement of a number of its members, Temple was exceptionally supportive of the work of the Columbian Council, later the National Council of Jewish Women. The Council held all its meetings on Temple premises. The Temple leadership encouraged its social service activities by including its important settlement work with immigrants and its outreach in religious education to the many small immigrant communities through the Southwestern Pennsylvania Religious School Association. The work of the Council further emphasized the establishment and growth of nonreligiously based institutions serving immigrants, in which the vast majority of Rodef Shalom members participated, frequently in founding or leadership roles. Beyond the involvement of members individually, the Temple itself directly supported through institutional allocations or designated fund raising Pittsburgh's Federation of Jewish Philanthropies, various overseas relief agencies, the Hebrew Institute, and a number of immigrant synagogues in the small towns of Western Pennsylvania.

"Gates of the Season" and "Gates of Shabbat" - two of three books translated into Russian by Alex Nayberg, commissioned by Dr. Jacob in 1988

Bilingual Temple Bulletin 1991

Temple leadership trip to Kiev organized by Dr. Staitman 1993

163

The Sisterhood, started in 1906, also raised funds and did social service work directed toward immigrants. One of its earliest projects was providing college scholarships specifically earmarked for Eastern European immigrants.

Perhaps the most significant indicator of how immigrants had affected this congregation was the extent to which Rodef Shalom, its rabbis, and its congregants spoke out against the ever more restrictive government policies that ultimately closed the door to open immigration and thus this chapter of mass migration. The chapter closed, but no subsequent immigration would influence so appreciably the demographics and diversity of this congregation. What also stabilizes at this time is a pattern of response to immigration—a pattern of rabbinic leadership and activism, the response of both individual congregants and the institution itself, and the increasingly sophisticated education of the members around issues of immigration and immigration policy.

Even with the proliferation of secular, community-based agencies involved in immigrant resettlement and acculturation, many immigrants had come to rely on relatives or *landsmen*. This individualized effort was crucial in the early decades of this century; it is not surprising, consequently, that in the 1930s those German Jews who had an opportunity to flee Nazi Germany turned to their American relatives and *landsmen* to "guarantee their entry" into this country. Some of Rodef Shalom's most influential congregational families of German origin were involved in this activity. Yet, again, very little evidence of that effort appears in the Temple records.

As a whole, American Jewry during this period was not sufficiently organized, unified, or politically powerful to halt the Nazi onslaught or influence American policy. Yet congregants like Leon Falk, Jr., before the war, became personally involved in obtaining visas for refugees and supporting efforts to resettle them in the Dominican Republic. Similarly, David Glick, who worked with the National Committee for German Jews, went on extremely dangerous missions to both Germany and South America to negotiate for exit visas and to provide legal assistance to refugees. There is no contemporary account of Glick's missions, and only in 1968, at the time of the dedication of the religious school library in his honor, is this mentioned in the *Bulletin*.[46] Rabbis Goldenson and Freehof, however, aided in part by congregational funds, used both their influence and their connections to bring Jewish intellectuals, scientists, academics, and rabbis to this country, for some of whom they found positions at local universities. Both rabbis spoke out from the pulpit, educating their congregants and interpreting this dark period of Jewish history. Throughout the 1930s and during the war, the *Bulletin* is full of reprints of articles from the Jewish Telegraphic Agency and other sources chronicling the rise of Nazism and its subsequent destruction of European Jewry. Numerous appeals appear for support for refugee relief and, later, for material assistance for those Jews surviving and displaced by the war. Efforts were made to increase refugee quotas before and after the war.

Education went on in the Sunday School and in numerous congregational forums. Confirmands wrote about Nazi persecution in the *Shofar* and were exposed to the first-hand stories of several German refugee youngsters. A passing reference to the Friendship Club (an association of German refugees) indicates that space was given for its meetings, and an exception was made to religious school policy to allow refugee children to enter the school free of charge and at any time during the school year.[47] The congregation also extended free membership to the refugees.[48] Although the immigrants of the 1930s and some of the survivors a decade later did join Rodef Shalom, they did not have any appreciable impact on membership numbers. Most Holocaust survivors found the more orthodox synagogues in Pittsburgh more familiar and attractive. Far more important than the question of membership numbers, however, is the commitment of individual and institutional support evidenced at Rodef Shalom.

The final chapter of Rodef Shalom's history involving immigrants is perhaps the best documented in the source material, but also this wave of immigration from the Soviet Union, starting in the 1970s and continuing to this day, is perhaps most familiar to you.

What is interesting is the repetition of earlier patterns: the provision of English classes for immigrants echoing Dr. Mayer's Russian school, the moving sermons from our pulpit, and the inspired leadership provided by our rabbis; the use of congregational forums to educate our members and the community at large; the direct involvement in specific projects to aid immigrants by our Brotherhood and Sisterhood, as well as by individual congregants; and the raising and allocating of funds earmarked for resettlement efforts here and overseas, in some cases helping the immigrants themselves organize fundraising efforts to assist their Soviet brethren. As in the past, we extended congregational hospitality and membership to these immigrants without charge, but with some variations in the pattern.

As a community we relied initially on a governmental, institutional, and communal approach rather than on individual assistance to these Russian immigrants. Only more recently, because of changes in public policy, have the *landsmen* of these Soviet Jews been required to be more directly involved in resettlement. And advocacy on behalf of these immigrants has now extended to dealing not just with the ability to emigrate or to gain entry into this country, but now with the adverse effects on these immigrants brought about by our government's changes in welfare policies. Even while this immigration continues, albeit at a slower pace, we see the congregation's increasing interest and involvement in not only Jewish life, but in Reform Jewish life developing in the Former Soviet Union. This did not occur in previous periods of immigration.

But perhaps most significantly from my perspective, is that now, unlike previous immigrations, the issues surrounding Soviet Jewry are topics of our Board discussions and minutes. We went so far, on two occasions in the 1980s, as to elect refuseniks as honorary trustees of this congregation in order to give full voice to our solidarity and concern.[49] Perhaps not only have we become more sophisticated, but possibly we recognize that this may well be the last opportunity we have here at Rodef Shalom to record the history of a Jewish immigration movement. And now, with our typewritten minutes, there will be no problem about ink!

*When I chose this topic, I assumed it would be interesting and very straightforward. I knew something about American Jewish history, of which immigration is obviously a key component. I had grown up with a keen sense of my own family's immigrant roots, and I had personal experience. I taught English as a second language to Russian immigrants, and I had been a Jewish immigrant to England for ten years. Very unJewishly, I repatriated and brought with me an immigrant husband and two half-immigrant children. So the idea of delving into the immigrant experience was particularly appealing.

My method, I decided, was to immerse myself in the primary source material. To get the true flavor of what was to be a study of the specific interplay between Rodef Shalom and the various waves of immigration, I would concentrate on the archival material here at Temple. I spent days reading the bound copies of the *Temple Bulletin*, which date to the early 1920s, poring through old issues of the *Shofar*, which we have from the late 1920s. I rummaged in the basement looking at dusty records, sorted through old copies of the *Jewish Criterion* in the Falk Library, and the volumes and pamphlets of collected sermons of our rabbis dating from the turn of the century. The most fun was gaining access to the safe upstairs (not easily arranged) and reading some old cemetery records and the run of Board minutes from 1880 on. How appropriate, I thought, to be sharing office space with a young man who was coordinating the Brotherhood's legal assistance project for immigrants from the former Soviet Union. There I was looking for immigrant history, and there he was advising Vladimir or Marina on the telephone. The reading proved difficult; I was having some trouble deciphering Mr. Affelder's or later Mr. Spear's painstakingly handwritten copperplate script. To tell you the truth, I think one of my most interesting discoveries was about ink. For whatever it is worth, black ink fades a great deal more over time than blue ink, and sadly for my eyes and those of future researchers, blue ink was used very infrequently.

I found it all exceptionally interesting, but when I completed my searching, rather than feeling accomplished, I was still feeling decidedly uninformed. I knew a great deal about the records of this congregation, the chronology of events, the names of the personalities, the significant issues and decisions that preoccupied the Board. I knew next to nothing about immigration, certainly not directly. There was no documentation before 1880, more than likely lost in one of the many episodes of flooding at the old downtown site (probably just as well, as I had assumed they would be in German anyway). I wondered whether it was merely the absence of material or whether that absence was attributable to a negative or pejorative attitude. Was this confirmation of an elitist congregation uncomfortable with the mass immigration of impoverished and uncouth hordes of Eastern European Jews? Furthermore, considering our German origins, why was there so little reference to the arrival of Jews fleeing Hitler in the 1930s or to outreach to the Holocaust survivors who emigrated here after the war? Although there was certainly mention of the more recent activities welcoming and supporting the Soviet Jews, that seemed a bit too little and too late.

167

I started thinking, evaluating what material I did have and speculating on why what I had hoped for and wanted to find was missing. It occurred to me that I was probably looking for the wrong thing and probably imposing my own bias. What I had to do, I came to realize, was to put together a jigsaw puzzle made up of subtle dimensions of inference and fact, and then see what the picture looked like. I would like to share this picture with you, many of the facts and some, at least, of those inferences.

Notes

1. M. L. Aaron, "Rodef Shalom Congregation 1856–1956," 1956.

2. Florence Rosner, "The Past We Inherit, The Future We Create," Pittsburgh, 1989.

3. Solomon Freehof and Vigdor Kavaler, eds., *J. Leonard Levy, Prophetic Voice,* (Pittsburgh: Rodef Shalom Press, 1970), p. 27.

4. *Encyclopedia Judaica,* Jerusalem, Vol. 2, p. 809.

5. Ibid., Vol. 15, p. 1586.

6. Ibid.

7. Ibid., p. 1596.

8. Ibid.

9. Solomon Freehof, *Towards a United World,* New York, 1954, p. 13.

10. Jacob Feldman, *The Jewish Experience in Western Pennsylvania* (Pittsburgh: Historical Society of Western Pennsylvania,1986) p. 30.

11. Corinne Krause, *Isaac W. Frank* (Pittsburgh: Historical Society of Western Pennsylvania, 1984) p. 15.

12. Ibid.

13. Feldman, *The Jewish Experience,* p. 19.

14. *Jewish Criterion,* Pittsburgh, May 31, 1918, p. 98.

15. Feldman, *The Jewish Experience,* p. 34.

16. Ibid., p. 35.

17. Ibid., p. 28.

18. Aaron, *Rodef Shalom*, p. 2.

19. *Jewish Criterion*, p. 24.

20. Ibid., p. 26.

21. Freehof and Kavaler, eds., *J. Leonard Levy* (Pittsburgh: Rodef Shalom Press, 1970). p. 16.

22. *Jewish Criterion*, p. 24.

23. Feldman, *The Jewish Experience*, p. 73.

24. *Minutes Rodef Shalom Congregation*, November 6, 1881.

25. *Encyclopedia Judaica*, Vol. 15, p. 1608.

26. Ibid., p. 1596.

27. Ibid., Vol. 13, p. 568.

28. *Minutes Rodef Shalom*, April 3, 1881.

29. Simon Dubnow, *History of the Jews in Russia and Poland* (Philadelphia:J ewish Publication Society, 1918) Vol.II, p. 373.

30. *Encyclopedia Judaica*, Vol. 15, p. 1608.

31. Ibid.

32. Ibid.

33. Ibid., p. 1611.

34. Feldman, *The Jewish Experience*, p. 137.

35. Aaron, *Rodef Shalom*, p. 8.

36. Henry Feingold, *Zion in America* (New York: 1974) p. 120.

37. *Minutes Rodef Shalom*, October 13, 1946.

38. Ibid., March 30, 1890.

39. Ibid., September 6, 1896.

40. Ibid., March 2, 1901.

41. Aaron, *Rodef Shalom,* p. 7.

42. *Minutes Rodef Shalom,* June 6, 1909.

43. Ibid., March 26, 1911.

44. Ibid., January 11, 1926.

45. Aaron, *Rodef Shalom,* p. 8.

46. *The Temple Bulletin,* Rodef Shalom Congregation, Pittsburgh, January 24, 1968, pp. 3–4.

47. *Minutes Rodef Shalom,* January 28, 1940.

48. Ibid., June 8, 1941.

49. Ibid., April 8, 1986 and March 8, 1988.

AMERICANIZATION
TWO PERIODS IN OUR HISTORY

Susan Friedberg Kalson

Upon approaching this subject, I was struck both by the vastness of the topic and the overwhelming amount of archival material here at Temple. I therefore narrowed my focus to address the question of how two of Rodef Shalom's prominent rabbis dealt with the tension inherent in being "American Jews," Jews who happen to be American, and "Jewish Americans," Americans who happen to be Jewish. How did they advise their congregants on being both devoted Jews and fully participating American citizens? How did they guide the struggle to retain Jewish practice and identity in a country that offered dazzling secular freedom and opportunities? How did they, and their congregants, take their rightful place in a democracy in which they were still only a tiny minority?

To explore these issues, I will focus on two critical periods in our history. First, I will look at the early years of this century and the writings of Rabbi J. Leonard Levy, whose tenure coincided with the great influx of Eastern European immigrants and thus a radical change in the composition of the congregation. Next, I will explore the period of 1938–1945 to see, through the writings of Rabbi Solomon B. Freehof, how the congregation responded to the crisis of Nazism and the Second World War. Finally, I will briefly touch upon the issues that face us today. Having ended the twentieth century, what insight can we gain from our own past that will help us cope with the continuing challenges of being both American and Jewish?

By the time J. Leonard Levy arrived in Pittsburgh in 1901, Rodef Shalom was well established as one of this country's leading Reform congregations. But although the German and Polish Jews who founded the congregation were well into their second and third American generations, Rodef Shalom's orientation was still toward Germany. The English-born Levy became the congregation's first rabbi to preach in English, and he preached not only to the founding families, but also to the newly arriving Eastern European immigrants of a new age. Levy's optimistic, self-confident voice rings through his sermons; his congregants were living at a remarkable time, practicing the best of all possible religions in this best of all possible nations. In Levy's sermons we see his view of America, his attempts to expose his gentile neighbors to his beloved religion and to adapt Jewish practice to fit his new country. As Dr. Freehof once noted, Levy's great achievement was in "taking Judaism out of the backwater and leading it into the mainstream of American life."[1]

Throughout his tenure at Rodef Shalom, Levy took every opportunity to express his gratitude to his adopted country and to assert the role that Jews could play in national life. Levy believed that the United States was built on the same foundation as Judaism, and said that "freedom in America came from Puritans who based their beliefs on 'Old Testament'."[2]

Although he always argued for complete separation of church and state, the relationship that Levy envisioned between Jews and their country was a symbiotic one: America's freedom offered Jews a chance to flourish, not only economically, but as fully integrated citizens of a diverse nation. In turn, given such freedoms, Jews would act as patriots first, for their best interests would be entwined with those of the country.[3]

Levy wanted his congregants to take advantage of the uniquely American opportunity to have individual relationships with their government, rather than being treated as a group as had been true in Europe. Thus, he encouraged voting and denounced the "Jewish vote" as myth: "The true Jew in America will vote . . . for the issues which are apt to advance the best interests of America and humanity."[4] And he encouraged others to follow his lead in speaking out on issues of concern. Even when he felt that the American government could have done better, Levy always couched his criticism in words of glowing praise, "America, representing as she does the flowering of the political ideals of humanity . . . ought not to be confronted . . . with the grave problems that afflict us. We ought to have done better."[5] In America, unprecedented opportunity for real freedom existed, and he was determined that Jews would share in it fully.

Jewish "society" wedding 1920s

Hill district street 1920s

House of Shelter 1900

YMHA - Hill district

One means by which Levy worked to integrate Jews into American communal life, and thus avail themselves of all this country's rich possibilities, was by reaching out to his gentile neighbors. He believed that interacting with non-Jews would diminish anti-Semitism and strengthen the position of Jews in the larger society. As Dr. Freehof wrote in 1967, "Part of his faith was that Judaism could boldly argue its case in the forum of the world and be vindicated."[6] To accomplish this end, Levy spoke frequently at local churches and, in turn, invited Christian clergy to share his pulpit. This practice, which also included the initiation of interdenominational Thanksgiving Services,[7] had its critics, but Levy persisted, and he succeeded in forging real interactions between his congregants and the non-Jewish world around them. The pinnacle of his success came on May 29, 1909, with the visit to the congregation by the President of the United States, William Taft. In that moment, Levy had truly created a congregation of Jewish Americans.

Levy's successes were not without cost, however. Although he steadfastly asserted the primacy of Jewish faith and practice, he, along with many Jews, made choices in those years that dramatically changed the face of Judaism.

> It is only then to be logically expected, now the Jew lives in a new environment, in which freedom is the dominant and characteristic factor, that the Judaism of this time and country should be affected by the spirit of freedom. We may then well speak of an American Judaism, a Judaism that, true to every essential of the old faith, is yet in harmonious accord with the free spirit of this God-blessed land in which we live.[8]

Like many of his contemporaries, Levy took a strongly anti-Zionist stand. In Levy's case, this position grew out of his devotion to the United States. It was true that some Jews, particularly those in Eastern Europe suffered terribly for their faith; this was no reason to seek "to rebuild the city of Jerusalem."[9] Indeed, "our purpose as Jews is not to go back to our old land, but in the new world, to set ourselves on the side of liberty and justice and truth and right. . . This is our country and we need no other."[10] Whether he truly believed that

Milltown 1910

Garment factory 1920

Young workers 1910

all of world Jewry would someday share in the bounty of American life, he clearly felt that Zionism threatened something as precious to him as his Judaism. "As a Jew, I am a member of a religion; as a citizen, I am an American."[11] With Jews in America flourishing, there was no need for any alternative Jewish state.

Much closer to home, Levy also took a position that had great implications for the course of American Judaism. He had come to a congregation in Philadelphia that, like other American Reform congregations, had substituted a Sunday morning service for its Saturday shabbat observance. Levy was greatly concerned with the pressures on Jewish men in this country to work Saturday, and, as he put it, their "legal obligation not to work Sunday."[12] The institutionalization of the Christian Sabbath in American life forced Jews to make a choice between work and Sabbath observance and work inevitably won out. The result was that virtually no men attended services Saturday, only women and children being free to do so, and men were relegated to "receiving religion in concentrated form, twice a year, on New Year's Day and on the Day of Atonement."[13]

To counteract this trend, Levy proposed Sunday services, but in addition to, rather than instead of, the traditional Saturday ritual. He could see no other means of dealing with the problem and felt that it was better that a Jew should worship Sunday than not at all. " It is useless to deny that, for many hundreds of thousands of American Jews, the Sabbath of Israel is dead."[14] Thus a custom was begun, born out of necessity, which, in acknowledging the realities of the American work life, also helped to perpetuate a deference to work over religious practice. As Jews we might well have found liberty and opportunity in the United States. But in becoming Americans, as Levy's eager adoption of Sunday observance showed, we had to sacrifice practices fundamental to the meaning of being a Jew.

Levy's great strength stemmed in part from his unwavering belief that the Jews had as much to give to America as America had to give to the Jews. All the ideals of Judaism could be found in the ideals of this country; our presence could only strengthen our nation. "All we have and all we are will be offered to America – the knight-errant on the field of chivalry, the champion of universal democracy."[15] Levy could not have envisioned a time when American Jewish identity would have become so perfectly enmeshed with the identity of the culture around us that we would be in danger of disappearing all together, a time when we would have offered up so much of ourselves to America that we might assimilate into extinction.

Like Levy, Solomon B. Freehof was an English-born rabbi whose enthusiastic adoption of this country as his own was marked by a deep belief that the ideals of Judaism provided the underpinnings for the creation of the United States. Freehof continued the congregational tradition of outreach to the non-Jewish community and of frequent Sunday sermons on topics relating directly to American life. But Freehof lived in far different times than Levy and confronted challenges unknown in Levy's day.

Freehof was Rabbi of Rodef Shalom from 1934 to 1966 and Rabbi Emeritus until his death in 1990. His brilliant legacy includes volume upon volume of eloquent sermons on a wide range of topics. His writings of the years 1938 to 1945 give a sense of what it meant to be an American and a Jew during the war years and how he struggled to help his congregation cope with the greatest crisis faced by world Jewry since biblical times.

Freehof's writings of this period, in his Sunday sermons and in a weekly column in the Temple Bulletin, follow two distinct but interconnected strands. The first is an enthusiastic, ongoing embrace of this country, of the American system of government and the American way of life. The second is a more anxious series of addresses that focuses on our place as Jews in American life and in the larger world during this time of tremendous vulnerability.

In 1943, Freehof expressed a belief quite similar to that of Levy: the American system of government was a long-awaited realization of God's plan for man, created by founding fathers who "were fully and deeply conscious that their America was expressive of the ancient divine will."[16] But belief in both religion and the righteousness of government were sorely tested during the war years, and Freehof repeatedly returned to his theme in search of a guiding glimmer of hope. In 1939, Freehof railed against the mood of despair that was settling over the nation, turning to the example of Abraham Lincoln to "resurrect" the faith that things would improve, to be reminded that great leadership had once saved the country in time of crisis and could do so again.[17] In 1940, referring to the "shockingly silent" and demoralized American youth,[18] Freehof wrote that the challenge was to help that youth understand "that this country represents the great and final hope of human liberty . . . to revere it is one of the highest sentiments of which modern man is capable."[19]

Freehof saw that the absolute certainty in human progress that had marked Levy's generation so dramatically was being destroyed by the evil of Fascism, and he believed that the Jews could help guide America back to its fundamentally religious and optimistic roots. We must have faith, he wrote in 1941, that "liberty may slumber, but will awaken among all men."[20] Ancient Jews believed "completely in liberty and, therefore, in democracy," which was the "destiny of mankind."[21] By teaching others to overcome the prejudice and hatred aimed now at the whole nation, but in the past so often directed only at them, the Jews could play a special role in helping America beyond its sense of despair and helplessness.[22]

Through religion, Americans could combat the propaganda and prejudice with which Germany fueled its war efforts. Through "interreligious comradeship,"[23] religious prejudice had been wiped out in the United States; this same spirit, infusing a coming together of American government, press, and churches, could defeat war propaganda. Any triumph of evil on the contemporary scene could only be short-lived, for ultimately God would triumph and, as the founding fathers believed, faith in that eventuality could "irradiate our lives."[24]

But if Freehof saw American Jews and Judaism as a beacon for their country, he also touched on a much darker side of American life during this period. How should Jews behave in order to avoid the fate of their European brethren? How should they deal with the anti-Semitism bubbling up even in this land of liberty? Could their behavior, in fact, affect their destiny?

Freehof made clear that German anti-Semitism was far different from that encountered in the United States. Germany had an official "public policy of anti-Semitism," which meant that no matter how German Jews behaved, they would still be the victims of a governmental decree. [25] In the United States, however, anti-Semitism took the form of "certain inchoate, shapeless, vague feelings in the hearts and minds of many. . . . "[26] Because American anti-Semitism was personal rather than official, Freehof believed that the behavior of Jews could in fact "aggravate or allay whatever feeling actually exists."[27] World events had cast a spotlight on Jews everywhere, Jewish publicity was both "abundant and bad,"[28] with Jews repeatedly portrayed as victims and pariahs.[29] "This conspicuousness was dangerous, because "being conspicuous is the basic ground in which anti-Semitism plants the weed that the Jews . . .(are) also conquering and dominant."[30]

To counteract the negative light in which they were thrown, American Jews should behave as modestly and inconspicuously as possible. Jewish groups should avoid publicity rather than seek it out. Jews should spend their money quietly. In business, Jews should act with absolute integrity, giving up "certain advantages that others take."[31]

Furthermore, to avoid the charge that increased Jewish immigration would be burdensome to the nation, Jews must not only take care of their fellow Jews, but extend their philanthropy to the gentile community as well, making sure to spread their generosity well around, rather than confining it to Jewish causes, no matter how desperate.[32] As enthusiastic and optimistic as Freehof's embrace of American life was, the realities of the time were inescapable On the

179

national front, Freehof was working diligently to help bring European rabbis and scholars to safety at Hebrew Union College, and encountering tremendous resistance from the American State Department in the process.[33] At the same time, he was counseling his congregants to avoid drawing unwanted attention to themselves by keeping a low profile, working diligently at being good Americans, and waiting for the storm to blow over. And they should remember always Freehof's optimistic note, "The very fact that we can discuss these little details of behavior proves we are still one family. . ., of Americans."[34]

To mark the high holidays of 1945, Freehof preached two moving sermons on the subject of faith and the future. The end of the war had brought not only peace, but overwhelming grief and the knowledge that an even more "horrific" war was possible in the future.[35] Faith had been drained in gentile Americans and Jews alike. Freehof advised his congregants to turn to the example of the new president, Harry Truman, whose first public statement was "a heartfelt prayer,"[36] and to find again their religious faith. As Jews, he urged them to pray for "a new heart of courage, a new spirit of faith that we may live; and the world, we pray, shall grandly live in the strange future which beckons to us all."[37]

And what of Freehof's "strange future?" While he lived to see American Jews more fully assimilated than anyone in prewar America could have envisioned, what would he think of us today? Our pursuit of the American dream, of the life as fully legitimate citizens that J. Leonard Levy worked to create, has succeeded to a remarkable extent. Members of this congregation now populate the staffs of community hospitals, offices of integrated law firms, and halls of universities. We vote as individuals, we meet with presidents, we interact so easily with our gentile neighbors that we marry them at a rate that threatens our very existence. In the quest for life as "real" Americans, many of us have sacrificed our life as Jews. The problem we face is not the need to blend in, in order to cope with massive immigration as in Levy's day or Fascism and anti-Semitism as in Freehof's. Rather, it is the need to distinguish ourselves as Jews, to

180

Jewish Criterion 1918

DIRECTORY OF JEWISH ACTIVITIES

LADIES' AUXILIARY, JEWISH HOME FOR THE AGED.
Meets every second Wednesday in the month at the Home for the Aged, Breckenridge ave. President, Mrs. Henry Jackson; honorary president, Mrs. Browarsky; secretary, Mrs. M. Streng; vice-president, Mrs. Cass Sunstein; honorary vice-president, Mrs. Ashinsky; treasurer, Mrs. Max Weissberg.

GREATER PITTSBURGH SECTION, COUNCIL OF JEWISH WOMEN.
President, Mrs. Enoch Rauh, 5837 Bartlett st.; vice-presidents, Mrs. C. J. Fechheimer, Mrs. Sol. Fleishman, Mrs. C. M. Igel, Miss Hannah Marks; recording secretary, Mrs. S. Hoffheimer; financial secretary, Mrs. Leon G. Ball; treasurer, Mrs. Henry Finkelpearl; corresponding secretary, Miss Bira F. Stein, 924 Mellon st.

TREE OF LIFE.
Craft avenue, Pittsburgh. Services, Friday evening at sundown; Saturday morning at 9:00 o'clock; Rev. Maurice M. Mazure, Rabbi. Residence, 211 S. Dithridge street. Bell Telephone, Schenley 1645. A. Goldstein, sexton. Phone, Schenley 1584-J.

JERICHO LODGE, NO. 44.
Meets second and fourth Sundays at Century Building, Seventh Street, near Penn Avenue (Elevator Service). President, Harold L. Solomon; vice president, Henry Ravich; secretary, David H. Goldman, 8048 Jenkins Arcade; treasurer, Isaac Arnold.

UNITED HEBREW RELIEF ASSOCIATION.
Aaron Cohen, president; Irvin F. Lehman and Mrs. Josiah Cohen, vice-presidents; Robert Lewin, treasurer; A. J. DeRoy, secretary; Charles I. Cooper, superintendent. Rooms, 602-603 Washington Trust Company Building. Bell 'phone 3034 Grant.

ABRAHAM LIPPMAN LODGE No. 672.
Meets second and fourth Wednesdays at 8 p. m., Mannsmann's Hall, 5911 Penn ave., East End. President, Lou Beigel; vice-president, A. L. Cramer; secretary, M. Weisenthal, 3116 Juliet st.; treasurer, Henry Jena.

HEBREW FREE LOAN ASSOCIATION.
Morris Jackson, president; David H. Goldman and Louis Shomer, vice-presidents; Max Tapolsky, treasurer; Victor Kevey, secretary. Meetings held every Thursday evening at 8 o'clock, at 1220 Wylie avenue, city.

PITTSBURGH HOUSE OF SHELTER.
(1625 Locust St.)
Meets second Sunday of the month at the "Home." Bell 'phone, 2840-J Grant. Honorary president, Mrs. A. Bernstein; president, Mrs. Louis Gordon, Jr.; vice-president, Mrs. George Sapper; recording and corresponding secretary, Mrs. E. N. Finkelhor, No. 6 Forbes Cottage, Forbes street, Bell 'phone, Schenley 2288; treasurer, Mrs. L. G. Osgood.

SISTERHOOD OF RODEPH SHALOM.
President, Mrs. A. C. Lehman; vice president, Mrs. Aaron Cohen; treasurer, Mrs. A. J. Sunstein; recording secretary, Mrs. Joseph Jackson; financial secretary, Mrs. Fred Wolf.

SAAR SHOLEM LODGE, NO. 154.
Saar Sholem Lodge No. 154, I. O. B. B., meets first and third Sundays of each month at 10 a. m., fourth floor Moose Temple, 628 Penn avenue, City. H. A. Cohen, secretary, 24 Kenwood avenue, N. S., City. Bell phone, Cedar 1906-J; Jos. Goodman, acting president, 813 Liberty avenue, City.

MONTEFIORE HOSPITAL, 3000 CENTER AVENUE, PITTSBURGH.
President, Henry Jackson; vice-president, I. W. Frank; vice-president, Marks Browarsky; treasurer, M. Kingsbacher; financial and recording secretary, A. C. Speyer; Mrs. C. Hirsch, Superintendent.

LADIES' AUXILIARY SOCIETY, TREE OF LIFE.
President, Mrs. M. Krieger, 5545 Black st., Hiland 2375-R; vice-president, Mrs. H. M. Frankel; recording secretary, Mrs. M. Saville; financial secretary, Mrs. Simon Davis, Hiland 4388-R; treasurer, Mrs. J. H. Frank.

IRENE KAUFMANN SETTLEMENT.
(1835 Center Avenue, 'Phone 850 Grant.)
President, Louis J. Affelder; vice-president, Isaac W. Frank; treasurer, A. J. Sunstein; secretary, Miss Minnie Affelder; honorary president, Mrs. A. Leo Weil; head resident, Mr. Sidney A. Teller.

J. M. GUSKY HEBREW ORPHANAGE AND HOME.
(Perrysville Ave., North Side.)
President, A. L. Solomon; secretary, Louis Caplan, 328 Frick Building; superintendent, Arnold Deutelbaum; Bell 'phone, 182 Cedar, President, Ladies' Auxiliary Society, Mrs. Josiah Cohen.

HEBREW LADIES' HOSPITAL AID SOCIETY.
Meets the first Sunday of each month at 2 p. m., at the Nurses' Home of the Montefiore Hospital. President, Mrs. B. Davis, 318 Aiken avenue, 'phone, 8975 Hiland; recording and corresponding secretary, Mrs. M. A. Goodstone, 5800 Ellsworth ave., 'phones, Bell 6926 Hiland; P. & A. 1861-X; financial secretary, Mrs. H. N. Finkelhor, No. 6 Forbes Cottage; assistant financial secretary, Mrs. S. Seegman; treasurer, Mrs. Bennett Levy.

JEWISH HOME FOR THE AGED.
Henry Jackson, president; Jos. Kornblum, first vice-president; D. S. Osgood, second vice-president; Rabbi A. M. Ashinsky, honorary president; Marks Browarsky, honorary vice-president; Jacob M. Friedman, treasurer; Manuel Cohen, secretary; Rev. A. J. Newman, superintendent. Bell 'phone, 1520 Schenley; P. & A. 'phone, 2880 Main.

RODEF SHALOM
Fifth and Morewood avenues, Pittsburgh, Pa. Bell Phone, 1740 Schenley. Services Saturday and Sunday mornings at 10:30 o'clock. Jacob I. Meyerovitz, M. A., Acting Rabbi, residence, 5801 Bartlett street, E. E. Telephone, The Temple, or Hiland 6013-J. B. Callomon, superintendent, 553 Melwood street, East End, Pittsburgh. Bell 'phone

181

create anew an identity, a religious practice, a faith, that sets us apart from the non-Jewish world in which we now live so comfortably.

In Freehof's sermons of 1945, we find a call for religious renewal. Perhaps now is the time to answer that call. The threat no longer comes from external forces; instead it is the product of our years of melting away into the great American pot, of heeding too well the message of our rabbis to be good Americans while ignoring their equally potent message to be good Jews. For without the knowledge of our traditions and the practice of our faith we cannot live out the real lesson of both Levy and Freehof for this congregation of American Jews that through our religion we can enrich and strengthen both our country and ourselves.

Notes

1. Solomon B. Freehof and Vigdor W. Kavaler, eds., *J Leonard Levy: Prophetic Voice* (Pittsburgh: Rodef Shalom Press, 1970) p. 20.

2. Ibid., p. 179.

3. Ibid., p. 81.

4. Ibid., p. 83.

5. Ibid., p. 169.

6. Ibid., p. 24.

7. J. Leonard Levy, *President's Annual Report*, 1909.

8. Freehof, op. cit., p. 79.

9. Ibid., p. 56.

10. Ibid., pp. 56-57.

11. Ibid., p. 57.

12. Ibid., p. 52, as expressed here.

13. Ibid., p. 53.

14. Ibid., p. 54.

15. Ibid., p. 37.

16. Solomon B. Freehof, "Our Heaven-Rescued Land," Rodef Shalom Pulpit, *Temple Bulletin*, Vol. 9, No. 7, 1943, p. 36; hereinafter cited as RSP.

17. Freehof, "Is Our Youth Unfit for the Crisis?" RSP, Vol. 6, No. 5, 1940, p. 3.

18. Freehof, "Crisis?" p. 8.

19. Freehof, "Faith Bewildered," RSP, Vol. 7, No. 1, 1941, p. 15.

20. Freehof, "Minds Confused," RSP, Vol. 7, No. 2, 1941, p. 20.

21. Freehof, "Minds," p. 20.

22. Freehof, "Hearts Bowed Down," RSP, Vol. 7, No. 3, 1941, pp. 37-39.

23. Freehof, "How to Defeat Propaganda, " RSP, Vol. 4, No. 7, 1939, p. 45.

24. Freehof, "A Just Cause Wins," RSP, Vol. 9, No .5, 1943, p. 9.

25. Freehof, "To the American Jews: How to Behave," RSP, Vol. 4. No. 6, 1939, p. 20.

26. Ibid., p. 20.

27. Ibid., p. 20.

28. Freehof, "Jews in the Headlines," RSP, Vol. 5, No. 3, 1940, p. 1.

29. Ibid., p. 2.

30. Freehof, "How to Behave," p. 22.

31. Ibid., p. 26.

32. Ibid., pp. 26-30.

33. Michael A. Meyer, "The Refugee Scholars Project of the Hebrew Union College," Bertram Wallace Korn (ed.) *A Bicentennial Festschrift for Jacob Rader Marcus* (New York: KTAV, 1976), pp. 362-72.

34. Freehof, "How to Behave, " p. 30.

35. Freehof, "A New World," RSP, Vol. 12, No. 1, 1945, p. 7.

36. Freehof, "A New Heart," RSP, Vol. 12, No. 2, 1945, p.12.

37. Ibid., p. 15.

THE ZIONIST DEBATE

Barbara Burstin

At the First World Jewish Congress, in 1897, Theodore Herzl called for the establishment of a Jewish state in Palestine. He had been galvanized into action by the raw hatred of Jews he witnessed during the Dreyfus trial in France. If Jews were not accepted in France, the land of the Enlightenment, then where could they find a home? With this move, Herzl initiated the modern Zionist movement that was to culminate in 1948 with the establishment of the state of Israel. Jews were to celebrate the rebirth of the Jewish homeland at the same time that they mourned the overwhelming losses suffered in the Holocaust. For fifty years Zionists had struggled to secure their dream. The road had been clogged with roadblocks set up primarily by the non-Jewish world, but some hurdles were erected by groups in the Jewish world as well. The story of this conflict over Zionism, arguably the most divisive and strident in American Jewish history, is a fascinating chapter in the development of the American Jewish community. Although various traditional Jewish elements opposed Zionism, the ranks of the opponents were filled with those who identified with the Reform movement, led by most, but not all, the Reform rabbis.

Reform Jews saw the world in very different terms than did the Zionists. They were convinced that the future of American Jewry was linked not to some far away Jewish state, but to a spiritual renewal in America and that the mission of the Jews was to bring peace and justice to all, throughout the diaspora, wherever they lived. The world was moving toward a better tomorrow in which Jews would be accepted and able to carry out this mission. They rejected any notion that Jews were insecure, that they needed to separate themselves in their own territory. Nationalism, particularism, separation were not for Jews. They were theologically misguided, and, practically, would create ill feeling among gentiles because they seemed to call into question the loyalty and patriotism of Jews in America. America was the homeland of those Jews in America, their promised land. This profound difference in ideology and outlook was only reinforced by the social and economic gulf between Zionist and Reform adherents in terms of background and class. The Reform movement was the bastion of the older, more established, German Jews in America, whereas Zionism was in the opening decades of the twentieth century the passion of Eastern Europeans and Eastern European immigrants to America. The battle lines were sharply drawn, and people who crossed the divide did so at their own risk.

It is in this context that I want to look at the three rabbis who presided at Rodef Shalom throughout the first half of the twentieth century. J. Leonard Levy led the congregation between 1901 and 1917, when he died suddenly of pneumonia in the influenza epidemic. Samuel Goldenson took over and remained chief rabbi until 1934, when he left to go to Temple Emanuel in New York City. Dr. Solomon B. Freehof was his successor and was the spiritual leader throughout the 1940s and beyond. How did each respond to the challenge of Zionism? These three wise men together spanned the years of the great Zionist debate in America. Their thoughts and comments can be read as expressions of Reform thinking and the changes they saw. They struggled throughout the first half of the twentieth century to confront and reconcile a world that increasingly belittled and mocked their expectations for progress and universal brotherhood. A look back at their responses can afford real insight into the gauntlet Zionism laid down to Reform.

To understand the intellectual climate of Reform Judaism in the late nineteenth century and the foundation on which Reform response to Zionism first rested, an appropriate and fitting place to begin is in Pittsburgh in 1885. That was the year that Kaufmann Kohler issued a call to Reform rabbis, eighteen of whom came, to draw up a statement of principles on Reform Judaism. Dr. Lippman Mayer, who had been called to the pulpit of Rodef Shalom in 1870 and who was to be one of the participants at this gathering, asked the Board of Trustees of Rodef Shalom to cooperate in hosting the conference. The conference itself was held at the decade-old Concordia Club in Allegheny, now known as the North Side. Rabbi David Phillipson, who actually was only twenty-three at the time and the youngest participant at the meeting, recalled in a talk he gave in

Zionist parade 1918

The *Jewish Criterion* 1918

1935 that the Pittsburgh Jewish community was "keyed up to a state of excitement." He described Dr. Mayer as "the genial rabbi" who welcomed his colleagues in a spirit of fine fellowship.

The rabbis in Pittsburgh optimistically looked out at the world through rose-colored glasses and saw in the modern era "the realization of Israel's great messianic hope for the kingdom of truth, justice and peace among all men . . . ." They asserted that Jews "were no longer a nation, but a religious community, and therefore expect neither a return to Palestine . . . , nor the restoration of any of the laws concerning the Jewish state." They said a lot more, too, about their belief that only those moral laws that tend to "elevate and sanctify our lives" are binding and other assertions that infuriated more traditional Jews. One Orthodox rabbi from Baltimore compared the rabbis assembled at Pittsburgh "to pygmies attempting to pull down the Washington monument." Although the Reform platform aroused the ire of many non-Reform Jews in America, it also served to lay the groundwork for the forthcoming battle with Zionists. Just twelve years after the adoption of the Pittsburgh Platform, Theodore Herzl issued his call for a Jewish state. In response to that, the organization of Reform rabbis, the Central Conference of American Rabbis (CCAR), set forth its disapproval of the Zionist objective. The attempts to establish a Jewish state

> show a misunderstanding of Israel's mission, which from the narrow political and rational field has been expanded to the promotion among the whole human race of the broad and universalistic religion first proclaimed by the Jewish prophets. Such attempts do not benefit, but infinitely harm our Jewish brethren where they are still persecuted, by confirming the assertion of their enemies that the Jews are foreigners in the countries in which they are at home, and of which they are everywhere the most loyal and patriotic citizens. We reaffirm that the object of Judaism is not political nor national, but spiritual, and addresses itself to the continuous growth of peace, justice and love in the human race, to a messianic time when all men will recognize that they form one great brotherhood for the establishment of God's kingdom on earth.

The swords were thus drawn.

In Pittsburgh, in 1901, when J. Leonard Levy became rabbi of Rodef Shalom, an active group of Zionists was in the city, cells of Eastern European Jews that had rallied to the cause of Herzl. After the first Zionist Congress held in Basel, Switzerland, in 1897, a group of teenagers organized themselves into the Herzl Club. In April 1898 a group of young men organized the Tiphereth Zion Society, which soon numbered in the hundreds. Other Zionist groups sprang up. The sixth annual convention of the Federation of American Zionists was held in Pittsburgh in 1903, and by 1904 the Zionist Council of Pittsburgh was formed and purchased the Zionist Institute on Center Avenue in the Hill. Zionism was a growing movement in the city.

What was Dr. Levy's response? Was he among the majority of Reform rabbis that opposed political Zionism or was he among the very few Reform rabbis, like Stephen Wise and Judah Magnes, who favored it? In a lecture on Zionism that Rabbi Levy delivered at Rodef Shalom in January 1902, he made his views very clear. He affirmed that the idea of a Jewish home in Palestine was not a dream, "but a nightmare and a regression . . . . To think, that all these ages of struggle, that all these centuries of effort, nobly borne, should terminate by our going back, disheartened, discouraged, broken in spirit and body to Palestine." Yet Levy, like many other Reform rabbis, did not totally dismiss the notion of a spiritual center for Jews in Palestine that had been advocated by Achad Ha'Am:

> If Zionism is an attempt to uplift the Jew, to help him attain the rights of men, if it is an effort to reintroduce the spiritual strength of Judaism to the Jew; if it is an endeavor to make of the Jew a productive laborer; if it is a resolve to colonize the Jew in Palestine and other lands, then Zionists may claim me as a follower. But when it comes to owning Palestine, I dissent.

Levy clearly could not include any nationhood concept in his understanding of what is a Jew. His emphasis was on Judaism as a religion, not on the Jews as a people. He stood firmly on the Pittsburgh Platform. His solution to the torrents of anti-Semitism that Jews in Eastern Europe faced was that Jews must stand and fight and die where they are, if need be, in order to teach men that God is One, that God demands righteousness as the highest expression of religion . . . . Our purpose as Jews is not to go back to our old land, but in the new world, to set ourselves on the side of liberty and justice and truth and right and to teach that aspect of religion which will enable men to accept the Divine Fatherhood and establish a human Brotherhood. Our realm is not Palestine, but a spiritual one. We need no political kingdom, no arms, no special territory of our own, no special country in the Orient.

A 1907 sermon revealed that Levy had not changed his mind:

In all kindness, but in all sincerity, I regard Zionism as the greatest political blunder committed by a section of the Jewish people in two millennia . . . . Zionism is not only not the panacea, but if seriously continued for some years, will as surely divide Israel as the Messianic claims instituted concerning a young Jew nineteen hundred years ago separated our people into opposing camps. I have heard it said, that we, who refuse to countenance this physical, material Zion proposition, are cowards. Politely, but emphatically, we return the compliment to those who utter it. To slink away to Palestine is more cowardly than to face a world in arms. Four thousand years of agonizing are not going to end in ignominious flight back to Palestine. Let those indulge it who will! But as for me and those I may be able to influence, we will die with our faces to the enemy, not with our backs toward them . . . . Israel's destiny is to live in the soul of an uplifted humanity, not to be buried alive in the Orient, even in the glorious city of David! To think that Zionism would provide safety for persecuted Jews was nothing more than a delusive hope.

Levy maintained that view until his death in 1917; yet when he died, among the many, many expressions of condolences was one sent by the Zionist Council of Pittsburgh. The Council took note of the many lectures that Levy had given to various Zionist organizations that he had "most willingly" assisted in the raising of funds for various Zionist enterprises, including the Palestine Welfare Society to provide all kinds of aid to the Jewish people in Palestine. They referred to him as a "self-sacrificing Jewish educator," who by his teaching contributed to "Spiritual Zionism" and noted that he had "assisted the cause of Zionism in many ways though not affiliated with it." To these

Young People's Zionist League
1920

NEXT ZIONIST CONVENTION
IN PITTSBURGH.

For the third time, Pittsburgh will
be host to a Zionist Convention. In
1903 the Sixth Annual Convention of
the American Zionist Organization
was held here. Many in the community will remember the outstanding features of that remarkable convention week, as for instance the "discovery" of Dr. J. L. Magnes, then
a shy boy orator; the memorable and
stirring mass meeting at the Bijou
Theater with Prof. Richard Gottheil
in the chair. Judge Cohen on the program and the mixed choir singing the
Shir Hamalos and the Al Naharos Bo-
vel; the Turner Hall banquet with A.
Leo Weil's toast of "Watchman What
of the Night;" and not least of all,
the great outpouring of the community at the lawn fete at Kenwood
Lawn.

Seven years later, in 1910, the convention paved Pittsburgh a return
visit, the American Zionist Organization having then chosen this city for
the celebration of the Bar Mitzvah

Josiah Cohen and the 1903
Zionist Convention

Pittsburghers, who were by and large Eastern European immigrants, Levy, the spiritual head of the powerful Reform temple of the German Jews, had demonstrated his sympathy for the oppressed no matter where they were from and his concern for Jewish life in Palestine. He gained their appreciation and respect though he never approved of the political goal of a Jewish state.

Samuel Goldenson held the reins at Rodef Shalom from 1917 until 1934. He was a national leader among rabbis, and in 1934 and 1935, he was president of the CCAR. Throughout, Goldenson remained a hardliner on the issue of Zionism. At a time when the anti-Zionist position of the CCAR was coming under increasing attack from within the ranks, with more and more rabbis feeling in sympathy with the Zionist cause, Goldenson held firm to his anti-Zionist view. In 1935 he opposed the so-called "neutrality" resolution that was passed by the CCAR and that for all intents and purposes canceled the anti-Zionist position of the CCAR dating back to the late nineteenth century.

The "neutrality" resolution stated that the acceptance or rejection of the Zionist position should be left to the conscience of the individual members of the CCAR themselves and that the CCAR should take no official position one way or the other. Goldenson acknowledged the great debate that was taking place within the Reform movement over Zionism at a time when Hitler's persecution of the Jews was already fearfully under way. But this debate he felt was nothing less than an attempt to reinterpret the nature of Judaism and "to demote the religion of Israel from the high and exalted place that it has always occupied in the life of the Jew." Although he was sympathetic to the plight of the Jews in Europe facing Hitler, he argued that "the malady is a moral and spiritual one and the cure can only come from raising the general standard of ethical thinking," which he felt rabbis and their Jewish flock must continue to do. He admitted that he was not offering an immediate solution to the problem of virulent anti-Semitism, but that placing a priority on Zionism as a secular pursuit "would only diminish the Jewish spiritual quest which was its paramount mission."

Goldenson not only was concerned with the religious life of Jews in America, but believed that as secular and political values grew stronger in Palestine itself, it would come at the expense of greater spiritual values and that Palestine even run by Jews would become just like any other state. Goldenson's unswerving views against Zionism led him to become, in 1943, one of the early supporters of the only Jewish organization ever established to oppose Zionism, the American Council for Judaism. But this occurred nine years after he left the pulpit at Rodef Shalom.

When Solomon Freehof took over at Rodef Shalom in 1934 he was a rising star in the Reform movement. His participation and leadership in the early 1940s (he was president of the CCAR for two years beginning in 1944) came at the height of the wars between Zionist and anti-Zionist both in the CCAR and in the larger community. Thus, a look at his thinking and action not only is relevant to the history of Rodef Shalom, but also sheds light on the internal struggle within the CCAR and beyond. Freehof's efforts to find a middle ground and calm the troubled waters ironically pitted him against his predecessor at Rodef Shalom, Samuel Goldenson. In 1942, for example, Zionists both within and without the CCAR sought to lobby for the establishment of a Jewish army from Palestine. This army would have lent weight and symbolism to the Zionist campaign for a Jewish state. A resolution in support of this proposed Jewish army was presented at the CCAR convention in 1942. Freehof, as the habitual mediator and unifier, tried to table the whole discussion and have the debate stricken from the record. He believed that no matter which way the vote went, there would be dissension and dissatisfaction that would serve only to divide the CCAR. His resolution to table failed, however, and the CCAR went on to vote in favor of the Jewish army proposal. Goldenson was among the twenty-seven rabbis who wanted to be put on record as opposing the resolution. He fervently believed that voting for such a motion would contradict the officially neutral position on the issue of Zionism that the CCAR had adopted in 1935.

In 1943 both Freehof and Goldenson were involved in the discussion at the Conference on Zionism. The issue had reached such stridency and urgency that a special session was devoted to the subject of the "compatibility of Zionism with Reform Judaism."

The Pittsburgh Platform was clearly no longer the prevailing philosophy of the majority of the Reform rabbis and, in fact, had not been for some time. Zionism was increasingly capturing the imagination of the Reform movement as opinions changed under the crushing weight of the persecution and murder of the Jews in Europe. Moreover, within the ranks of the Reform movement itself were many Eastern European Jews who had never identified with the philosophy and outlook of the older German Jews. At the end of the CCAR session, a committee was appointed to prepare a resolution for the Conference under the chairmanship of Dr. Freehof.

Dr. Freehof presented two resolutions to the Conference. The first stated that the Conference declares that it discerns no essential incompatibility between Reform Judaism and Zionism, no reason why those of its members who give allegiance to Zionism should not have the right to regard themselves as fully within the spirit and purpose of Reform Judaism. That resolution carried the Conference. Freehof and his committee then presented the second resolution, which drew the ire of Rabbi Goldenson, among others. The second resolution called for the dissolution of the American Council for Judaism, which a group of Reform rabbis, including Goldenson, had established in 1943 to oppose the Zionist effort to establish a Jewish state.

Goldenson defended the ACJ, arguing that an organization was needed to counter the "Jewish nationalist philosophy" of Zionists. He protested the charge of treason made against the rabbis who supported the ACJ and argued that, in our democracy, all have a right to their opinions. He argued that the CCAR did not have a moral or legal right to urge the ACJ to disband and that although he, too, was in favor of unity in the ranks, that should not mean total conformity.

Despite his plea, the CCAR adopted the resolution presented by the Freehof committee 137 to 45, with Freehof voting in favor of it. Goldenson, needless to say, was opposed. Freehof, in July 1943, wrote an article for *Liberal Judaism* that affirmed his belief that a Reform rabbi could be either a Zionist or an anti-Zionist as he so chose. He felt such a statement to that effect was necessary at the CCAR to "rectify a wrong" when the Conference in the past had denounced Zionism. He, himself, did not express any personal views on the issue of Zionism. When he went on in the same article to support the call for the dissolution of the ACJ, he again did not take issue with that organization's basic point of view. Rather, he justified his call for dissolution on his belief that the ACJ threatened to split the CCAR along "party lines."

After the war, in November 1945, in two consecutive Sunday morning sermons at Rodef Shalom, Dr. Freehof gave his advice first to the Zionists he knew who were among his congregants and then a week later to the anti-Zionists who were also in his Congregation. In these two talks he revealed much about his own temper and outlook on the issues. In his talk to Zionists, he talked about how Jews are a family, which means they help each other and they also quarrel with each other. He deplored the fact that the quarrel had continued even in the face of the recent tragedy of the Jews during the war in Europe. "Surely the time has come," he pleaded, "for reconciliation, for mutual patience, for overcoming of misunderstandings." He spoke about how for the first time in American Jewish life there was an organized anti-Zionist movement so that now we have both "intense Zionists and ferocious anti-Zionists, and between the two, Jewish communities are being torn apart." He went on to say that although it would be unfair and unrealistic to ask a Zionist to give up his dream, what they should do is tone down their rhetoric. He felt that many non-Zionists became anti-Zionists because of the loud and vociferous protests of the Zionists. But beyond that, when a Zionist speaker gets up and says we must cure the homelessness of the Jewish people, he is not speaking for the American Jew who does not consider himself in exile. For Freehof, that was the rub that was causing such protest by anti-Zionists.

195

What Freehof suggested was an "American Zionism" that would fight for Jewish independence in Palestine but would recognize that "we are part of the American nation and this is our beloved home."

In his talk to the anti-Zionists just a week later, Dr. Freehof began by commenting how "almost every fight which we have had in the last twenty-five years has been, at bottom, a Zionist/anti-Zionist fight, with no compromise seemingly possible. Every great drive, every dispute in the welfare funds, every argument in every city on communal matters has the immovable Zionist and the unchangeable anti-Zionist." He deplored what he called extremism on both sides. He argued that the number of "reasoned anti-Zionists or reasoned Zionists are few" and that there was a shrill level of debate. He complimented the Zionists, calling them remarkable and extraordinary, but cautioning that their style had to be reckoned with. "If your arteries are perfectly flexible and your nerves calm and glacial, if you can stand all sorts of wear and tear, be an active Zionist . . . . They use up 100% of nerve energy in the most bitter political disputes, and after that, by some miracle, they have another 100% left for Zionist work." The tragedy with the anti-Zionist movement is that all it has done so far is "to stick out its tongue at the Zionist movement.... It needs something to do other than just writing with chalk on the board fences of modern Jewish life. It needs a task, a task not for itself but for world Jewry."

According to Freehof, Zionists needed "to modify their philosophy"; anti-Zionists needed "to modify their program." Zionists needed "to bring America into their philosophy," and anti-Zionists needed to bring what he called "world Israel" into their program. "Once you have an anti-Zionist movement which has a specific task for world Jewry, a task pursued positively, you will have a movement worthy of great respect and a movement that will make life more liveable for all of us . . . . Let each do its positive work and leave the decisions to history." In conclusion he called for an end to the great acrimony between the Zionists and the anti-Zionists. Both were

Rodef Shalom Israel Bond Dinner 1970

A portion of the Temple's Israel tour 1980s

necessary. The important thing was that American Jewry be united, since the health and vitality of world Jewry depended upon America.

Thus, Solomon Freehof tried to pick up the pieces after the Zionist controversy had torn American Jewry apart. He gave credit to both sides, spoke kind words to both sides, criticized both sides. The bottom line for him was that American Jewish community come together to get on with the important task of leading the rehabilitation of world Jewry in the wake of the Holocaust. He had witnessed first hand the rancor and division this issue had stirred for so long within the ranks of the Reform movement and in the American Jewish community. In the CCAR and in his own congregation in Pittsburgh, he sought to steer a middle course and build a bridge over troubled waters. He viewed the zealotry of both sides with disapproval.

Dr. Freehof, for all his moderation, won few supporters among the Zionist causes in Pittsburgh in the 1940s. Those Zionists who counted themselves among his congregants remember what they describe as "a great silence." For the many ardent Zionists outside Rodef Shalom, the Temple was viewed as the headquarters of the enemy and Freehof its general. Yet Freehof had personal friends among Zionists in Pittsburgh and elsewhere. He was a committee member in 1940 when Pittsburgh hosted the 43rd annual Zionist convention, and he was close friends with the fiery Zionist Rabbi Abba Hillel Silver. In 1946, when Silver spoke to the Pittsburgh Zionist District, Freehof accepted an invitation to introduce him. Freehof did not turn his back on Zionist support for Israel, nor did he deny the importance of rebuilding the Jewish homeland. He walked a tightrope within his own congregation and on the national level, seeking to smooth out the rough edges on each side and find the usable center.

Now, fifty years later, it is interesting to reflect on the concerns of all three rabbis. Although the great Zionist debate is over and the Jewish state firmly established, some of the same concerns have again come to the fore. Can Jewish unity be achieved? What will be the nature of the state? What will be the relationship of the state with its neighbors? What is its relationship with America and with

American Jews? These issues continue to challenge and perplex. Moreover, the concern that all three rabbis felt about the spiritual nature of Judaism and the need to rekindle that spirit among American Jews is certainly a great issue. The question is being asked whether it is time again to focus energy and resources on the religious and cultural life of America, to give American needs a greater priority. The Reform rabbis more than one hundred years ago argued that Jews in America had a mission, to be a light unto the nations. Horrible events intervened to turn many from that priority to what was seen as a more defensive posture, to establish a Jewish refuge. Now, in the wake of the success of that mission, the old clarion call of the Reformists might yet be heard again. There will clearly be a debate—there always is in the Jewish community—but the words of some rabbis from our past, particularly from Rodef Shalom, seem more compelling today than ever before.

THE LITURGICAL WRITINGS OF J. LEONARD LEVY: THE JUDAISM OF AN AMERICAN REFORM RABBI

Ruth Langer

PREFACE

On his seventieth birthday, my grandfather Marcus Lester Aaron gave to each of his grandchildren a copy of *J. Leonard Levy: Prophetic Voice.* In the letter that accompanied the book, he wrote:

> Doctor Levy came to Pittsburgh as Rabbi of Rodef Shalom congregation in 1901, when I was not quite six months old. He died in the spring of 1917. I was a member of the last class that he lived to confirm. I had the privilege in subsequent years of studying under other great teachers; no teacher had a greater or more sanctifying influence on my life than J. Leonard Levy. His memory has been a living presence to me through all the years.

This essay is dedicated to the memory of my grandfather Marcus Lester Aaron, a man who strove all his life to carry out the ideals of his teacher and to teach them to his family.

THE MAN HIMSELF

> My religion is based upon the acceptance of the Eternal God as my Father and upon my treatment of my fellowman as my brother. To work in hope; to accept the past in gratefulness and to strive to add to the good for the future; to be honest in all my dealings and expressions; to worship the truth; to be loyal to my country and to my ideals; to seek salvation through character; to treasure the truth of Scripture and to labor to advance Israel's God; to live that I may die regretted and to die in the faith that I may live after death;—this is my religion.[1]

Not every rabbi has so carefully thought through his personal philosophy that he can summarize it in one paragraph, print it on a little card with his picture in the corner, and distribute it to the members of his congregation. Few rabbis who do this will find their little card framed and hung with love in many homes of their congregants. Dr. Joseph Leonard Levy was a rabbi who was so loved and respected by his community that in this way—and in many others—he was able to enter their homes and profoundly influence their lives.

J. Leonard Levy was born in London, England, on November 24, 1865, one of fourteen children of Rabbi Solomon and Elizabeth Levy.[2] At age nine, he entered the preparatory department of Jews' College; at age sixteen he began theological studies there concurrently with secular studies at University College. He received his A.B. from the University of London in 1884 and completed his studies and was ordained a rabbi by the spring of 1885.

Levy began his formal service to the Jewish community on April 26, 1885, when, at age nineteen, as the youngest ordained English-speaking rabbi, he was elected rabbi of the Bristol Hebrew Congregation.[3] He was very successful and gained a reputation as a teacher. At this time, however, he began to read books "practically forbidden" and "began to understand that orthodoxy erred in making certain rites and ceremonies a fixed, integral part of Judaism."[4] Engagement with theories of evolution[5] aided this process. When he was called to the B'nai Israel Congregation in Sacramento in 1889, shortly after his marriage to Henrietta Platnauer, he was thus more than ready to leave the orthodox rabbinate and religiously conservative England.[6] During his almost four years in Sacramento, he became fully committed to the ideology of American Reform Judaism.[7]

After turning down an offer with double the salary to accept a position in San Francisco, in 1893, Levy went to Philadelphia to be the associate rabbi of the Keneseth Israel Reform Congregation. He chose to come east because he

> realized that to come east meant to succeed men like Einhorn and Hirsch, and to work with a colleague whose reputation had already become international and whose services on behalf of Reform Judaism were a matter of common knowledge throughout the United States.[8]

Levy remained in Philadelphia, working as Joseph Krauskopf's associate until he was called in 1901 to Congregation Rodef Shalom in Pittsburgh. While in Philadelphia, his organizational abilities as a scholar and pastor as well as his oratorical abilities were well appreciated. He was active in community affairs, both interfaith and civil. He founded the Philadelphia Sterilized Milk, Ice and Coal Society and the Home of Delight, a slum settlement house. Here we see the first still extant evidence of Levy's emphasis on social welfare. In Philadelphia, he also joined Krauskopf in publishing and distributing his Sunday sermons, a custom he brought to Pittsburgh. He also pursued scholarly activities, translating *Tractate Rosh Hashanah*, "the first volume of the Babylonian Talmud to appear in English in America."[9]

Levy's decision to leave Philadelphia and accept the call to Pittsburgh was not easy.[10] Although there is some evidence that with Levy's growing professional maturity, he had developed his own following, and rivalry had developed between him and Krauskopf,[11] Pittsburgh at that time was, at least from an East Coast perspective, a real backwater. Where Philadelphia's community was politically liberal, Pittsburgh was still staunchly Scottish Presbyterian conservative.[12] Where American Reform Judaism was strongly established in Philadelphia, Pittsburgh had an indebted congregation of only one hundred twenty (some sources say one hundred fifty) families who had never known an English-speaking rabbi.[13] Levy came to Pittsburgh ready to accept the challenge of building and molding a congregation and community whose condition he described to his Philadelphia friends as "from a Jewish standpoint . . . appalling."[14]

In this endeavor, Dr. Levy (he received an honorary D.D. from the Western University of Pennsylvania in 1902)[15] was entirely successful. The congregation grew phenomenally from the very beginning, outgrowing its new building in three years.[16] The resulting larger building, still in use today and a registered historical landmark, was built in 1907 but was not dedicated until it was paid for, just at the time of Dr. Levy's sudden death from pneumonia resulting from influenza on April 26, 1917. Its sanctuary is dedicated to his memory.

In sixteen years, Congregation Rodef Shalom was transformed. It instituted Sunday services six months of the year in addition to the regular shabbat services and published the sermons delivered there, distributing them by the following week. Like their peers in Philadelphia, a special group of young adults called "The Seekers"[17] met with Levy in his home Sunday afternoons to talk about his sermons, discuss current events, and study philosophy. Levy's publications for Rodef Shalom went well beyond sermons, filling the liturgical and educational needs of the congregation. Our focus here will be his liturgical writings.

Levy's influence in Pittsburgh extended far beyond the walls of his congregation. Representing the Rodef Shalom Board of Trustees, A. Leo Weil eulogized his rabbi saying that when Levy came to Pittsburgh there was no Jewish representation in civic, commercial, social, or philanthropic life. During Levy's tenure in Pittsburgh, this changed dramatically. "The Jew of our city has become not only more respected and respectable, but also more self-respecting. Much of this is due to the leadership of Doctor Levy."[18] Among other achievements, Levy was a trustee of what became the University of Pittsburgh, as was his predecessor. He worked hard to foster interfaith understanding. His Sunday services were attended by large numbers of non-Jews; in the same year he organized and hosted the first interreligious Thanksgiving service in Pittsburgh.[19]

He is remembered as never being afraid to speak his mind and to challenge the values and lifestyles of the community. Issues that he addressed, not only from the pulpit, but also in the community, included a bill to ensure that widowed mothers would receive pensions; a program to build model tenements; and a reinterpretation of the state's requirement of daily Bible reading so that in Pittsburgh only Proverbs, a doctrinally neutral book, would be read. He was also a leader in Pittsburgh's fight against tuberculosis, encouraging sick Jews and others to seek cures. He coined the term and was a chief proponent of "euconomics," the combination of the study of economics with the concerns of human welfare. In Pittsburgh's industrial boom, these messages were doubly important and doubly threatening. Levy claimed that his life was threatened no less than fifteen times, and he was called "the most dangerous man in Pittsburgh."[20]

On the national scene, Levy was a member of the Board of Governors of Hebrew Union College, on the executive board of the Central Conference of American Rabbis, and active in the Synagogue and School Extension of the Union of American Hebrew Congregations. He traveled extensively, both in the United States and abroad, and himself estimated that he addressed at least 500,000 people in the year before his death.[21]

His eulogies depict an erudite person as well as a wonderful rabbi. He had broad knowledge of theology, philosophy, history, and literature and was fluent in German, French, Italian, Latin, Greek, Hebrew, and Sanskrit. His mind was termed encyclopedic. All of this, as well as talents as a preacher and teacher, was combined with a commitment to high ideals, a pleasing personality, sensitivity to others, and generosity. In addition, he was a sportsman and enjoyed photography, horticulture, architecture, and the arts.[22] We also know that he had some talent for music and verse, as several of the hymns printed with his services and in his hymnal have either his settings of the verse of others or his verse set to music. His death at age 51 was unexpected. An estimated 15,000 people attended his funeral.

LEVY'S JUDAISM

What was the Judaism of this rabbi? Today, we have two major sources, his collected sermons[23] and his liturgical writings—our focus here. The first editions of his services all appeared in his first three years in Pittsburgh. They were subsequently issued, reissued, and distributed around the country, but his notes introducing the new editions indicate few changes. The religious thought represented in these volumes, therefore, coming from a relatively brief span of time, is very unified. By virtue of his willingness to reissue the books without major changes, we can assume that even if his philosophy grew and changed, he still found the sentiments expressed in his services acceptable.

THE LITURGIES THEMSELVES

The liturgical writings of J. Leonard Levy include *A Book of Prayer* (1902), a collection of thirty services for use during one year's cycle of Sunday services; *The Children's Service for Use in Religious Schools* (1902), a collection of four services, twenty supplementary services, and a hymnal; *Memorial Service for the Day of Atonement (1902); Home Service for Hanukkah (1903); Haggada* or *Home Service for the Festival of Passover* (1903); *The Children's Service for Rosh Ha-Shanah (1904);* and *The Temple Hymnal,* (4th edition 1922).[24] Levy, no doubt, modeled his liturgical writing at least in part on the pattern set by Krauskopf in Philadelphia. There, Krauskopf, hired in 1887 as the first English-speaking rabbi of Congregation Keneseth Israel, had no available Reform English liturgies. Consequently, shortly after his arrival in 1888 he published *The Service Ritual,* advertised as "used at the Sunday Service at the Temple . . . composed of thirty completely different English services, including Hymns, suitable for Friday evening or Sunday morning services, and also for home services." In 1892, shortly before Levy's arrival, he issued his *The Service Manual,* described as "A book of prayers, meditations, responses and hymns differing each Sabbath and each holiday."[25] Levy, hired as the first English-speaking rabbi in Pittsburgh, no longer needed to create his own liturgies, but obviously saw this as part of his rabbinic role.

What do these liturgical writings teach about the Judaism of this rabbi, born and educated in British Orthodoxy yet a teacher of and committed to American Reform Judaism? Several themes stand out as representing significant breaks from the Judaism of Levy's youth. First, he adopted American Reform Judaism with all the passion of the converted. Ceremonialism and traditional forms were unimportant parts of his religion, although observance of holidays and prayer never lost their prominence. Rationalism and scientific knowledge were sources of religious truth and required that tradition meet their standards. The promise of America was a glowing dream, and the solution of its social problems was a prime concern of his Judaism. This, and the spreading of Judaism's message, were the mission of the Jews and the meaning of their dispersion. Only by working for a better world could humans hope to bring the Messianic Age.

Most striking about each of these services is their lack of traditional structure. The reason for this was quite simple. Levy considered the structure in itself less important than the principles originally expressed through it.[26] Especially if this external form did not fit Levy's purposes or if it seemed incomprehensible and meaningless to the modern Jew, it was dispensable. As he says in the preface to the *Home Service for Hanukkah:*

> If I can succeed in getting the Jewish mothers of Pittsburgh to maintain the old observance in a new form; if I can arouse a little enthusiasm for the Maccabees and their struggle in the breasts of a few of our children, I shall feel thoroughly recompensed for my labor in behalf of the children I love.[27]

This service is indeed in a "new form." The traditional Hanukkah blessings are entirely missing, as are any traditional readings. The service opens instead with a few short prayers, derivative of the traditional evening service, which function to set the mood and express the essential themes of Judaism (the unity of God and the prophetic call for social justice). In this section, we find the only Hebrew in the entire service, the first line of the *Sh'ma* without any vowels. The candles are lit, but a prose paragraph replaces both the traditional blessing and the prose passage, *hanerot halalu,* that explains the function of the lights. Levy's new text explains the historical background of the holiday and its inspirational message for us, omitting all elements of the miraculous. Following this, the ritual relates the story of Hanukkah as told in I Maccabees, divided into responsive readings over the eight nights. The service concludes with the singing of "Hanukkah Hymn," which, although employing the

HAGGADAH

OR

HOME SERVICE

FOR THE FESTIVAL OF

PASSOVER

BY

RABBI J. LEONARD LEVY, D. D.
OF THE CONGREGATION RODEF SHALOM
PITTSBURGH, PA.

SEVENTH EDITION
1922

PITTSBURGH:
THE RODEF SHALOM CONGREGATION
FIFTH AND MOREWOOD AVENUES

HOME SERVICE FOR THE SABBATH EVE.

By

Rabbi J. Leonard Levy, D. D.

(The table being arranged for the evening meal, there should be placed upon it some lighted candles, a cup of wine and a loaf of bread. If it is preferred a small glass of wine can be placed before each one present. All being seated the reader shall recite the following:)

Now the children of Israel shall keep the Sabbath, to observe the Sabbath throughout their generations, as an everlasting covenant. It is a sign between God and Israel forever. (Exodus xxxi., 16, 17).

May our home be sanctified, O God, by the light of Thy presence. May it shine upon us in blessing. In every condition may we feel that if Thou art with us, we can never be moved or harmed. May this Sabbath bring us peace in our relations with our fellow-men and one another, and may our souls ever find rest in Thee, our God and Father.

These lights are a symbol of God's law; may we each week promise to walk by its light, fulfilling the will of our Father in heaven.

The wine is an emblem of life; as we drink from the same wine, so may we promise to share together the duties and burdens of life, in love and truth.

The bread is a token of God's bounty; as we eat of it, may we feel how good God is, and may we always strive to prove ourselves worthy of His Fatherly love. Amen.

(The wine should then be drunk by each person, and the bread should be broken and each partake of it. The parents should then lay their hands in blessing on the head of each child present.)

HOME SERVICE

FOR

'HANUKKAH

WRITTEN FOR

Congregation Rodef Shalom
PITTSBURGH, PA.

BY

RABBI J. LEONARD LEVY, D. D.

FIFTH EDITION

PITTSBURGH, PA.
1916

common melody of *Maoz Tsur,* is by no means a translation of that text. This service requires the family, as a group, to concentrate on the meaning of the act of lighting the candles and observing Hanukkah; probably in response to the growing American elaboration of Christmas celebrations, it elevates the Jewish holiday above its traditional status.

We find a similar introduction to the *Home Service for the Festival of Passover.* Although Levy presumes that people would hold a *Seder* without his intervention, he is concerned about the quality of that experience. In the "Preface to the Sixth Edition," he states that because few can read Hebrew and the existing English translation "is scarcely adapted to present-day life and thought," he is attempting "to adapt the old form of the Service to modern use" and to take the themes of the Haggadah and give them a modern dressing.[28] The resulting service includes no Hebrew at all, no blessings for the wine or ritual foods, no dwelling on the plagues or the miraculous events of the Exodus itself, no continuation after the meal, and no ritual eating of the *matzah* or *karpas.* The children ask a revised set of four questions as only one of a series of questions that continue throughout the ritual. The participants do still drink four glasses of wine, although all before the meal. The cups have new meanings, however, consistent with the overall message of the service, which has become largely a paean to Liberty, especially as it is found in America. Levy adds to the traditional service a description of Moses' role in the Exodus,[29] a lengthy explanation of Sinai as the purpose of the Exodus,[30] and an enumeration of the benefits that Torah and Judaism's teachings have brought to the world. The aspects of Passover as a spring festival come in only at the end, tied to a discussion of human immortality. This is probably an attempt to combine the future-oriented ending of the traditional Haggadah with an interpretation of the spring festival that instead of commemorating the Temple sacrifices, recognizes the theme of physical resurrection of the earth in the spring.

Levy's synagogue services are similarly untraditional in structure and content. The congregation continued throughout his tenure, however, to use David Einhorn's *Book of Prayers for Jewish*

Congregations—but in English[31]—on Sabbaths and holidays.[32] This prayer book, although it changes the wording of several prayers and shortens many of them, maintains a basically traditional structure. Most of the prayers are present in Hebrew, and the English translations are often placed so awkwardly that it would be difficult for the congregation to follow them. This book obviously met the needs of the congregation, however, for Dr. Levy did not write a replacement, and everything indicates that had he felt the need, he would have.[33]

In contrast, although Einhorn's prayer book does contain a weekday service, Levy early on published an entirely new prayer book for his Sunday services. When we compare the structures of the two books, the reason is readily apparent. Einhorn's weekday service, like his Sabbath Service, probably takes at least half an hour to read. It is traditional in structure, although it does contain significantly less Hebrew than the rest of the book. The focal point of Pittsburgh's Sunday service was the sermon or lecture that Board minutes record as having begun 25 minutes into the service.[34] For this reason the service needed to be shorter, and, because it was also attended by many non-Jews, the prayers had to be accessible and educational to them.

In *A Book of Prayer*, Levy drops all semblance of traditional structure, retaining in Hebrew only the first line of the *Sh'ma* and the first response of the *Kedushah*, both out of their traditional contexts, and the *Kaddish*. The thirty services in the book have in common only these two lines, the paragraph preceding the *Sh'ma*, and their basic organization of proem, hymn, glorification, thematically driven "Old Testament Readings" consisting of selected verses "for Rabbi, Congregation and Choir respectively," a prayer based on the theme of these readings, a Scriptural reading to be chosen by the rabbi, memorial prayers and *Kaddish*, the lecture, and a benediction. Like most Reform liturgies of this period, including all of Levy's, this text places a heavy emphasis on meeting the needs of mourners and spends much time discussing philosophies of death.[35] Levy dedicates each service to a discrete theme, about half of which could be classified as ethical and the rest as theological. Over the course of a winter Sunday Service season, these expose the worshiper to the most important themes of Judaism.[36]

In *The Children's Service,* the need for brevity and communication is even greater, so it leads to an abandonment of traditional liturgical structure. Considered of greatest significance for the children, and hence common to all services, are the Ten Commandments (not according to the usual Jewish numbering!). These are followed by ten more commandments on themes relevant to the children's lives, varying from service to service, a shortened version of the Sunday service's paragraph preceding the *Sh'ma,* and the first line of the *Sh'ma* itself in Hebrew. The four services in this format are on different themes, designed to be followed by a supplementary service on one of twenty themes about ethics or the pertinent holiday. Thus, although the children were taught some basic home liturgy in religious school,[37] they learned more ethics through their school worship services than they did synagogue skills.

REVELATION

For Levy, the ultimate source of these all important ethics was the Bible and revelation, but his liturgical statements about revelation are somewhat ambiguous. Although he speaks often, especially in his *Haggada,* about the importance of Sinai for Jewish and world history, he never specifically states that the Torah was given there by God. He writes instead that *Moses* "gave them, at Sinai, the first laws that were to govern them . . . ."[38] Levy's equivocal language was deliberate. He wrote elsewhere, in defense of Reform theology, that if the Bible's inspired status means

> direct and personal dictation by God, as it were, into the ear of His chosen prophets...then prophecy, reduced to its last analysis, is nothing more or less than the function of an amanuensis, of a stenographer who receives the dictation of God . . . . Alas, that such a theory should have been invented to bolster up the Scriptures! If the Bible is so great that they thought that only God could have written it, how much greater does it become if human

beings wrote it! I believe, and Reform Jews teach this belief, that the Bible, from cover to cover, is the work of man. We wish to relieve God from the responsibility of being the author of many of the horrible things attributed to Him in the Bible.[39]

Revelation continued after Sinai up to today. God speaks to us in nature as well as through books,[40] and

man's mind has been illumined by the rays of wisdom with which [God] didst illumine the chosen of the earth, the prophets and seers, the philosophers and teachers, the thinkers and writers, the inventors and discoverers of all lands, who thought [God's] thoughts after [Him].[41]

Rational thought thus becomes a source of revelation, and modern sources of knowledge become sources of Jewish knowledge. These ideas are by no means unique to Levy, but their explicit expression in printed liturgy is more unusual.

This elevation of reason provides a theoretical basis for many of Dr. Levy's innovations. Within the prayer book itself, he criticizes both Orthodox Judaism and anyone else unhappy with his liturgical changes:

Grant, O God, that we may fully understand that Thou are best worshiped by those who follow the dictates of conscience rather than the appeals of convenience, for Thou, O God, desirest truth more than fashion and reason more than credulity. Give us eyes to see that mercy is more than sacrifice, sincerity is more than form, uprightness more than ceremony, justice more than custom, right more than rite. Let not our respect for what our fathers held dear blind us to our duty of acquiring more light and broader views of truth.[42]

Levy believed in progressive revelation, where the teachings of the past must be continually evaluated in light of current knowledge. The eternal core of the teachings must always be preserved, but its presentation may change in order to communicate it to today's world. This interpretation of revelation also stresses that the Judaism of the previous generation was not wrong—for them. Levy, although a committed Reform Jew himself, had respect for the tradition of his parents, for what *his* father held dear.

AMERICA

The move from Orthodoxy to Reform was not the only significant change in J. Leonard Levy's life. He also became an American. The importance of his new country and his unbounded patriotism is quite evident in several of his services. Again, we must remember that this is the age when America was the "promised land" for many Jews, both the recent refugees and the established Americans who gloried in their civil liberties and the relative absence of persecution. Levy participated in this fully.

Although most of his explicit patriotic statements are in the *Haggada,* which we shall examine below, we do find references to "our country" creeping in unexpected places, particularly in the child-oriented services. The Hannukah candle lighting ends:

> Many hundreds of years have passed since the brave Maccabees fought for God, their religion, and their homes; but we remember their example, and tonight we promise, like them, to be true to God, to our religion, and to our country.[43]

and the reading for Sukkot in *The Children's Service* contains the rhetorical question:

> Have you not much to be thankful for? Youth and hope are yours; a free land and a chance for education are yours . . . .[44]

In the opening prayer of the *Haggada,* Levy wrote:

> We are thankful to God for the goodness He has shown us, for the blessings of health and home, of friends and country.[45]

It is noteworthy, though, that the "prayer for the country" appears in only a few of the Sunday Services and is fully absent from the English translation of Einhorn's prayer book.[46] It is possible, though, that

214

A

BOOK OF PRAYER

BY
DR. J. LEONARD LEVY
RABBI OF "CONGREGATION RODEPH SHALOM"
PITTSBURGH, PA.

SECOND EDITION

PUBLICITY PRESS, PITTSBURGH
1902

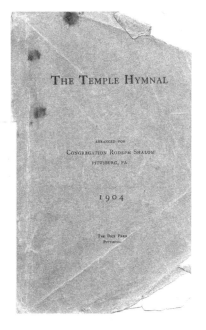

THE TEMPLE HYMNAL

ARRANGED FOR
CONGREGATION RODEPH SHALOM
PITTSBURG, PA

1904

THE DIKE PRESS
PITTSBURG

THE

CHILDREN'S SERVICE

FOR USE IN

RELIGIOUS SCHOOLS

BY
RABBI J. LEONARD LEVY, D. D.
CONGREGATION RODEF SHALOM
PITTSBURGH, PA.

THIRD EDITION

PITTSBURGH, PA.
NATIONAL PRINTING COMPANY
1913

215

this was simply read by the rabbi. The theme also appeared regularly in Levy's sermons.[47]

The *Seder* itself is permeated with Americanisms. Moses presented Pharaoh with a "Declaration of Independence"[48] and after Moses' death, "the Israelites lived in Palestine under a republican form of government."[49] These references are not merely an attempt to use language children would understand and relate to; throughout the *Seder* Levy points to the similarities between Jewish and American history and indicates the Jewish origins of the most cherished American ideals. He transforms the setting of the *Seder* so that it, too, transmits this message. His preliminary instructions state: "The family should assemble around a table, in the center of which there should be placed an American flag, some unleavened bread, a few flowers, . ."[50] The subsequent liturgy explains the meaning of the flag here:

> Our chief reason for keeping the Passover is to be found in the fact that on the day on which Israel left Egypt, "Liberty" was born. The sacred light of "Freedom" was then kindled and with God's help, it shall never go out.[51]

After five pages of discussion of liberty, a child asks, "Where do we find civil, political, and religious liberty united today?" and the leader replies:

> Here in America.... To us the United States of America stands as the foremost among nations granting the greatest liberty to all who dwell here. Therefore, we grace our table with the National flag.[52]

The Jews gave the world the ideal of liberty, and with Sinai, the ideal of liberty under law.[53] The Jew, therefore, has special reason to be proud of being American; no other country has so well fulfilled Jewish ideals.[54]

SOCIAL JUSTICE

This is not to suggest that Levy was uncritical about his new country. Finding much in America, and particularly in the industrial society of Pittsburgh, that needed improvement, Levy felt strongly that it was the Jew's ethical duty to work for the perfection represented in American and Jewish ideals. The recognition of the enormity of the problem is expressed in his *Memorial Service for the Day of Atonement:*

> To obtain supplies to meet the needs of the household involves constant toil. In the sweat of the brow do we eat bread; only by hard labor and unstinted effort do most of us seem able to procure sufficient to stay hunger's pangs. Work, almost without rest, is a constant condition of life. In mines, behind the forge, on the fields, in the factory, in store, in office, a slavish devotion to daily toil is needed to meet the requirements of a progressive civilization. By thrift and by self-denial we may accumulate a competence for the days when age will press on us with its heavy burden, when sight will begin to fail, and limbs to totter, and mind to act slowly. Even then through the criminal misconduct of others our possessions may be wiped out of existence overnight and our fancied security prove to be the shadow of a dream.[55]

A dominant figure in Pittsburgh philanthropy during Levy's tenure there was the retired industrialist Andrew Carnegie, whose *Gospel of Wealth* taught that wealth carries with it significant social responsibility.[56] Levy was intolerant of those who believed otherwise. Wealth in itself was not bad, but it should be used to enable the person to become a blessing to society. The idea that Jews, especially wealthy ones, have social responsibilities, pervades the liturgies. It is a particularly prominent statement in the one paragraph present in all the Sunday morning services, the one paragraph in the service the regular participants must have known practically by heart:

> Our God, who art in heaven, may the unity of Thy name be proclaimed throughout the world. May the kingdom of right-eousness be speedily established on earth. May we accept whatsoever Thou sendest us, saying: This is from the Lord; let Him do what seemeth right. Remove our sins far away from us and forgive us according to Thy loving kindness. Help us to be pure of heart and clean of hands. May we deal with our fellowmen as Thou, God, dealest with us, doing justice, loving mercy, seeking equity. May we always bear ourselves as though we felt that Thou God

dost see us. May we add to the good in the world and strive to overcome the evil. Grant us sustenance for the soul and body and cause the work of our hands to prosper. We humbly pray Thee to be with us in all the ways we go, and may we sanctify Thy name in life and death through the words of our holy teacher, "Hear O Israel, the Eternal is our God, the Eternal is One.[57]

The opening prayers of the *Home Service for Hanukkah* express this emphasis on social justice quite simply and forcefully:

He has shewed thee what is good and what the Lord requires of thee: to do justice, to love mercy, and to walk humbly with thy God. Depart from evil and do good; seek peace and pursue it; and thou shalt love thy neighbor as thyself; I am the Lord.[58]

Because of their repetition eight nights in a row, these words become a part of the person who recites them. The thought has nothing to do with *Hanukkah,* but everything to do with Levy's all-embracing religious vision.

In several of the Sunday services, Levy becomes even more explicit and even openly critical of the materialists of his day:

It is because of Thy great mercies, O God, that we are not consumed. We forget Thee while following the desires of our own hearts, enchanted by the attractions that meet our gaze. We spend our money for that which is not bread, and drink waters that are not drawn from the wells of salvation. We make our own will our law, setting aside Thy commandments and even refusing to follow Thy holy precepts. We do that which we ought not to do and leave undone that which we ought to do. We are sinful, erring creatures and it is out of the wealth of Thy loving kindness that we are spared unto this day.... May we leave the ways of evil and follow Thee. May we set aside selfishness and hardness of heart, stiff-neckedness and all manner of uncharitableness . . . .[59]

A confirmed capitalist that did not devote time and money to charitable pursuits must have squirmed inwardly at this condemnation. Many rabbis or ministers would have hesitated to use such strong language, but Levy's commitment and character allowed him to

218

express himself freely and effectively. Solomon B. Freehof credits Levy with helping to lay the spiritual foundation for organized Jewish charities.[60]

In his liturgical writings Levy moved beyond condemnation of materialists to suggest concrete alternatives:

> May we not limit our worship to silent meditation or enraptured contemplation, but may we wisely and righteously transform the wishes of our hearts and the concepts of our minds into noble deeds dedicated to the good and welfare of our fellow-men.[61]

> May we resolve to fulfill the law of love, to cheer the sorrowing, to sustain the failing, to help the poor and suffering, to plead the cause of the widow and orphan, to inveigh against all intolerance and bigotry and to become the champions of liberty.[62]

Prayer and good intentions are not enough; we must also act, and these actions in turn are a form of worship eminently acceptable to God. These are "the sacrifices, whose sweet savor is ever pleasing to [God] and whose usefulness will always be blessed of [God]."[63]

JEWISH MISSION

Hearkening to the prophetic call for justice was not just something Jews should do because it was the ethical way to act. According to Dr. Levy, the Jews have a mission, and with that mission, a duty. He said that it is "our duty to live by our beliefs, so that, by our example, others may learn to respect them, and, in the end, accept them."[64] The beliefs of the Jews are necessary to the happiness of mankind."[65] Instead of looking backward and forever harping on the misfortunes of our people, we should look forward and work for the future.

In his memorial for Levy at the 1917 Conference of the Central Conference of American Rabbis, Rabbi Rudolph I. Coffee quotes Dr. Levy, saying, "[W]e spend too much time permitting ourselves to degenerate into a people with a grievance, instead of realizing that we are a people with a mission."[66] Jews fulfill their mission not only passively by living by the true tenants of their religion, but also actively by aggressively reaching out to the world:

> Like warriors of old may we go forth with the sword of truth, the shield of justice, the armor of righteousness and wage a holy war against all the causes that keep men's minds in bondage, their souls in slavery and their hearts in chains . . . . As Thou art One, so may mankind's unity be established.[67]

Levy's personal sense of mission had at least two elements. One, expressed more explicitly in his sermons (but inherent in the structure of the Sunday services and, particularly, in their rephrasing of the Lord's Prayer, cited above), was the need to answer Christian missionaries and present Jews with a strong modern foundation for their own faith.[68] If this also made Judaism more attractive to Christians, then this would only enhance the second element of that mission, the hastening of the arrival of the Messianic Era. This he states explicitly in one of the Sunday services, saying, "May we understand that only by duty fulfilled in small as in great things, and by loving service to mankind, can we hope to draw near the blessed era of the Messiah."[69] He continues with an elaboration of the nature of this era, saying among other things:

> Not until hate and malice have disappeared, not until schools take the place of prisons and temples of learning supplant penitentiaries, not until all superstitions and ignorance, all evil and corruption are destroyed, not until Thy holy name is praised by all men all the world over and Thy absolute unity is acknowledged by all Thy children . . . not until then can we believe that Messiah has come.[70]

This time of the Messiah will be a time of peace, of understanding, of goodness, of universal education, of freedom, of friendship, and of universal worship and recognition of the unity of God. In other words, it will be a utopia where neither Jews nor anyone else need worry about persecution. In his liturgical writings, however, Levy did not explicitly reject the idea of a personal Messiah. As with the question of revelation, he leaves his language somewhat ambiguous, at least to a later ear. As we see in the brief citations here, although he describes the characteristic classical Reform idea of the Messianic Age, he also uses the word "Messiah" without qualification. His sermons, however, leave no doubt that his personal theology did not include expectations that an individual human would come as Messiah to transform the world.[71]

DEATH AND IMMORTALITY

Levy's messianic belief, and indeed his entire very rational theology, includes no supernatural intercession beyond that which comes as revelation through the minds of humans. Miracles play no part; the Messianic age will be for those alive at that time. He never mentions resurrection of the dead.[72] Levy did, however, devote a relatively large amount of his liturgy to his theories of life after death and of immortality. Rejecting David Einhorn's *Yom Kippur* Memorial Service, which concentrates mostly on the emotions of the congregation remembering its loved ones, Dr. Levy writes one that follows the model set by Joseph Krauskopf that is fully twice as long. Its fifty-six pages are filled with long philosophical expositions of the meanings of death and immortality.[73] But Levy goes beyond Krauskopf's models in the short Sunday services where he devotes about one quarter of their liturgical time (excluding the lecture and the hymns not printed with the service) to the *Kaddish* and its introduction. Levy also devotes the last sixth of the *Haggada* to a discourse on immortality.

There can be several possible reasons for this heavy emphasis on death, typical of the age across American culture.[74] Dr. Levy may have been a man bothered by his own finitude and fascinated with the phenomenon of death. This may explain to some extent why he drove himself so hard and slept only four hours a night.[75] It is also possible that, just as he felt it imperative to provide a solid basis for countering Christian missionaries on other issues, he found it necessary to give his congregants a proper Jewish theological understanding of death, a fundamental hinge in the Christian claims to superior salvation.

Certainly what he expresses in his liturgical writings is an attempt to give a rational basis to a concept of immortality:

> The learning of the ages supports this belief, as the hope of humanity trusts it. The latest discoveries of science support it. If the principle of the Conservation of Energy is correct, as we believe, then it affords strong presumption in favor of the Immortality-Belief, to which we give expression in this Memorial Service, held in honor of our beloved dead. Life is a mode of energy. Energy is indestructible, therefore life is indestructible. Force or energy may be transformed, therefore life may be transformed; but, if life is energy and energy is conserved to all eternity, then so, too, must life be . . . .[76]

> It is sweet to hope and rational to believe that though our loved ones are gone, they are not forgotten, and that they live on in another existence . . . .[77]

We today may question the logic of his arguments, but, living in an age of rationalism, Levy felt driven to provide himself and his congregants with a way to accept a belief in immortality. His constant defensive reiteration that this belief is rational may indicate that this belief was being challenged as irrational. It is not knowable whether his "scientific" proof was effective.

Maybe because he was a bit unsure himself about a supra-mundane immortality of the soul, Levy also offered a theory of immortality on earth:

> [T]he influence of our example remains even when we are gone . . . . Truth, honor, honesty, cleanness of hands and purity of heart, wherever practised [sic] will gain for us immortal influence here on earth just as beyond the grave there is life forever with God.

> Our dead do not die, until we kill them by forgetfulness. They live on in us and through us, even as we shall through our children . . . In this sense our loved ones never die, for they live in hearts and lives left behind.[78]

His two theories do not contradict one another, but Levy feels no need to demonstrate the rationality of the second. It was not under attack because it was intuitively obvious to all.

CONCLUSION

Levy's personal statement of religious faith with which we began this study, gave pithy voice to the major themes that appear in his liturgical writings: the concern for others or social consciousness; the future orientation and working toward the Messianic Age when all will worship God; the worship of the truth in the demand of rationality and the reverence for revelation; the American patriotism; and the concern for immortality both with God and on earth. Every theme also received further exposition in his published lectures, setting an agenda for his congregation, his city, and his world. Although the intervening century has challenged elements of Levy's teachings most deeply,[79] twenty-first century Jews have much to cherish in the teachings of the man who transformed Rodef Shalom into one of the great pulpits of American Judaism. The continued vitality of his congregation under his successors is also a piece of Levy's immortality.[80]

Notes

1. *The Temple Bulletin: J. Leonard Levy Memorial Issue* (Pittsburgh: Rodef Shalom Congregation, April 19, 1967), p. 7; and Solomon B. Freehof and Vigdor W Kavaler, *J. Leonard Levy: Prophetic Voice* (Pittsburgh: Rodef Shalom Congregation, 1970), p. vii. This volume unfortunately does not indicate the sources of most of its materials, but most words cited here are Levy's own, unless otherwise indicated. Levy concluded his Sunday lecture "My Religion," delivered November 19, 1905, with this paragraph (Series 5:3, p. 19). The text of the sermon does not indicate if he was quoting an earlier publication.

2. His brother Meyer also came to America and served as a rabbi in California. Meyer's biographical sketch in the *American Jewish Year Book 5664*, 1903–1904, p. 75, identifies Solomon as rabbi of the Boro' Synagogue in London. Edna Levy Barach's oral history records that her grandfather was rabbi of the Great Synagogue on Duke's Place. See *My Voice Was Heard*, Ida Cohen Selavan, ed., for the National Council of Jewish Women, Pittsburgh Section (New York and Pittsburgh: Ktav and NCJW, 1981), p. 35. The family was Sephardic and had arrived in England via Holland. The tape of the oral history interview, from November 3, 1975, records in

addition that Solomon himself was born in England. Some details were also confirmed in a private interview with Barach in 1985.

3. Freehof and Kavaler, p. x, citing the *National Encyclopedia of American Biography*. Freehof and Kavaler unfortunately do not indicate the sources of most of their materials.

4. Levy, in Freehof and Kavaler, p. 44.

5. Jerrold Goldstein, *Reform Rabbis and the Progressive Movement*, M.A. Thesis, University of Minnesota, 1967, p. 19, suggests that his reading of Spencer and theories of evolution created religious turmoil for him.

6. Levy, in Freehof and Kavaler, pp. 42, 44.

7. According to Barach's oral history, Levy's brother Meyer, already serving in California, had recommended him to the Sacramento congregation, which was seeking an English-speaking rabbi, then a rarity in the United States. Two members of that congregation traveled to England and approached Levy in Bristol.

8. Levy, in Freehof and Kavaler, p. 44.

9. Freehof and Kavaler, p. xi. Possibly in the *New Edition of the Babylonian Talmud*, original text edited, corrected, formulated, and translated into English by Michael L. Rodkinson (New York: New Talmud Pub. Co., 1896–), although library catalogue entries do not acknowledge him.

10. See what is apparently his parting address to the Philadelphia congregation, Freehof and Kavaler, pp. 45–46.

11. Barry S. Kogan, *"The Mind of Rabbi J. Leonard Levy,"* Term Paper History 303, Hebrew Union College-Jewish Institute of Religion, Cincinnati, 1969, n.p. Krauskopf was only seven years older than Levy.

12. Freehof and Kavaler, p. 48. Levy describes Pittsburgh as "this rock-ribbed, iron-bound, conservative community" where "many Pittsburghers, like their ancestors, must have imagined that Jews were like the coal in the surrounding hillsides, only fit to be burned."

13. Freehof and Kavaler, pp. 45–49.

14. Freehof and Kavaler, p. 46.

15. As reported in *The Jewish Criterion* 15:2, June 20, 1902, p. 9.

16. *The Jewish Criterion* 15:9, August 8, 1902, p. 3. In response to many requests for copies, Levy reprints here an article about himself from *The Jewish Chronicle* that reported that Levy attracted overflow audiences both Saturday and Sunday mornings, no matter what the weather.

17. Modeled after Krauskopf's "Society of Knowledge Seekers," founded in his first year in Philadelphia, 1887–1888. See Marcolm H. Stern, "National Leaders of Their Time: Philadelphia's Reform Rabbis," in Murray Friedman, ed., *Jewish Life in Philadelphia 1830–1940* (Philadelphia: ISHI Publications, 1983), p. 186.

18. The congregational minutes for May 19, 1917, record that Weil, a member of the board, was requested to speak at the Memorial Service held by the Eastern Council of Reform Rabbis. The excerpt, Freehof and Kavaler, pp. 2–3, is almost certainly from this address, as Weil mentions that he is substituting for the president of the congregation and that the Board of Trustees had approved his text. (A generous over statement made as part of the eulogy; Dr. Mayer, his predecessor, had established a firm basis for Levy's efforts. Editor's note)

19. Levy's published sermons evidence significant concern with interfaith matters. Many address (and refute) points of Christian theology. Others obviously try to explain Judaism more clearly to Christians or those influenced by it. Anti-semitism and answering Christian mission are also frequent concerns.

20. Solomon B. Freehof, "The Classic Reform Leader: A Centennial Tribute," November 28, 1965, in Freehof and Kavaler, p. 17.

21. Levy, in Freehof and Kavaler, p. xii, in an address on April 15, 1917.

22. A. Leo Weil, in Freehof and Kavaler, pp. 2–3.

23. Published by the following week's service throughout the thirty-week Sunday service season. In Philadelphia, Levy and Krauskopf alternated weeks, and the congregation published their sermons together. Levy himself lectured almost weekly in Pittsburgh. For an analysis of some of Dr. Levy's sermons, see Kogan. Freehof and Kavaler also contains thematically organized extracts. Levy also regularly published columns in the *Jewish Criterion,* a Pittsburgh newspaper that functioned as a weekly Temple bulletin under his editorship.

24. The Klau Library at Hebrew Union College in Cincinnati has original editions only of the two High Holy Day services. These services are of lesser quality and may not have received such broad use.

25. Advertisements found at the back of Levy's first regular Sunday sermon in Philadelphia, October 8, 1893. I have been unable to obtain a copy of Krauskopf's *Service Ritual.* Einhorn's *Olat Tamid* was not translated from the German until 1896; the first edition of the *Union Prayer Book* was not published until 1892 (with a more widely accepted edition in 1895). By the time Levy arrived in Pittsburgh, all these English liturgies were available to the congregation.

26. Compare Krauskopf's preface to his *Service Manual:* "The fixed Order of Worship has been departed from in this *Manual,* but merely in form. The spirit of the traditional service has been sacredly preserved. Its devotional sentiment has been brought nearer to the modern mind by the use of a number of the most approved liturgical aids" (p. 1). Levy's departures from traditional structure are often even more radical than those represented in this volume.

27. Rabbi J. Leonard Levy, D.D., *Home Service for Hanukkah* (Pittsburgh: Congregation Rodeph Shalom, 1910), p. 3.

28. Rabbi J. Leonard Levy, D.D., *Haggada* or *Home Service for the Festival of Passover* (Pittsburgh: The Rodef Shalom Congregation, 1922), p. 3.

29. The traditional Haggadah deliberately emphasizes that it was God who saved Israel, to the point that Moses is mentioned only once and in passing.

30. The traditional Haggadah mentions Sinai only in its segue from the actual exodus to the ongoing celebration of the Exodus in the Jerusalem Temple.

31. Translated by Julie Einhorn from the German *Olat Tamid* (1896, and reprinted in 1913). Congregational minutes record authorizations for the purchase of Einhorn's Saturday and High Holy Day services on October 8, 1916, and December 3, 1916. Levy's daughter recalls that her father changed the congregation's liturgy from German to English. See *My Voice Was Heard*, p. 49.

32. M. L. Aaron, "Rodef Shalom Congregation: One Hundred Years," in *Centennial and Dedication Festival Recollections, 1856–1956* (Pittsburgh: Rodef Shalom Congregation, 1956), n.p.

33. Congregational minutes for June 5, 1904, however, order the printing and adoption of Levy's book of Sabbath Readings and Sabbath Services. There is no indication that this was carried out— but it does point to Levy's having composed such a text.

34. Rodef Shalom Temple Board Minutes, October 13, 1901, discussing protocols for latecomers to the 10:30 Sunday services. One had rights to one's own pew until 10:45. No one was to be admitted once the lecture began at 10:55.

35. Where Krauskopf's *Service Manual* radically alters the *Kaddish* text, however, adding extensive references to death (mostly from biblical verses that he includes in Hebrew—not translated to Aramaic), Levy maintains a much more traditional text, adapting the *kaddish derabbanan* to refer to the dead instead of scholars. His English translation, in its interpretation of the Aramaic text, also addresses the mourners directly.

36. Dr. J. Leonard Levy, *A Book of Prayer* (Pittsburgh: Publicity Press, 1902), p. 6. According to his introduction (which contains themes similar to those found in the introductions to his occasional liturgies, quoted above), these services were composed, week by week, during Levy's first year in Pittsburgh specifically to meet the needs of the Pittsburgh congregation. His obvious model—and the volume he chose *not* to adopt in Pittsburgh—was Krauskopf's *Service Ritual*.

37. See selections on "Prayers," in Rabbi J. Leonard Levy, D.D., *Textbook of Religion and Ethics*, Pittsburgh, n.p., 1903.

38. *Haggada*, p. 10. This is a shift in emphasis from Deut. 4:44, "This is the Torah which Moses placed before the children of Israel." By the eighteenth century, Ashkenazic liturgical use of this verse had added to it "according to the instructions of God through Moses," in order to remove precisely the ambiguity that Levy entertains.

39. Freehof and Kavaler, pp. 49–50.

40. *A Book of Prayer*, p. 269.

41. Ibid.

42. *A Book of Prayer*, p. 196.

43. *Home Service for Hanukkah*, p. 6. Although this passage does not mention America specifically, its context, with its discussion of freedom-fighting, certainly suggests this reading. It is doubtful if any of Levy's congregants understood "our country" to refer to anything but America.

44. Rabbi J. Leonard Levy, D.D., *The Children's Service for Use in Religious Schools* (Pittsburgh: Press of John Crawford Park, 1921), p. 23.

45. *Haggada*, p. 6.

46. It does appear in the German original, pp. 22–23.

47. See, for instance, Levy's sermons: 5:4, "The Jew in America," especially 6:5, "The Making of an American"; 12:16, "Americanism" (in a series on Religion and Social Theories); 12:24, "The Dawn of Liberty"; others, like "The Hall of Fame," April 15, 1917 (published in the *Jewish Criterion,* based on stenographical transcription, without Levy's corrections because of his fatal illness), and many more on local and national issues of the time address more in passing the uniqueness of America.

48. *Haggada*, p. 9.

49. Ibid.

50. Ibid., p. 4.

51. Ibid., p. 20.

52. Ibid., p. 25.

53. Ibid., p. 21.

54. On this phenomenon in American Jewish life, see Jonathan D. Sarna, "The Cult of Synthesis in American Jewish Culture," *Jewish Social Studies* 5:1–2 (1998–1999): 52–79, and especially his discussion of Levy, pp. 62–63.

55. Rabbi J. Leonard Levy, D.D., *Memorial Service for the Day of Atonement* (Pittsburg: Congregation Rodeph Shalom, 1902), p. 11.

56. Carnegie's publications on this theme began with an article, "Wealth," *North American Review*, June 1889, and continued with a book of essays published around the time he sold the Carnegie Steel Company to focus on philanthropy, *Gospel of Wealth,* 1900.

57. *A Book of Prayer,* pp. 9–10, and each service following. See also the shortened form in the *Children's Service for Use in Religious Schools,* p. 7, and the three services following. This prayer is an obvious attempt to provide a Jewish equivalent to the Christian Lord's Prayer. Levy's congregants were probably familiar with the Christian prayer from their participation in American civic life and educational settings. The attempt to provide a Jewish equivalent is itself interesting.

58. *Hanukkah,* p. 5, concatenating Micah 6:8, Psalms 34:15, and Leviticus 19:18.

59. *A Book of Prayer,* p. 25.

60. "A Man of Ideals: Sermon Delivered on the Fiftieth Anniversary of the Death of J. Leonard Levy, Sunday, April 23, 1967," in Freehof and Kavaler, p. 25.

61. *A Book of Prayer*, p. 277. See, too, for instance, pp. 12–13.

62. *Haggada*, p. 38.

63. *A Book of Prayer*, p. 13.

64. *Haggada*, p. 12.

65. *Haggada*, p. 13.

66. Rabbi Rudolph I. Coffee, "Joseph Leonard Levy: Memorial Address," *Central Conference of American Rabbis Journal*, No. 27, 1917, p. 241.

67. *A Book of Prayer*, p. 45.

68. Sermons too numerous to list address Christian doctrine explicitly. Many on other topics show a concern about the reality of living in Christian society. *The Jewish Chronicle*'s reprint from *The Jewish Criterion*, 15:9, August 8, 1902, p. 3, refers to Levy's published lectures as the "missionary tracts of modern Judaism."

69. *A Book of Prayer*, p. 277.

70. *A Book of Prayer*, p. 278. This passage provided Levy's congregants with a neat response to Christian missionaries.

71. In a Sunday lecture on December 17, 1893, in Philadelphia, titled "What is the Messiah," he stated explicitly, "But the Messianic idea as interpreted by us to-day [sic], does not refer to a man at all." (Ser. 7, no. 12, p. 8, of the combined lectures of Krauskopf and Levy, Ser. 1, no. 6, of Levy alone). In Pittsburgh, on February 8, 1903 (Ser. 2, no. 16, p. 13, in a series on "Jewish Affirmations"), he presented explicitly the understanding of Reform Jews, that the biblically predicted *"political* Messiah" had been Hezekiah, and that "we do not expect a *political* redeemer to come again." He proceeds to refute Christian claims that Jesus fulfilled Messianic prophecies, the real focus of all his lectures on this theme. He concludes, "Israel, the servant of God is the Messiah to the world,...not manifested in one Jew but all Jews . . . in the . . . distant future . . . M essiah shall come" (p. 16). On December 22, 1907, in a sermon entitled "A Jewish View of the Messiah," he pointed to the disastrous consequences of Sabbatei Zevi's messianic claims, and suggested that Zionism was leading to similar disappointment (Ser. 7, no. 8, p. 14ff.). Compare also Ser. 14, no. 9, December 27, 1914, "If the Messiah Had Come," and Ser. 15, no. 7, December 19, 1915, "The Jews and the Messiah," where he does admit that not all Jews agree as to whether the term

Messiah means a person, time, condition, or a whole people (p. 11).

72. The Einhorn *Book of Prayers for Jewish Congregations* used by Rodef Shalom had altered the classic liturgical locus of this idea, the Hebrew and English second blessing of the *amidah,* to read: Thou art the source of all might and power; in Thee alone is safety. In Thy love, Thou sustainest the living; with infinite kindness Thou redeemest the souls of Thy servants from death spiritual . . . none of Thy words ever faileth. Be praised, O God, dispenser of life eternal.

73. Compare Krauskopf's *The Service Manual* (Philadelphia: Oscar Klonower, 1892), 11th edition, 1921, where the Memorial Service, in much smaller type, occupies 39 pages. The two services are similar in structure, although Levy includes more Scripture and more references to general culture. Although Levy does not follow Krauskopf slavishly, certain sections are obvious paraphrases of Krauskopf's texts. See, for instance, the opening hymn in both and the memorial prayers and their lead-in at the conclusion of the liturgy.

74. Colleen McDannell, *The Christian Home in Victorian America, 1840–1900* (Bloomington: Indiana University Press, 1986), pp. 98–99, describes the elaborate Catholic and Protestant practices. Some suggest that this was heightened for Jews by the fact that so many had left parents behind when immigrating, resulting in more elaborate memorial rites apart from the funeral itself.

75. A. Leo Weil's Eulogy, in Freehof and Kavaler, p. 2.

76. *Memorial Service*, p. 43.

77. Ibid., p. 45.

78. *Haggada,* pp. 35–36.

79. Although my grandfather used Levy's home rituals his entire life, he was forced to paraphrase the paeans to America during the Vietnam and Watergate eras. Levy's reliance on rationalism, his opposition to Zionism (not apparent in the liturgies, but clear in several lectures), his rejection of traditional forms are among those elements of his teachings not to survive the twentieth century.

80. This paper was originally written in 1985 as a term paper for History 56 at Hebrew Union College, Cincinnati. My gratitude to Jonathan D. Sarna, then my teacher, now also my husband, for his assistance with the historical background against which this revision reads Levy's religion.

THE RABBI AND THE ARTIST
J. LEONARD LEVY (1865 – 1917) AND
AARON HARRY GORSON (1872 – 1933)

Rina C. Youngner

Rabbi J. Leonard Levy and the artist Aaron Harry Gorson were separated by class, education, temperament, and life history. The only thing they shared was a determination to participate fully in American life at a time when ubiquitous and patronizing anti-Semitism separated Jews from the mainstream. Everything Levy did reflected his mission: to encourage full participation in American society by self-confident Jews. His relationship with Aaron Gorson, I believe, originated in this attitude. Gorson, on his part, was obsessed with being a painter. He ignored the fact that Russian Jewish culture rejected such a career. Even in America in 1900, to be Jewish and a painter was unusual. Levy influenced Gorson's life and artistic career at two important junctures: in 1900, Rabbi Levy made it possible for Gorson to study art in Paris, and because of Rabbi Levy, Gorson came to Pittsburgh in 1903 and gained a measure of success.

Levy and Gorson met sometime after the Rabbi came to Philadelphia in 1893. It was a very fortunate meeting for Gorson. Even though Rabbi Levy was in his early thirties, only seven years older than Gorson, he was already highly respected and widely known. Born in England, the son of an Orthodox rabbi, Levy had studied Jewish theology at Jews College, and secular philosophy, history, sociology at University College in London. He spoke four modern languages fluently and read Hebrew, Greek, Latin, and Sanskrit. He was polished in manners and a natural leader. Aaron Gorson, on the other hand, was born in the textile center of Kovno in the Russian Pale [now Kaunas, Lithuania]. His parents were poor and he received only an elementary education. He was intense and driven, rough and awkward in demeanor.

Both men were immigrants, but with a difference. Rabbi Levy had been invited to come to America to lead a congregation in California when he was just twenty-four years old. As his talents became recognized in the Reform Movement, he was asked to go to Philadelphia to be the associate rabbi at Knesset Israel. In 1901, he decided to come to Rodef Shalom in Pittsburgh. When Rabbi Levy arrived, the congregation was small and its aspirations limited. Under his leadership, Rodef Shalom built a historic temple building and grew in size and influence, both in the Jewish Reform Movement and in Pittsburgh's political and social life.

In contrast to Rabbi Levy's successful moves, Gorson left Europe among anxious Russian Jews escaping threats of pogroms; he came to America harboring the frustration of laying aside his talents in order to make a living. As a boy in Kovno, Gorson had fashioned scraps of paper into figures that the peasants bought when they came to town. But his parents and the ghetto culture of the Pale saw little value in this; he had to earn serious money instead of indulging himself. He left Kovno, having served a three-year apprenticeship with a tailor. In 1888, at the age of sixteen, he joined his brother in Philadelphia. Even though he immediately began working in the garment industry, and even though he married at the age of twenty-three, Gorson took art lessons at the Spring Garden Institute of Philadelphia and eventually – around the time he married – enrolled in night classes at The Pennsylvania Academy of Fine Arts. A student of Thomas Eakins, Thomas Anshutz, taught evening classes with the help of several assistants during those years. Of course, the demands of family, work, and poverty interrupted Gorson's attendance; he was enrolled from 1894 to 1896 and again in 1897–98. He was good enough to win some prizes in local shows and to get a commission to paint the portrait of former Philadelphia Mayor Ashbridge. This was probably the time, around 1898–99, of his first portrait of Rabbi Levy.

Jewish artists were almost nonexistent in America at that time. Ten to fifteen years later, the generation of Abraham Walkowitz, Max Weber, the Soyer brothers (all immigrants), began working in New York City. Gorson was a lone pioneer in this respect, and it was his

Self-Portrait

Mills Along the River

233

luck that his talent fit into Rabbi Levy's mission to encourage Jewish participation in the larger American society. The Rabbi gathered the money necessary to send Gorson to Paris for a year in 1900.

Paris attracted a concentration of artists; no other city gave them such importance and respect. The collaboration between the state institution of L'Ecole des Beaux Arts and the large number of private ateliers set up to teach art fed France's hunger for public and private art. All the world came to study art in Paris. Perhaps Levy's experience in London during his University years made it natural to think of sending a protégé to Paris. The idea of a Jewish artist was not unheard of to him.

The year that he spent in Paris was the only time Gorson lived in an artistic milieu. Certainly Philadelphia did not accord artists a central place; neither did Pittsburgh. Unlike L'Ecole des Beaux Arts, the privately owned studios were open to all; there were no entrance examinations, no qualifying tests. Students paid by the month. Gorson attended the Julian Acadèmie, a school that attracted many Americans. (He kept a tuition receipt for the four weeks from 19 March to 14 April in his scrapbook). The fee entitled him to work with twenty or thirty other people from 10:00 a.m. to 4:00 p.m. drawing and painting from a live model. Every two weeks, one or the other of two respected painters from L'Ecole des Beaux Arts came to the studio to critique the students' work. Jean Paul Laurens and J. J. Benjamin Constant alternated monthly during Gorson's time there. Years later, he told a reporter that Laurens though him a good colorist, but Gorson was warned to improve his drawing. Perhaps this is why Gorson also went to the Académie Colarossi in the evening, to practice drawing from the figure. Gorson kept a certificate issued on 23 May 1900, giving him permission to copy paintings in the Louvre and the Palais du Luxembourg Museum.

Gorson seems to have used every minute to learn and practice the basic techniques of painting. But he did not develop a distinctive style, nor did he experiment with distinctive subject matter while in

Paris. A decade later, a group of Russian Jewish artists lived in Paris. Marc Chagall and Chaim Soutine developed personal and Jewish iconographies and styles in their paintings. Amedeo Modigliani was also part of this loose group. Would Gorson have met them and been influenced by them if he had come ten years later? As it was, Gorson did what most students in Paris did: he studied and tried to assimilate academic technique. At the Louvre, he traced the development of the European painting tradition. At the Luxembourg, he saw contemporary works that had won prizes at the semi-annual salons, as well as paintings donated to the nation by collectors. At the Luxembourg Gorson would have seen some of Whistler's paintings.

Although it was Whistler's work that influenced Gorson, this did not become immediately evident. When Gorson returned to Philadelphia, he continued doing portraits – Rabbi Henry Berkowitz's portrait was done in 1901, and two portraits were awarded honorable mention at the exhibition of the American Art Society of Philadelphia in 1902. It seems that by 1903, however, Gorson realized that he could not subsist as an artist in Philadelphia. Thus he came to Pittsburgh, where his patron had moved. And indeed he got help.

Again, Rabbi Levy's intervention changed the course of Gorson's life. Gorson kept Dr. Levy's business card with the written message saying "Introducing Mr. Harry Gorson" in his scrapbook. A story in the *Post Gazette* by Thomas Seltzer in 1903 (also printed in *The Jewish Criterion* a publication started by Rabbi Levy), noted that Gorson had just finished a portrait of Rabbi Levy and had done two large paintings for Rodef Shalom: one of them depicted Moses pleading with Pharaoh. Another early commission came from Francis L. Robbins, President of the Pittsburgh Coal Company. Gorson was paid $500 to copy life-size portraits of Lincoln and Grant from White House paintings. (They are now at the Washington County Historical Society). In 1906, three years after coming to Pittsburgh, Gorson executed a portrait of Mrs. W.S. King, the wife of a glass manufacturer. It had a 40 x 50 inches gold frame and Gorson received $1,000 for it.

Even while Gorson was doing a brisk business in society portraits, he was thinking about the Carnegie International Exhibitions that had been taking place yearly since 1896, when the Carnegie Institute opened. A few Pittsburgh painters were always accepted each year. The similarity between the Pittsburgh Internationals and the semi-annual salons of Paris must have struck him, and like the competitive and assertive French artists who swamped the salons in Paris, Gorson began submitting paintings almost yearly, starting in 1904. He probably had a better chance of acceptance with landscapes than with portraits, and this may have motivated a change of subject. In 1904, he submitted "Pittsburgh Weather"; in 1905, "Pittsburgh Smoke." Both were rejected, but he was already focusing on the mills of Pittsburgh as his subject.

Ironically, industrial landscapes were almost nonexistent in Pittsburgh, the most industrial city in the world at that time! People bought paintings with subjects that took them away from industrial life. Thus, still lifes, portraits, rural and forest landscapes were acceptable subjects, not factories. With the annual International exhibitions, however, new ideas entered Pittsburgh art. The visiting European jurors of the early Internationals were thrilled by the sight of the Carnegie's Pittsburgh mills, especially at night. Fritz Thaulow, a Norwegian painter who lived in Paris, did at least five paintings of the Pittsburgh landscape in 1898, the year he served on the Jury of Awards for the Third Annual Exhibition. (The Duquesne Club owns an 1898 Thaulow pastel showing a steel mill by the river at night). A year later, the respected Pittsburgh painter, Martin Leisser, did two or three oil sketches of the J & L plant and Eliza Blast Furnaces on opposite banks of the Monongahela, but he did not work them up into finished paintings. In 1904 Joseph Woodwell, another respected local painter, submitted a small painting, *Back of the Iron Mills*, to the Carnegie International. Both Leisser and Woodwell created images of somber realism.

Gorson, remembering Whistler's rendering of the Thames and its factories shrouded in fog, took a different approach, one that

Pouring Iron

emphasized the play of light and dark, and smoke, mist, and reflections. At the turn of the century, when Pittsburghers "scurried through sooty streets, handkerchiefs clamped over noses and mouths to filter the dirty air,"[1] Gorson told the *Pittsburgh Press* reporter that the city had "scenes of grandeur and enthralling picturesqueness." He admired how "the muddy river water catches the gleam of the dying light and becomes. . . running gold."[2] Like Whistler, he gave musical names to his paintings – *Nocturne, Prelude.* In 1908, a painting of his, *Pittsburgh*, was accepted into the International. The reviewer noted that it was hung on line with the Gold Medal winner, an honor for Gorson. Immediately after, on September 26, 1908, Gorson had an exhibit at J. J. Gillespie and Co., Pittsburgh's premier private art gallery.[3]

In 1910, Gorson acquired another patron, Oliver Ricketson, the son of the owner of an assembly plant who had married the daughter of Tom Carnegie, Andrew Carnegie's younger brother. When Oliver Ricketson saw Gorson's paintings, he bought six right away, sending one called *Nocturne* to Andrew Carnegie in Scotland. Moreover, he commissioned Gorson to paint a portrait of his ten-year-old daughter, Lucy, and invited him to visit the family at Ricketson's Point in New England that summer.[4] Once Ricketson connected Gorson's paintings to the Carnegie name, all the steel magnates bought paintings: the names Jones, Oliver, Schoenberger appear on the list of buyers. In 1926, E. H. Gary wrote to Gorson that for many years he had enjoyed the painting *The Mill at Night*.[5]

Gorson experienced an explosion of recognition and success. He was now at the center of the city's art activity. When the Associated Artists of Pittsburgh was organized in 1910, Gorson was a founding member. He was now a colleague of James Bonar, the first president of the society and an amateur painter. He had been brought from Dumferline by Andrew Carnegie in 1884 at the age of twenty to work as a mechanical engineer in the Carnegie plants. By 1896, Bonar owned a company that built and sold steam appliances. Gorson was also a colleague of Johanna Woodwell Hailman, daughter

238

of the artist Joseph Woodwell. She had married the engineer and steel manufacturer James B. Hailman. Yet, although Gorson was part of the art scene, he was not a part of the social scene. He worked all day, every day.

For almost a decade, Gorson was busy. He showed at seven Internationals, exhibited at the Corcoran Gallery, at the National Academy of Design, and at the Art Institute of Chicago, The City Art Museum of St. Louis, and the Rochester University Art Gallery. In 1913–14, he taught at the Stevenson School of Art in Pittsburgh, and he had regular shows at J. J. Gillespie and Wunderly Galleries. In 1917, Gorson had a solo exhibition as part of the annual Associated Artists show, where he showed twenty-seven paintings: twenty industrial landscapes and seven portraits, including "J. L. Levy" as a violinist.

Rabbi Levy had provided the means for Gorson to become a successful artist: in Philadelphia, he raised the money to send him to Paris; in Pittsburgh, he allowed Gorson to use his name as a reference, and he encouraged his congregation to buy paintings from Gorson. It is possible that Gorson met other artists through Levy as well. For example, Jean-Emile Laboureur, a visiting French artist, wrote his parents that he had a fine dinner and conversation at the Levy home. Though Laboureur does not mention Gorson, Rabbi Levy's name connects these two artists. Levy gave Gorson the opportunity to develop a career as a painter. Ricketson and the steel magnates, on the other hand, swamped him with success. They wanted his pictures of the steel factories along the river at night, images of factories that glamorized and dramatized the industrial landscape. The laborers and their homes, the sooty and smelly air, the grit of the engines and trains, these are absent from Gorson's paintings. If they had been there, his paintings would not have been as popular.

Johanna Hailman, James Bonar, George Sotter, Christ Walter, all local painters, were inspired by and painted their versions of Gorson's vision, but they also painted other subjects. Gorson

239

narrowed his focus to the industrial landscape, seen from one perspective – the dramatic and the beautiful. As time passed, Gorson settled into compositional formulas. Whereas he had begun by seeking different industrial sites and revisiting familiar ones at different times of day, now he relied on his photos and sketches in his studios. He favored night scenes and repeated the same composition over and over again. By 1920, he had exhausted his natural market among the steel manufacturers. He bitterly acknowledged that he had outlived his popularity and moved to New York, seeking a new art scene, new sights, new subjects. But he could not break loose. He wrote to a friend that "those damned Pittsburgh subjects" haunted his imagination, even in New York.[6] In 1922, he showed sixteen paintings at the John Levy Gallery; nine of them were Pittsburgh scenes. He was reviewed somewhat favorably by Royal Cortissoz, a prestigious critic for the *New York Times*, but that did not help him much.

When he died suddenly of double pneumonia after an operation at Mt. Sinai in October 1933, it was in Pittsburgh, not New York, that a memorial show was mounted. The proceeds of the show at Gillespie's went to his widow and children. Will Hyatt, then president of the Associated Artists of Pittsburgh, pointed out that although Gorson was not the first, he was in his time, the best painter of factories, "this despite a monochrome palette, a oneness of view point." Indeed, Gorson started what might be called "the Pittsburgh school" of painting industry when he began painting dramatic spectacles of blazing light against the night sky, reflections in the river, and blocks of buildings on the shore.

Rabbi Levy helped Gorson at critical times in his life and Gorson certainly acknowledged his indebtedness with portraits and paintings. Levy had to rejoice in Gorson's moment of success, but not all his expectations were fulfilled. Gorson was not a "proud Jew." He did not draw attention to his Jewishness. Many people, even today, are surprised to learn he was a Jew.

240

Notes

1. Ruth L. Wilson "Painters of Pittsburgh. . . Aaron Harry Gorson," *Pittsburgh Press* "Roto," July 1977, p.18.

2. Charles Gillespie, "Pittsburgh the Beautiful: Artist Finds Inspiration for Pictures Amid the City"s Smoke and Gasses," *Pittsburgh Press Illustrated Sunday Magazine.*

3. Gillespie, "Pittsburgh the Beautiful," p.13.

4. Gorson Documentation File, Spanierman Gallery, New York.

5. See *"Art and Artists,"* Pittsburgh Bulletin, 4 June 1910, p.13 and two unsourced and undated clippings in the Gorson documentation File, Spanierman Gallery, New York. The painting in Scotland is now in Dunfermline and is known as *Blast Furnace, Carnegie Steel Company, Pittsburgh*, listed in Mick Gridley, *A Catalogue of American Paintings in British Public Collections,* (Exeter, Eng.: American Arts Documentation Centre, University of Exeter, 1974).

6. Gorson to Reverend Leiseder, January 1923, quoted by Ruth L. Wilson, *"Painters of Pittsburgh,"* p.18.

A FAMILY OF LEADERS:
THE AARON FAMILY THROUGH FOUR GENERATIONS

Frances Aaron Hess

When Rabbi Jacob asked me a year ago to speak about the role of my extended family at Rodef Shalom Temple throughout its one-hundred-forty-year history, I had no idea how much fun I would have poring over ninety-two years of Temple minute books and perusing the wealth of archival materials stored in my parents' house. I have learned so much about my own family and have developed an even deeper sense of pride in the family's role in the American Reform Jewish world. It is not easy to speak about the accomplishments of one's own relatives, but I shall let the records speak for themselves. For fifty-one of the eighty-three years from 1889 to 1972, family members served as president of the congregation: my great-great uncle Abraham Lippman, 1889–1910, my grandfather Marcus Aaron, 1930–1941, and my father, Marcus Lester Aaron, from 1953 to 1972. An Aaron, from Marcus to Marcus II, played a critical role in the selection of all Rodef Shalom's rabbis from Dr. Levy in 1901 to Dr. Staitman in 1997.

The family's ties to Rodef Shalom go back to its earliest years. Meyer Hanauer, one of my great-great-grandfathers, came to Pittsburgh in 1850 from Wiesenfeld in Bavaria and was a member of the congregation from its very beginning. After his death on August 18, 1882, the Temple Board passed a resolution:

"Resolved that through his long membership of this Body he has earned our sincere and earnest gratitude by his devotion to the best interest of our community as well as by his efforts in behalf of our congregational success."[1]

LOUIS ISRAEL AARON (1840–1919)
AND PHILLIP HAMBURGER (1849–1921)

Two of my great-grandfathers, Louis Israel Aaron and Phillip Hamburger, served on the board of Rodef Shalom. Born in Moschin in the Prussian province of Posen in 1840, Louis Aaron joined Rodef Shalom in 1860 when he arrived in Pittsburgh. He was elected to the Board of Trustees in 1887 and served until 1895, with the School

Committee his principal interest. In 1897 he was appointed to the Committee of Three, along with Phillip Hamburger and Emil Wertheimer, to secure $35,000 in funds for the new Temple. The minutes, passed by the Temple board after Louis I. Aaron's death on December 31, 1919, describes his pivotal role in the Congregation:

> We have learned with profound sorrow of the sudden demise of Louis I. Aaron, one of the oldest members of this congregation, whose continued interest and influence in its behalf during a period of fifty years and over has largely aided in its remarkable progress through all these years. Not only by his liberal contributions to the cause we represent, but by his personal sincerity and his exceptional example as a constant attendant at divine worship, he has practically demonstrated his love of Judaism and its inherent principles."[2]

A very successful business man, first in dry goods, then the grain and malting business, and, finally, pottery, Louis I. Aaron was "one of the leading public-spirited Jews of the city of Pittsburgh. . . Devoted to Judaism, his able, energetic and intelligent support was given to substantially every Jewish activity in the city of Pittsburgh."[3] He was one of the organizers of the Hebrew Benevolent Society of Pittsburgh and was its secretary for many years. He was one of the organizers and the secretary of the United Hebrew Relief Association. He was a director of the Federation of Jewish Philanthropies and the Jewish Free Loan Society. He was very active at the Gusky Orphanage and Home from its founding and for many years thereafter. "He was instrumental in the organization, financing and management of the Hebrew Institute of Pittsburgh, which without his enthusiastic support and large money contributions would not have come into existence."[4]

Another great-grandfather, Phillip Hamburger, was born in Hammelburg, Bavaria, in 1849. He came to Pittsburgh in 1867 to join his uncle Meyer Hanauer and eventually married his daughter, Fannie. Active in business as a distiller, he devoted a great deal of time and energy to Rodef Shalom Temple. He served on the Temple board

Philip Hamburger

Louis Israel Aaron

245

for forty years until his death in June 1921. He was a member of the Finance, Cultus (later known as Worship), and Building committees, and was chairman of both Finance and Cultus. He frequently represented Rodef Shalom at UAHC (Union of American Hebrew Congregations) Councils (as biennials were then called). He was the fourth-highest bidder for seats at the new Eighth Street Temple in 1901, and he donated a window for that temple in memory of his late wife, Fannie Hanauer Hamburger. That window is the front left window of our present sanctuary. The memorial resolution adopted by the Temple board in 1921 stated:

> Rarely has a man served the cause of Judaism with more fidelity and earnestness. The interest which he had in the Congregation was always manifested in readiness to give personal service and to contribute of his means generously to its support. There was no problem connected with the congregational life congregational which he did not take seriously to heart and concerning which he did not give his colleagues on the Board his fullest and frankest judgment."[5]

ABRAHAM LIPPMAN (1838–1910)

My great-great-uncle Abraham Lippman, whose sister Mina was the wife of Louis I. Aaron, was one of the major figures in the history of Rodef Shalom. Born in Memelsdorf, Bavaria, in 1838, he emigrated to the United States at the age of thirteen, settling in Pittsburgh by 1860. In 1880, after a very successful career in commerce, he retired to devote himself to the poor and the needy. He was first elected to the Temple board in 1884 and served for two years. In March 1889 he was elected president of the congregation and served in this capacity for twenty-one years until his death on March 21, 1910. The congregation thrived under the leadership of this "sweet, simple, honorable, kindly, just, peace-loving man."[6] At the dedication of the new temple on Eighth Street in 1901, Abraham Lippman spoke of his role at Rodef Shalom Temple:

> For nearly thirteen years I have labored hard and faithfully for all things relative to congregational matters, and have felt a keen delight in its great strides and successes. When I take a retrospect

246

over the past forty years, I am filled with pride at the stupendous advancement that has been effected among us. . . . May God strengthen me in my purpose to uphold the beautiful motto inscribed over the portals of the Temple Rodef Shalom[7] – "Seek Peace and Pursue It."[8]

His presidential address in March 1909 conveyed his continued pride in the congregation:

> We have, as a congregation, been unusually successful, and while complaints reach me, on all sides, about congregational conditions in other cities, I am happy to say that I look forward to the future of this Congregation without the slightest fear.[9]

At the annual meeting in March 1910, just eight days after Abraham Lippman's death, Judge Josiah Cohen, his successor as Temple president, proclaimed:

> The history of Rodef Sholem cannot be written without his name appearing large on the pages which record the event of the past four decades. He loved the House of God and worshiped therein with pious fervor and reverential spirit. . . He will be missed by all who love the congregation to which he was attached with so true and unselfish a purpose.[10]

At the memorial service held on March 27, Rodef Shalom's rabbi, Dr. J. Leonard Levy, summed up Abraham Lippman's significance to Rodef Shalom Temple:

> It was this congregation that was to him a source of the highest joy. Lippman and Rodeph Shalom will always be associated one with the other. We have had former presidents of this congregation who did excellent service for Rodeph Shalom, but he was the President par excellence. It was Abraham Lippman who was President at the time when the new era began for this congregation. What joy he found in the little building on Eighth street! How nobly he stood for the broader Judaism to be presented by this broader and larger Temple! How generously he gave of his means as a contribution toward this, our present building.[11]

Abraham Lippman was very generous to the congregation. He

made substantial monetary contributions to the Temple and made a number of no-interest loans when the Temple treasury was short. He provided funds so that after his death his pew should be assigned free of charge to deserving widows for whom membership and taxes would be a hardship. After the unassigned pew system and the abolition of dues and taxes on pews made this provision unnecessary, the funds were transferred in 1938 to the Religious School Building Fund. While president, Abraham Lippman remembered the children in the religious school at Hanukkah and was responsible for the distribution of fruit at Succoth. After his death, his nephew, Marcus Rauh, continued both traditions in his uncle's memory – candles at Hanukkah and apples at Succoth – and so it continues right down to the present.

After his death, Abraham Lippman was memorialized not only by Hanukkah candles and apples but by a memorial plaque in our sanctuary and a Memorial Chapel at West View Cemetery. This chapel, built in 1911–12, was a gift to the congregation from four nephews, Charles Israel Aaron, Marcus Aaron, Abraham Lippman Rauh, and Marcus Rauh "as an appropriate mark of love and esteem to the memory of our late departed."[12] In 1945, the Temple board found it necessary to raze the chapel, since it was in serious disrepair and was no longer used because of the current preference for funeral parlors. In 1946, President Eugene B. Strassburger appointed a committee, chaired by Vice President Marcus Lester Aaron, to recommend a suitable memorial to Abraham Lippman in the main building of the Temple. That was not finally accomplished until the building expansion of 1956, when the school library on the main floor was named for Abraham Lippman.

MARCUS RAUH (1859–1940)

One of Abraham Lippman's nephews, Marcus Rauh, served on the Temple board for thirty years, 1910–1940. He was first elected to fill the vacancy created when his first cousin, Marcus Aaron, moved up to vice president when Vice President Josiah Cohen became

248

Marcus Rauh

A. Lippman.

Dinner in honor of Abraham Lippman on the occasion of
the fiftieth year of service to the congregation 1910

249

president after the death of their uncle Abraham Lippman. Marcus Rauh played a very active role on the board as chairman of the Membership Committee from 1911 to 1926 and chairman of the Religious School Committee from 1916 to 1931, when he became honorary chairman until his death. He also served on the UAHC Executive Board from 1910 to 1940, and was one of its vice presidents from the mid-1920s until the late 1930s, when he became an honorary board member.[13]

Marcus Rauh's importance to Rodef Shalom was evident in the resolution the board passed after his death:

> In the passing of Marcus Rauh, the city of Pittsburgh, the Pittsburgh Jewish Community and especially Rodef Shalom Temple have sustained a great loss. The entire community has been bereaved, yet our loss here at Rodef Shalom seems more grievous, for his life and work within the Temple seems to us to have been the source of the inspiration which made him so useful a citizen in all other fields.
>
> The Jewish faith, so deeply instilled in him by righteous and God-fearing parents, guided his life from the very beginning . . . . Hardly ever, unless ill health prevented it, was he absent from the service of prayer and devotion. As the Temple meant so much to him in the early formative years of his life, he desired to build up a similar love for Judaism and the temple in the hearts of the entire younger generation . . . .
>
> We of the Board of Trustees mourn his loss particularly. He was associated with the Board for thirty years. During the long period of unbroken companionship, we learned to revere his gentleness of mood, to respect his keenness of mind and to be influenced by his truly religious spirit.[14]

The Temple board placed a memorial plaque to Marcus Rauh in the sanctuary.

MARCUS AARON (1869–1954)

The tremendous accomplishments of my grandfather Marcus Aaron, both at Rodef Shalom and on the national Jewish scene, were the outgrowth of his very thorough grounding in American Reform Judaism. As stated in the Rodef Shalom Board of trustees resolution at the time of his death in 1954:

> But all that he did in every walk of life and in every field of service was an outgrowth of his religious faith and the ideals which it proclaimed. From the very beginning he was devoted to our Reform movement in Judaism. He proudly recalled that as a lad he witnessed that famous gathering of Reform rabbis in Pittsburgh that wrote and proclaimed the Pittsburgh Platform. He remembered the names of those leaders and the words that they spoke. That doctrine that they preached, that of our ancient faith voicing itself as a superb ethical influence, deeply impressed his youthful mind and became the unfailing guide of the man throughout his long and splendid career.[15]

Although he was very active with Homer Laughlin China Company and served on the Pittsburgh Board of Education from 1911 to 1942 and as its president from 1922 to 1942, he still devoted his heart and soul to Rodef Shalom for more than fifty years. He began as a teacher in the religious school in the 1890s. As a thirty-year-old, his first major role at Temple was to serve on the Committee of Nine and as its secretary, 1900–1901, to "devise plans and ways and means to provide for the building of a new Temple and for the election of a successor to our present Rabbi (Dr. Lippman Mayer)."[16] After the committee brought in its recommendation for a new building at the Eighth Street location rather than a move to Allegheny,[17] Marcus Aaron was appointed to the Building Committee, along with his father-in-law, Phillip Hamburger. He served as assistant to the chairman, Samuel Wertheimer, and as secretary to the committee. Thought to be too young to be elected a Temple trustee in 1901, he was first elected an honorary trustee and appointed as chairman of the Pew Committee and as member of the Worship Committee. He played a crucial role in the sale of seats for the new Eighth Street Temple, which rendered the new Temple totally debt free. The very next year, 1902, he was elected a regular trustee.

He immediately assumed an active role as a board member, making many motions at board meetings to move the action along. He played the leading role in negotiating the sale of the Eighth Street Temple in 1904. At the congregational meeting called to approve the sale, he argued:

> A Temple should not be a club with a limited membership and a waiting-list. Every Jew in the community be he ever so humble should feel that in our Temple he is welcomed either as a member or seat-holder but for the present we have reached our limit, we have no room for new members, seat-holders or the children of members. Such a condition is intolerable and ought to be quickly corrected.[18]

He first served as chairman of the Site Committee for the new Temple on Fifth Avenue and then as chairman of the committee of five that supervised the building of the new edifice.

Marcus Aaron served as first vice president of Rodef Shalom for twenty years, from the death of President Abraham Lippman in 1910 to the death of President Josiah Cohen in June 1930, when he was elected president. He held this position until June 1941, when he resigned because of ill health. The Board moved to accept his resignation only if he were elected honorary president for life.

In the early twenties, he played a strong leadership role in the successful campaign to get Rodef Shalom to adopt an unassigned pew system. At the national meeting of the UAHC in Buffalo on April 25, 1921, in a speech that was reprinted in full in the *New York Times* and lauded by an editorial, he declared:

> Our congregations have generally been financed by methods that would hardly be justified in a social club. On the outside we inscribe the motto: 'My house should be a house of prayer for all people.' Inside the temple we have a mental reservation: "For such as can afford to pay."
>
> So long as there is a single reform Jewish congregation where property rights are evidenced by private ownership of pews,

Marcus Lester Aaron, Marcus
Aaron, Louis I. Aaron

Marcus Aaron

involving as it does a rich man's corner and a poor man's section, we are maintaining "an abomination in the sight of the Lord."[19]

As Marcus Aaron confessed in his presidential speech at the 1934 annual meeting, he had been responsible for bringing three rabbis to Rodef Shalom. Talking about the selection of Dr. Solomon B. Freehof in 1933, he said:

> I had been quite successful in several such attempts at Highway Robbery. Together with Judge Josiah Cohen, I had persuaded Dr. Levy to come to us from Philadelphia, thirty-three years ago and by the power of my right arm (as the Chairman of the Special Committee for the Selection of a Rabbi) I had brought Dr. Goldenson to Pittsburgh from Albany sixteen years ago, so I was delegated by the Committee to go to Chicago and kidnap Dr. Freehof.[20]

Dr. Freehof confirmed Marcus Aaron's powers of persuasion when he seconded the motion electing Marcus Aaron honorary president for life

> stating that when he came to Pittsburgh, it was solely because of Mr. Aaron's persuasion and that he did it largely at that time because Mr. Aaron was known as one of the outstanding lay leaders in Jewish life and that he felt that when he came he was really coming to "Mr. Aaron's Congregation."[21]

One of the promises Marcus Aaron made to Dr. Freehof when he agreed to come to Pittsburgh was that adequate school facilities, which had been a crying need for over ten years, would be provided in the very near future.[22] Considering religious education for all Jewish children absolutely vital, he provided the vision and leadership to see this project to completion at the cost of over a half-million dollars without any permanent indebtedness. At the 1934 Annual Meeting, he proclaimed:

> We can no longer neglect proper housing for our school children, and I recommend that we proceed to correct the greatest blunder of our congregation in all its history at the earliest possible moment. If we cannot find the money to erect and pay for such a

building, we prove ourselves utterly unworthy of the self-sacrificing, spiritual leadership that has been, and is, ours.[23]

When the new religious school building was dedicated on Hannukah 1938, he thanked the congregation and its rabbi for "this undertaking, so vital to everything we stand for, particularly to our most precious possession – our children and the community's children – those who will soon take our place as the members of Rodef Shalom Congregation."[24]

Marcus Aaron brought great glory to Rodef Shalom through his active involvement with the national institutions of Reform Judaism. When Dr. J. Leonard Levy died in March 1917, Marcus Aaron was elected to take his place on the Board of Governors of Hebrew Union College. He served until 1930, when he was succeeded by his son, Marcus Lester Aaron. Marcus Aaron also served as an active member of the Executive Board of the UAHC from 1913 until 1941, when he was elected an honorary member for life. In his speeches at UAHC Councils and at temples in the East and Midwest in the 1920s, he was a tireless and articulate advocate for the importance of Jewish education, the need for regular attendance at worship services, the necessary partnership of lay leaders and rabbis in furthering the cause of Judaism in America, and the importance of adequate financial support for both the UAHC and the Hebrew Union College. His challenge to the Twenty-Seventh Council of the UAHC in Buffalo was:

> We have the remedy in our own hands. We only need take our business of being Jews more seriously. We need to bend all efforts – to unite all loyal hearts in a systematic organized movement – in a relentless campaign of education to infuse more Jewishness into our business life, to put new vigor into the Jewish home, school and pulpit; to train the young for active service in the synagogue; to bring within its folds those who have drifted away, and within its influence those of other beliefs.[25]

After Marcus Aaron's death in June 1954, the Temple Board placed a plaque in his memory in the sanctuary. At Dr. Freehof's suggestion in September 1956, the Rodef Shalom Board of Trustees named the Garden Court in memory of Marcus Aaron, "... who served this congregation so long, so well, and so faithfully."[26] Trying to persuade his son, Marcus Lester Aaron, then president of Rodef Shalom, why this memorial was necessary, Dr. Freehof argued:

> Our congregational building has become an historic evidence of the families who have served it so devotedly. Our building has honored the name Falk and the name Lippman and the name Cohen. It would be historically untrue if the name Aaron were not permanently a part of the building.[27]

As the board said in its memorial resolution: "This Temple was his life work, this was his blessing, and here he will be eternally remembered . . . . . A great man has left us; a glorious recollection remains."[28]

MARCUS LESTER AARON (1900–1994)

Carrying on the tradition of his father, Marcus Lester Aaron, involved with Homer Laughlin China Company for more than sixty-five years, still devoted a lifetime of service to Rodef Shalom and to Reform Judaism on the national and international scene. His extraordinary commitment to Reform Judaism came not only from his own family but from the rabbi of his youth, his teacher and mentor, Dr. J. Leonard Levy. As my father wrote to his fourteen grandchildren when he gave each one a copy of *J. Leonard Levy: Prophetic Voice* on his seventieth birthday, "No other teacher had a greater or more sanctifying influence on my life than J. Leonard Levy. His memory has been a living presence to me through all the years."[29] Dr. Levy's one-paragraph statement, *My Religion*, was the creed by which my father lived and which he taught to his four children:

> My religion is based upon the acceptance of the Eternal God as my Father and upon my treatment of my fellow-man as my brother. To work in hope; to accept the past in gratefulness and to strive to add to the good for the future; to be honest in all my dealings and expressions; to worship the truth; to be loyal to my country and to my ideals; to seek salvation through character; to treasure the truth of Scripture and to labor to advance Israel's

256

purpose; to do justice, to love mercy and to walk humbly before God; to live that I may die regretted and to die in the faith that I may live after death; – this is my religion.[30]

In the twenty years between my father's return to Pittsburgh in 1923 from Princeton University and Harvard Law School and his election to the Rodef Shalom Board of Trustees in 1943, he played a prominent role in the national and international organizations of Reform Judaism. In January 1925, he was invited to the National Federation of Temple Brotherhood's (NFTB) first biennial in St. Louis to participate in a symposium on *How to Develop and Maintain the Interest of Our Young People in Judaism*, representing the young man's point of view. After the biennial, he received invitations to speak at the annual conference of the New York State Federation of Temple Sisterhoods that April and at a Friday evening service at Temple Beth El in Steubenville in December. He was also asked to serve as vice chairman of the NFTB's National Committee on Student Welfare.

His speech on *Judaism and the Synagogue: The Young Man's Viewpoint* at the UAHC's Thirtieth Council's conference on *The Perpetuation of Judaism* in January 1927 was a ringing call for ritual and prayer book reform. According to the *Cleveland Plain Dealer*, "debate centered around the address of Marcus [L.] Aaron, Pittsburgh, a business man, still under 30, who asked the august body of mature minds to strip reformed [sic] Jewish ritual of the 'things we don't believe.'"[31] Dr. Goldenson asked him to give the same talk at a Rodef Shalom Sunday service on February 5, 1927, and he also delivered a sermon at the Pittsburgh YM&WHA weekly Friday night service in late March. Rabbi and Mrs. Morris S. Lazeron invited him to speak at the Baltimore YM&WHA on "Youth Challenges the Synagogue" in December 1927. As a result of his Cleveland speech, he was also asked to chair the NFTB'S National Committee on Youth Education to see what needed to be done in youth and adult religious education.

His 1927 Cleveland speech also led to his being appointed one of five UAHC representatives to meet with five rabbis from the Central Conference of American Rabbis (CCAR) to work out a plan for prayer book revision. At the meeting of this Preliminary Committee on Prayer Book Revision in March 1930, the minutes record that "Mr. Aaron felt more strongly than he did then [in Cleveland in 1927] that a revision of the prayer-book in keeping with modern thought and practice was essential to the future of Judaism."[32] He also served on the subsequent UAHC Committee on Revision of the Prayer Book. In 1935 he served two terms on the UAHC's Board of Managers for the Department of Synagogue and School Extension. Throughout the 1930s he served as the UAHC'S representative to the World Union for Progressive Judaism's International Youth Committee and was a member of the World Union's governing body.

Marcus Lester Aaron served on the Board of Governors of Hebrew Union College for forty-five years, 1930–1975, and then continued participating as an honorary governor until his death in April 1994. In 1970, at the time of my father's seventieth birthday, President Nelson Glueck wrote:

> As a faithful member of the Board of Governors of the Hebrew Union College-Jewish Institute of Religion you have stalwartly supported during the thirty-nine years of your service in this office the programs which have resulted in our College's growth to international stature and influence . . . . Thoughtful, devoted, generous, you have been an encouraging participant in our development, and I am sure in many other projects of great spiritual value.[33]

Although Marcus Lester Aaron had taught in the Rodef Shalom religious school in the 1920s and had also frequently represented the Temple at the national level, his fifty years of active participation in congregational leadership did not begin until 1943, when Rodef Shalom increased the size of its board from sixteen to twenty and he was elected to one of the four new positions. In 1946 he was elected a vice president and served as chairman of the Worship Committee until he was elected Temple president in 1953. As chairman, he spoke out year after year forthrightly and eloquently for the need for greater attendance at services other than the High Holy Days. He also argued very cogently that Temple membership should be open to all; there should be no ceiling on the size of the congregation.[34] Arguing for the proposed rotating seating plan for the High Holy Days, he "reiterated the position . . . that the new plan was, in effect, an extension of the unassigned pew system and that it promoted the idea that the place of worship was entirely secondary and subordinate to attendance of public worshiping."[35] Ever the democrat with a small "d," as was his father before him, he believed there should be no charge to congregants for the use of the Chapel or Temple because "the Temple was to be a house of worship for all people and that the more frequently the members used the facilities of the Temple, the better relations there would be between the institution and its members."[35]

In March 1953, the Temple board's Slate Committee recommended Marcus Lester Aaron as president of the congregation, "believing he would measure up to the high standards of the past presidents of the congregation."[36] During his nineteen years as president, the congregation thrived. As stated in the unanimous board resolution drafted by Dr. Walter Jacob at the time of his retirement in March 1972, "during those years, a new building was added to the Temple, major improvements in the older structures were undertaken, the program of the Congregation and its membership vastly expanded."[37] Just as his father had been the driving force behind the new buildings on Eighth Avenue and Fifth Avenue and the 1938 Religious School Building, so Marcus Lester Aaron presided over the 1953–1956 building program that culminated in the Rodef Shalom Centennial and Dedication Festival, May 10–13, 1956. He served as chairman of the Building Fund-Raising Committee that secured the $960,000 in capital funds needed for this enterprise.

While president, he wrote the history of Rodef Shalom that was first published at the time of the Temple's Centennial celebration and was updated in 1976. He was also responsible for Rodef Shalom's publication in 1974 of *World Problems and Personal Religion:*

Sermons, Addresses, and Selected Writings of Samuel H. Goldenson, which was sent to every member of Rodef Shalom Congregation in Pittsburgh and Temple Emanu-El in New York City and the entire Reform rabbinate. This was a labor of love in memory of his beloved rabbi and friend. Again, like father, like son, Marcus Lester Aaron served as chairman of the Pulpit Committee that recommended the election of Dr. Walter Jacob as rabbi when Dr. Freehof retired. He presided with great "dignity"[38] and "outstanding statesmanship"[39] over the May 1, 1966, congregational meeting at which Dr. Jacob was elected.

During the nineteen years my father was president, he gave infinite attention to all details. He attended practically every Temple committee meeting in those two decades. He wrote every communication that went out over his signature – every letter, every speech as president, every letter accompanying the High Holy Day tickets, every congregational appeal for funds for the UAHC and Hebrew Union College-JIR,[40] every memorial and testimonial resolution issued by the Temple board. Each speech, whether a welcome to new members or an annual meeting address, was written with the greatest of care and reflected a deep Reform Jewish spirituality, a commitment to the loftiest ethical principles, and a nobility of language. At the conclusion of his presidency, the board published his presidential addresses as "a gift in recognition of his spiritual and devoted leadership of Rodef Shalom."[41]

In these Annual Meeting messages, year after year, he set forth his high ideals for the congregation and its mission:

> Here at Rodef Shalom we have taken great pride in a great congregation, blessed as no other congregation has been with the leadership in our own time of Dr. J. Leonard Levy, Dr. Samuel H. Goldenson and Doctor Freehof himself. No other congregation, we like to think, has had the privilege which we have had, and for that privilege we are deeply grateful.
>
> One thing is clear, however, no congregation lives on privilege. No congregation can live on its past achievement or on past and

Marcus Lester Aaron

Marcus Aaron II

Temple Board 1980s

261

present blessings. Our future must be prepared today . . . . What we need above all is consecration of spirit – dedication of mind and heart and soul. Only with such dedication may we hope to build a future for this Congregation worthy of its great tradition.[42]

In the concluding paragraph of his 1965 message, he reminded the congregation that:

It is our task in this Congregation to raise up a new generation, dedicated, as were our fathers, to the cause of religion, to the service of God and of man, to the vision of a better future – better because we have tried to make it better – better because we have given of ourselves. The task requires loyalty, consecration, and intelligence on our part – a supreme personal commitment. "And the work of righteousness shall be peace; and the effect of righteousness, quietness and confidence forever" (Isaiah 32:17). The goal may be distant; but the future depends on us. Let us face that future undaunted and unafraid.[43]

Even his pleas for funds, whether for the Building Fund of the 1950s or the Five Year Capital Campaign in the 1960s, were pitched on the loftiest plane. "When you are called upon to give, we hope that you will give in proportion to the high objective that we seek. We are asking for money; but we have not become materialists. We know that the objectives of faith are those immaterial and ultimate realities which glorify life and give it meaning, and to those objectives with your aid we shall dedicate this building."[44] In his yearly appeal for the support of the UAHC and HUC-JIR, he never failed to remind the congregants of Rodef Shalom's historic role in the national institutions of Reform Judaism. Rodef Shalom Temple had been one of the founding congregations of the UAHC in 1875, and a Pittsburgher, Henry Berkowitz, was one of the four members in the first class of rabbis ordained at Hebrew Union College in 1883.

What my father asked of others in generous response to Rodef Shalom's financial needs, he more than demanded of himself. Following the family tradition of munificent support of the Temple, he assumed more than his fair share of responsibility for the financial well-being of the congregation. After Marcus Rauh's death in 1940,

262

he carried on the tradition of apples and Hanukkah candles in Abraham Lippman's memory.

My father's style of presidential leadership is aptly described by Walter E. Ellman in a letter written after the conclusion of his eight-year term on the temple board:

> I wish to take cognizance of the wise and truly inspiring leadership of Lester Aaron, whose imprint has been indelibly stamped on the Temple Board, and whose constant example has continually established a standard of dedication and loyalty for all the Trustees to emulate. I think we all owe him an especial vote of thanks for the spirit of democracy, with which all board meetings are run. There is never any pre-mature[sic] end to debate, never an attempt on the part of a ruling clique to ride roughshod over the rest of the Board.[45]

The tributes to my father on the occasion of his seventieth birthday in 1970 are a moving testimony to his particular contributions to Rodef Shalom. Dr. Freehof wrote:

> There could not have been a president with more of those qualities which strengthen the mind and heart of a rabbi. His deep respect for the rabbinate as an institution, his complete devotion to Temple worship, his embodiment of that high social idealism brought to the world by the biblical prophets, all these characteristics of his strengthened me and made my rabbinate a joy.[46]

The Board of Trustees resolution proclaimed:

> In many ways Marcus Lester Aaron is characteristically and uniquely himself. The central element in his personality is his commitment, his sense of complete devotion to a cause; and our Congregation has been blessed by the fact that his complete public commitment has been given to Rodef Shalom Temple and to its ideals. Others may and do understand the importance of the public religious services as a creative force to communal spirituality. But to him public worship is more than that: It has been a personal devotion. It has been for years a source of inspiration and encouragement that the President of the Congregation, in spite of

263

many busy affairs to call upon his time, has almost never missed a single service in our sanctuary.

But we are sure that it is rare that such practical knowledge should be completely permeated with a deep spirituality. The practical problems of the Congregation were never allowed to obscure its religious aims and its devotion to the will of the Eternal God.[47]

As Rodef Shalom trustee for life from the time of his retirement as president in 1972, Marcus Lester Aaron continued his active and devoted service to the congregation until 1993. At the time of his death in April 1994, the lay and rabbinical leaders of Rodef Shalom paid him tribute in *The Jewish Chronicle*: "He was a trustee of the Congregation for fifty years and its president for nineteen years, following in the footsteps of his uncle, Abraham Lippman and his father, Marcus Aaron. He led with learning, wisdom, and complete devotion to Judaism. His personal piety and deeply held convictions inspired those who followed him."[48]

MARCUS AARON II (B. 1929)

The family tradition at Rodef Shalom continues today. In 1991, my brother, Marcus Aaron II, a lawyer and president of Homer Laughlin China Company, as were his father and grandfather before him, was elected to the Temple board. From 1992 to 1994 he served as chairman of the Worship Committee. In 1994 he became assistant treasurer and also served as chair of the Budget Committee, a position he still holds. In February 1996, he was elected treasurer of the congregation. Carrying on the family tradition of involvement in the rabbinical search process, Pete, as he is known, served as co-chairman of the Committee on Rabbinical Succession that nominated Dr. Mark Staitman in the spring of 1996 to succeed Dr. Jacob as Rodef Shalom's rabbi. He later became an honorary trustee.

CONCLUSION

If the Aaron family legacy of one-hundred-forty years is to continue, then the members of Rodef Shalom Congregation must pick up the torch and carry it forward. Marcus Lester Aaron phrased the challenge boldly in a speech to a joint workshop of all the Temple boards in October 1971:

> We have come to a critical point in the long history of our faith from Abraham to the present day. The responsibility for that faith cannot be delegated to others; it cannot be delegated to our Rabbis. That responsibility is ours, your and mine.
>
> If we – you and I – neglect public worship, Judaism will wither and die. If we – you and I – neglect the study of our history and our religion, Judaism will not survive. If we – you and I – are indifferent to the imperatives of the moral law, we shall not be Jews except in name.
>
> To build a future for ourselves and a better world for all men, we need the faith, the education, the intelligence, and the commitment – the dedication above all else to God and to goodness.
>
> What does that require of us as members of Rodef Shalom Congregation?
> 1. It requires regular weekly attendance at public worship.
> 2. It requires study of our history and our religion – not merely for our children but for ourselves. Without education the past will be forgotten and the future will be lost.
> 3. It requires understanding and commitment to the moral law – the practice in human relations of a living faith.
> 4. It requires conscious dedication to the building of a better world. We do not ask a perfect world. We ask only that each of us in proportion to his ability shall make that world just a little better because of our dedication to Judaism as a living faith. If such is our conscious commitment, we shall bring new life and strength to Rodef Shalom Congregation and shall add new meaning to an ancient vision.[49]

ACKNOWLEDGMENTS

I want to thank Dr. Walter Jacob for asking me to prepare this paper and for all his advice and support. I am very grateful to the rabbis and staff at Rodef Shalom for all the assistance they gave me as I searched through the Temple archives. My brother, Marcus Aaron II, and my sister, Elinor Goldmark Aaron Langer, gave me great help and encouragement from start to finish on this rather daunting project. Thanks, too, to Louise B. Stern and Dr. Ronald B. Sobel for their invaluable editorial help.

Notes

1. *Minutes of Congregation Rodef Shalom*, August 27, 1882.

2. *Minutes Rodef Shalom Congregation*, January 4, 1920.

3. A. Leo Weil, "Louis I. Aaron," *Publications of the American Jewish Historical Society*, No. 28, 1922, pp. 257-8.

4. Ibid., p.258.

5. *Minutes Rodef Shalom Congregation*, June 12, 1921.

6. Dr. John A. Brashear, Judge Josiah Cohen, Rabbi J. Leonard Levy, D.D., *Abraham Lippman, A Tribute*, Pittsburgh, 1910, p.16.

7. The Temple's name is spelled in various forms in the documents of 1880-1910, Rodef or Rodeph; Shalem, Sholem, or Shalom. Only after 1911 does it seem to be consistently spelled as Rodef Shalom.

8. *Jewish Criterion*, Vol. 13, No.14.

9. *Minutes Rodef Shalom Congregation*, p. 243, March 28, 1909.

10. Ibid., March 27, 1910, p. 277.

11. Dr. John A. Brashear, Judge Josiah Cohen, Rabbi J. Leonard Levy, D.D., *Abraham Lippman, A Tribute*, Pittsburgh, 1910, p.19.

12. *Minutes Rodef Shalom Congregation*, March 26, 1911. Letter from Charles I. Aaron, Marcus Aaron, Abraham Lippman Rauh, Marcus Rauh to President Josiah Cohen.

13. I was unable to find the precise dates of his UAHC vice presidency.

14. *Minutes Rodef Shalom Congregation*, March 8, 1941.

15. Ibid., June 29, 1954.

16. *Minutes of Congregation Rodef Shalom*, March 26, 1900.

17. According to Marcus Lester Aaron, his father, Marcus Aaron led the movement to keep the Temple in Pittsburgh, rather than to move to Allegheny. He saw the trend to be for the Jewish community to settle in the East End of Pittsburgh. Under Abraham Lippman plans were all set to go to Allegheny until Marcus Aaron upset the plans. Marcus [L.] Aaron, *Pittsburgh Section, National Council of Jewish Women Oral History Project*, Tape 1 of 5, February 10, 1975.

18. Ibid, December 27, 1904.

19. Marcus Aaron, "What A Layman Can Do for Judaism, " *New York Times*, May 29, 1921.

20. *Minutes Rodef Shalom Congregation*, October 28, 1934.

21. Ibid., June 8, 1941.

22. *Minutes Rodef Shalom Congregation*, May 9, 1937.

23. Ibid., October 28, 1934.

24. Marcus Aaron, *Remarks by Marcus Aaron, President of the Rodef Shalom Congregation of Pittsburgh upon the Occasion of the Dedication of the Dr. J. Leonard Levy Auditorium and of the Religious School Building*, December 18, 1939.

25. Marcus Aaron, "What a Layman Can Do for Judaism," *New York Times*, May 29, 1921.

26. *Minutes Rodef Shalom Congregation*, September 18, 1956.

27. Rabbi Solomon B. Freehof, D.D., *Letter to Marcus Lester Aaron,* September 19, 1956.

28. *Minutes Rodef Shalom Congregation*, June 29, 1954.

29. Marcus L. Aaron, *Letter to Edward W. Roston, Jr.*, October 8, 1970.

30. J. Leonard Levy, *My Religion.*

31. *Cleveland Plain Dealer*, Tuesday, January 18, 1927, p.5.

32. *Prayer Book Revision Committee Minutes*, March 11, 1930.

33. Dr. Nelson Glueck, *Letter to Marcus L. Aaron, September 28, 1970.*

34. *Minutes Rodef Shalom Congregation*, October 13, 1946.

35. Ibid., March 31, 1952, special board meeting.

36. Ibid., October 12, 1947. Letter from Marcus L. Aaron.

37. Ibid., March 14, 1972.

38. Louise Freund, *Letter to M. L. Aaron*, May 2, 1966.

39. Leonard Weitzman, *Letter to M. L. Aaron*, May 4, 1966.

40. In 1950 Hebrew Union College merged with the Jewish Institute of Religion, henceforth to be known as Hebrew Union College-Jewish Institute of Religion or HUC-JIR.

41. *The Temple Bulletin*, Rodef Shalom Congregation, March 22, 1972, No. 29.

42. M. L. Aaron *Presidential Addresses*, Pittsburgh, pp. 28-29.

43. Ibid., p. 40.

44. Ibid., p. 6.

45. Walter E. Ellman, *Letter to Vigdor W. Kavaler*, March 27, 1970.

46. Solomon B. Freehof, *Testimonial on the 70th Birthday of Marcus Lester Aaron*, October 8, 1970.

47. The Board of Trustees of Rodef Shalom Congregation, *Honoring the 70th Birthday of Marcus Lester Aaron*, October 8, 1970.

48. *The Jewish Chronicle of Pittsburgh*, April 24, 1994, p. 24.

49. M. L. Aaron, *Presidential Message to Joint Meeting Workshop, Board of Trustees, Sisterhood, Brotherhood, Junior Congregation*, October 10, 1971.

BUILDING THE BIBLICAL BOTANICAL GARDEN

Irene Jacob

When the Tutankhamen Exhibit traveled to the United States, millions saw the splendor of daily life in ancient Egypt, and they began to appreciate the great civilizations of the Bible. The exhibit whetted the appetite for more information—not only in museums, but in a living setting. The Rodef Shalom Biblical Botanical Garden represents a modest effort in that direction.

Our biblical ancestors depended on nature; every aspect of their life was dependent on plants: food, clothing, shelter, medicine, as well as the luxuries of life. When we understand this, then the pages of the Bible come to life in a new way. A good bit of this lore has been recovered through the scholarly efforts of the last century—for instance, archaeological discoveries in Israel, Egypt, and Mesopotamia have shown us how wheat and barley were transformed into bread—but few of these studies have become available in a popular, accessible setting. The Rodef Shalom Biblical Botanical Garden undertakes this task each summer.

This will be a brief history of the garden. When my husband and I wrote a book, a guide to *"Gardens of North America and Hawaii,"* we found in our research that only a few such gardens existed, so we decided to plan a biblical botanical garden.

A third of an acre adjacent to the Temple was available as a site. We began with a hand-drawn outline of a garden shaped like the Land of Israel with a hint of its topographical features. The first draft, on brown wrapping paper, was unrolled before a potential benefactor, as the venture would depend on generous support. When the donor reacted enthusiastically, we went further. This was not to be a pretty garden with some biblical plants and a few statues, but a garden designed along botanical lines.

My research into biblical plants had begun before 1983, when, as Education Coordinator at Phipps Conservatory, I initiated a small winter exhibition there on biblical plants. This led me to greater and extensive research, and eventually my husband and I were asked to write on flora for the four-volume *Anchor Bible Dictionary*.

We were ready to begin construction in 1986. The work connected with the garden went far beyond research. Professionals built three ponds, a stream, a beautifully designed waterfall, two bridges, a pavilion, and walkways. The soil needed careful preparation. Those tasks were largely done by the two of us along with a few volunteers.

When we started to seek sources for plants, it turned out to be a national and international search. A few could be grown annually from seed, but for some plants, like sugar cane, we had to find a source willing to provide us with starter canes each season. As we traveled across the country on tasks totally unrelated to the garden, we visited obscure nurseries and often returned home in the dead of winter with carefully packed plants such as cinnamon, which we hoped would survive the plane ride, and the cold welcome to Pittsburgh.

The first winter brought its own set of problems as we scrambled to keep our plants alive, but we soon became aware of another problem. Mediterranean plants such as the mandrake do not bloom in summer as no rain falls in Israel from May to November. Yet given Pittsburgh's climate, summer had to be our season. To give the garden the splash of color, that the public would want, we included plants with biblical common names such as Joseph's Coat and Jacob's Ladder, and provided distinctive labels.

To attract repeat visitors, as those who come to museums, we wanted the garden to offer something new each year. So, from 1988 onward, we pursued a different theme each year. We knew that the research alone would be considerable and that thorough study would be necessary.

Our first theme was suggested by our own visits to Israel. There we learned that 90% of the plants currently grown in Israel are

Garden gate to the pavillion

Bridge from the pavillion to the
garden

271

not native. Our first exhibit in 1988, *"Forgotten Immigrants: Plant Introductions to Israel through 2,000 Years,"* demonstrated how plants brought to Israel had become almost native there. Perhaps the best example is the *opuntia,* which Israelis call the *"Sabra,"* a prickly cactus native to Central America and introduced to Israel in the early 19th century. The plant has become so much a part of the country's culture that native Israelis call themselves *Sabras,* that is, prickly on the outside, sweet on the inside.

The popularity of this special exhibit encouraged us to turn to plants used in medicine in Mesopotamia, Egypt, and Israel. The Bible is only incidentally interested in medicine. The illness and injury of various individuals were reported, but only in its historical context. The sole exception was the detailed concern with preventive medicine displayed by Leviticus. There we have extensive material on hygiene for settled areas, during warfare, quarantine to prevent the spread of communicable disease, and personal cleanliness. Attention was also given to diet and its effect on health, particularly meat.

Physicians rarely appeared in the Bible, and we possess no parallels to the Egyptian medical papyri or the prescriptions and medical tablets of Mesopotamia. Such works may some day be found by the archeologist, but at the present time biblical medicine must be reconstructed from what we know of the surrounding nations and from the much later talmudic traditions. Although the Talmud was produced in written form between the fourth and sixth centuries, long after the Bible, it contains considerable older material.

A replica of the oldest medical document – a clay tablet, written with a reed stylus in cuneiform script, the oldest medical "handbook," which lay buried for almost 4,000 years – accompanied the display.

Considered the best physicians of the ancient world, the Egyptians wrote detailed prescriptions for many major diseases, as well as common ailments caused by stings and animal bites. Some of these were recorded in the Ebers Papyrus, a document written more than three thousand years ago, which mentioned about nine hundred prescriptions derived from 85 plants. These plants include sesame, the seeds of which contain an oil similar to olive oil, which was used in ointments, or asafoetida, whose root produces a brownish gum, which was used internally for stomach problems and externally for eye diseases.

The Egyptians also had some knowledge of mold cultures – antibiotics – which were the precursors of penicillin. "Bread in rotten condition" was described for poultices. Incense, frankincense and myrrh – mentioned frequently in the Bible – when burned produce phenol carbolic acid, the germ killer introduced into operating rooms in the nineteenth century. The incense not only served a religious purpose, but helped with plagues, flies, and vermin.

The exhibit ended with a three-day symposium led by scholars from the United States, Israel, and Germany. The papers were published in the book, *The Healing Past—Pharmaceuticals in the Biblical and Rabbinic World,* by Brill of Holland, the foremost scientific publisher in Europe.

This exhibit was followed the next year with a show on medicinal plants from the late biblical period; we dealt with those mentioned by classical authors such as Josephus, Theophrastus, Dioscorides, Galen, etc., and others who lived from 460 B.C.E. to 100 CE. The ancient Greeks had an extensive knowledge of medicinal herbs, but we must not think that they necessarily discovered them. The Greeks were "the spoiled darlings of history," who took the discoveries of others, including Mesopotamia, Egypt, and pre-Hellenic nations, and adopted them.

The Garden was to enhance our appreciation of the value of some of their treatments. We now realize that plants, such as periwinkle, butcher's broom, or squirting cucumber, really do possess healing properties. Most modern physicians know little of ancient plants and their medicinal properties, but they are again being studied by European pharmaceutical companies.

The Garden joined the celebration of the 500th anniversary of Columbus's arrival in America with *"New World Plants in Europe and Israel."* We showed how profoundly agriculture and gardens throughout the world were influenced by Columbus's voyage. While European botanists of the Middle Ages dealt with only 700 varieties of plants, after 1500 the Americas added five thousand new plants. This agricultural revolution brought potatoes, corn, tomatoes, beans, peppers, pineapples, and many other plants into general use in Europe and Asia and led to an enormous population explosion in those countries.

Let us look at a few familiar items that are a gift of the American continent. Vanilla is the most important flavoring substance the Americas have contributed to the world. It is the only economically useful member of the orchid family.

Cortez tasted an avocado in 1519. Its Aztec name *"Ahucatl,"* means "butter from wood," The English name for it was derived from the Spanish modification *"abogado."* Avocadoes were introduced to Florida from Mexico in 1833; by 1908 they were grown in Israel and are now a very large export product.

Our most common annuals such as marigolds, zinnias, begonias, and petunias are South American and were not known to us before 1492.

The common zinnia traces its origins to Mexico. So strong is the Mexican connection that Mexican bandits figured in the history of the zinnia's discovery. As the story went, Johann Gottfried Zinn, a professor of medicine and director of the Botanical garden at the University of Goettingen in Germany, was searching for interesting new plants in the mountainous wilds of Mexico in the 1750s. Suddenly, he noticed some unfamiliar purple blooms. They had almost finished blooming, so he gathered a sackful of fading flowers in the

Young date palms in the desert

Irene Jacob trimming the papyrus in
the stream

hope that their seeds had ripened. Out of the bushes came bandits who attacked him and grabbed his sack. They were about to murder him when the leader opened the sack and found nothing but a mess of dead flowers. They immediately released him, apparently believing it bad luck to kill the feeble-minded.

Since the introduction of the zinnia to Europe, the plants, with their original purplish single-petaled flowers and stiff stems, have been extensively hybridized into a wealth of garden varieties

The American explorers added thousands of plants and enriched our lives far more than the gold that the Spanish sailors sought.

As usual, we had our annual lecture series, which included a speech on "The Glorious History of the Latke" (a Jewish potato-cake).

The garden was particularly sweet smelling when we dealt with "Fragrance through the Ages: Perfume, Incense and Cosmetics from the Bible to the Present." The Egyptians, as early as 3200 B.C.E., were the first sophisticated society to employ cosmetics The Egyptian practice of burying their dead with their household treasures has left us an invaluable picture of their cosmetics. The tomb of Pharaoh Menes contained, alongside jewels, ivory, and gold, jars of perfumed ointment, kohl eye color, rouge, pomade, and lip color made from plant materials.

In Egypt the perfume industry was entirely in the hands of priests. The walls of the temple at Edfu provide both pictures and formulae for various perfumes. The religious texts also mention that deities enjoyed perfume; for this reason they were manufactured in temples.

The most famous use of perfume in the Bible occurred in the Esther story; she was treated with oil of myrrh for six months and other perfumed oils during the remainder of the year before being presented to King Ahasuerus. Then "she obtained grace and favor in the sight more than all the virgins."

Perfumes of all kinds for men and women were listed in the Song of Songs, "The smell of your garments is like the smell of Lebanon." Special plants for this exhibit included roses, jasmine, and tuberose.

Incense offerings, especially from myrrh and frankincense, were important in biblical Jewish worship as they were in the rest of the ancient world that worshiped through sacrifices. Incense offerings were described in detail in the Five Books of Moses. We cannot trace the development of incense rituals, but we do know that the right to participate was restricted to priests. Scholars have disagreed whether incense and perfume began in sanctuaries as a way of pleasing deity or as a pleasant aroma in the home, which was then transferred to the sanctuary. In any case, the sweet smoke of burning incense rising heavenward became a symbol of the link between people and their God. Iincense, undoubtedly, also kept the sacrificial rituals from smelling badly as hundreds of animals were slaughtered in the sanctuary.

Have you ever asked yourself what our lives would be like without the use of dyes? The language of color has enabled us to express our feelings and emotions, as happiness, grief ,and love. Our Exhibit "The Ageless Art of Dyeing—Colors in Nature from the Bible to the Present" dealt with this subject. The art of extracting colors from plants originated in China and India and passed to Babylon and Assyria, and from there to Egypt. Earlier, primitive people used crushed leaves, flowers, berries, and bark of trees; such colors soon faded. We possess a profusion of multicolored material from ancient Egypt's tombs. The ancient Egyptians had a strong preference for white but were not averse to color. The royal tombs and temples were colorfully decorated. Houses excavated at Tel el Amarna contained pillars painted red; the capitals were green and the ceilings many different hues. Color plays a more important role in Egyptian writing than anywhere else in the ancient Near East as we can see from the multicolored hieroglyphics. Some signs were assigned the colors associated with the object: reddish brown to male figures and pale yellow to female; reed baskets or lotus plants were green; animals were yellow, as was linen: sky and water were blue. These, in other words, more or less followed nature. Other signs were provided with a color convention with no relationship to the real object, so blue was used for bread and for thrones.

The most color-drenched coat of biblical times must have been Joseph's. Later, when Moses led the Israelites from Egypt, they carried the knowledge of dyes with them, "And they made upon the skirts of robe pomegranates of blue, purple and scarlet and twined linen."

The ancient craftsmen carefully guarded the secrets of their profession, so what remains concealed still far exceeds what we know. Ancient writers recorded that there were once nearly a thousand different sources of natural dyes, but because of the secrecy surrounding their recipes, many of them have been lost forever. We know less about dyes in the various Mesopotamian lands than in Egypt, as fragile cloth material was rarely preserved in large quantities, but fragments do exist.

Both the Jerusalem and Babylonian Talmuds indicated that the craft of dyeing was highly considered. Those who practiced it were identified through a badge that consisted of colored wool worn behind the ear. Jewish and Syrian dyers were considered the best in the Roman Empire. A number of dye factories have been excavated in ancient Israel at Tel Dor and in other locations.

In 1995 we highlighted "Grain and Bread: From Ancient Israel to Ethnic America," and the galleries of the temple showed a pictorial history of grains, including copies of ancient tools such as grinding stones, sickles and threshing boards. We exhibited a stamp collection that demonstrated the importance of grain for dozens of nations around the globe. The stamps celebrated advances in agriculture and grain production as well as the people connected to it. The collection was prepared by Marian Finegold, who is also a docent in the Garden.

We take our morning toast or luncheon sandwich very much for granted and rarely think of the complex history of grains – kernels from sheaves of wheat, barley, oats, rye, millet, and sorghum. Apart from rice in the Far East and central Asia, bread constitutes the largest human dietary source of nutrients.

Until cereals were domesticated in 7000 B.C.E., people depended on hunting. By the time the Book of Genesis was written, wheat and barley had become the dominant cereals of the Mediterranean area. The Hebrew word for bread, *lehem*, occurs nearly 300 times in the Hebrew Bible. In Mesopotamia and Egypt there were 250 types of bread. The peoples of biblical times generally lived subsistence lives, and a failure of the grain harvest meant famine. No wonder the Bible so often reflected on the blessings of bread. In ancient times, barley was so important that the calendar was adjusted to accommodate its growth. If it was not far enough along to harvest, a month was added to the year–creating a leap year.

The law of ancient Israel required that the corners of grain fields be harvested by the poor. The Talmud defined the amount to be allocated; it was to consist of at least 1/60. The poor who harvested the corners of the field were forbidden to use knives or sickles in order to prevent violence.

The discovery of leavened bread has been attributed to the Egyptians, and the action of yeast was first attested about 1500 B.C.E., when a baker may have left the dough in the sun and then discovered that the dough had fermented. The first bread was unleavened, although it had little in common with the modern *matzah*. Because the bread was thicker and came from the fire hard, it would have been difficult to cut and divide; thus, the words "breaking bread."

Greece, in contrast to the Near East, depended largely on imported cereal, because of its poor soil. Thus Athens, with its half million people, had to import more than 1 million bushels of grain annually. The best bakers in Rome were Greeks. In 168 B.C.E. following the victorious campaign against Perseus, the bakers who traveled with the Greek army, were taken as slaves. Even today many Italian bakers have Greek names.

As we follow the history of bread, we might remember that in the English Middle Ages, bread was used to form platters called trenchers, which soaked up the fat from the meal. After the food had been eaten, the trenchers went to the servants or dogs. In England, wheat remained a luxury until the seventeenth century. Until then, rye formed 40% of English bread. Rye is still popular in Russia, Germany, Sweden, and Denmark.

By 1880, France was the largest bread-consuming country in the world. Napoleon's armies were fed the best bread, unlike the British navy which ate ship's biscuits – often full of weevils. A British baker at that time wrote: "Where one man dies by chances of war, two are lost to the nation eating ship's biscuits."

Columbus brought wheat to the Western Hemisphere in 1493. Later, the Pilgrims brought seeds to New England but found it difficult to grow as they were not experienced farmers. The preparation of suitable land was an additional obstacle. It was wooded, and even when trees were cut down, it was still full of stumps.

The Civil War played an important role in the development of wheat cultivation in the American Midwest. This part of the country had land to spare and after the passage of the Homestead Act in 1862, farmers streamed westward. The North therefore had an advantage in feeding its armies. The South, on the other hand, continued to grow cotton and was often hard put to produce enough food for its population. Its cheap slave labor also restricted development of tools more complicated than the shovel and hoe. Another factor in the growth of northern agriculture was its industry, which developed agricultural machinery, like Cyrus McCormick's reaper. Similar

Lily and lotus pond

The stream

advances have continued. A century ago it took more than sixty-four hours per acre to prepare the soil, plant, cut, and thresh the grain. Now the same amount of work takes less than three hours.

The North also had the good fortune of a series of poor harvests in Europe, and especially in England: these lords had to import huge quantities of wheat from the Union, so, in 1862, the north exported over 400 million bushels of flour compared to only ten-thousand in 1859.

Wheat continued to progress at the turn of the century; plant scientists began to produce new varieties artificially from parent plants selected for desirable traits – greater yield, resistance to diseases and insects, a shorter growing season, better milling and baking qualities, shorter straw to reduce the opportunities for wind and weather to flatten it and make harvesting more difficult. Today, most of the varieties grown commercially in the U.S. were unknown even 20 years ago.

Following wheat in 1996 we did a retrosepctive of the first decade and also turned to the delightful subject of "Progress and Change in Ancient Medicine and Agriculture," with a major symposium to which we invited the following scholars, listed with their topics: Dr. Marvin Powell (University of Southern Illinois) – *Diet and Deficiencies in the Ancient World*; Dr. Robert Biggs (University of Chicago) – *Cures from Babylon – How Good Were They?* Dr. Robert Rittner (Yale University) – *What Mummies Don't Tell Us and What They Do*; Dr. Oded Borowski (Emory University) – *From Manna to Chicken Soup – Diet and Disease.* These lectures expanded the earlier medicinal and agricultural exhibits.

Despite computers, writing materials remain vital to our daily lives. The ancient advance from clay tablets to papyrus represented a major change and permitted all kinds of new developments to which we turned in 1997 with the topic "From Papyrus to Paper." The older forms of recording on clay tablets were discussed briefly, but the major emphasis was on the unusual papyrus plant and on the large

Waterfall with lilies and alium

Child with etrog

283

major emphasis was on the unusual papyrus plant and on the large variety of plants later used to produce paper, especially in modern times.

Papyrus is among the most versatile of plants and was widely used for everything from housing and items of clothing, to boat building of some of the heavy crafts used to haul building material for the pyramids. As wood was scarce and papyrus plants plentiful, especially in the Nile delta, it proved to be a most useful material. Interesting as all of the other uses may be, the most enduring contribution of this plant was its use as a readily available writing material. Along with parchment, more widely used in the northern lands, it served as the chief material for anything which needed to be written until the invention of paper was transferred from China to the West by the Arabs in the tenth century. Even after this time, it remained in use. Possibly from as early as 3000 B.C.E. – in other words for four thousand years this material was used throughout the western world.

The paper industry that followed the Chinese and later Arab pattern depended heavily on another plant, flax, as it was manufactured from linen. During the nineteenth century we again find Egypt playing a major role accidentally. After the discovery of a large number of mummies in excavated tombs, the endless roles of linen in which they were wrapped were often shipped to paper mills and supplemented the rags collected in European and American cities as a source of paper.

Efforts to expand the plant sources led to the exploration of a long list of plants – many of them grown in the Biblical Garden for this exhibit. Eventually wood pulp became the principle source of paper; it was inexpensive and permitted the vast expansion of newspapers, popular mass fiction, and the use of paper for packaging, personal items, clothing, containers, etc. All of this remains so to our time.

Irene leading a tour of nuns

The grape arbor

285

The exhibit was augmented by a show entitled "Paper and Jewish Paper" in the Gallery; the use of paper from the time of the Cairo Genizah, through early Jewish printing and the expansion of Jewish literary output after 1800 was part of the exhibit. There was a special display of stamps and Jewish post-cards and greeting cards.

Following these years of serious topics, we decided to take on something more light-hearted and took "The Story of Beer – Liquid Bread," as it is the oldest alcoholic drink, already brewed by the Sumerians some 6,000 years ago. Beer plays a role in the Gilgamesh Epic and was regulated by the Code of Hammurabi. The Bible includes it among the alcoholic drinks under the general term *shekhor*. In contrast to wine, it does not play a major role in the biblical texts, but archaeological excavations have demonstrated that it was a significant drink among the ancient Israelites and the city states of ancient Palestine. It is also mentioned in the Talmud.

Mesopotamia boasted sixteen major varieties of beer and possibly as many as 700 different brands. Sweet substances, herbs, spices, and fruit were added for additional flavor. The additives used were featured in this special Garden exhibit. Techniques of brewing were discussed and compared to modern methods through several special programs.

Our viewers discovered that hops (*Humulus lupulus*), which we consider so essential to beer, are a late part of the beer-making process. The ancient people of the Near East brewed beer because the grains upon which it is based were plentiful. It was not only an intoxicating drink of pleasure, but also a simple way of providing a more varied diet and vitamin B_{12}. As a heavy, paste-like drink, it is a dietary supplement.

The role that breweries played in American history and in the development of Pittsburgh was explored through a special presentation. The local newspapers were intrigued by the show and carried lovely articles that described it. Many of our visitors took home Karen Herzog's delightful book of recipes, *Cooking with Beer*.

Our exhibit on "The Thread of Life – Textiles from Plants " in 1999 dealt with the large array of plants used through thousands of years for the production of cordage and clothing. Wool and fibers seem to have developed simultaneously. In the ancient Near East there was considerable experimentation with various fibers. Linen made of flax *(Linum usitattissimum)* was the most widely used fiber. The exhibit dealt with the complicated process of growing, harvesting, and processing flax. It provided an opportunity to demonstrate the art of spinning and weaving which has not changed very much through the ages.

The production of linen was shown to be complicated; it as well as other fine fibers were part of a labor intensive industrial process. The detailed knowledge provided by Egyptian wall paintings and miniature scenes was displayed.

Cotton was introduced to Egypt as early as 12,000 B.C.E., but it seems to have been used chiefly for oil; references to textiles appear only in the 2nd century B.C.E. and subsequently became an important item of trade.

As the need for clothing and textiles for other uses is world wide, so a large number of fibers were used by different cultures throughout the world. They were explored and many of them were grown in the Garden.

The accompanying exhibit "2000 Years of Jewish Costumes" was shown in the Gallery and a series of lectures that dealt with fashions in ancient Israel and Egypt as well as medieval Jewish garb were given. A large number of illuminated medieval manuscripts show clothing of all groups in Jewish society.

The year 2000 saw us return to diet as we had a display and a series of lectures on "King Tut's Vegetable Garden." The variety of vegetables was greater than imagined and played an important role in the health of the ancient world. Each of the lands, Egypt, Mesopotamia and Israel , with their differing climates, grew different vegetables. They were often grown together with other plants in order to use every available piece of land.

In contrast to grain, which can be stored relatively easily, many vegetables must be consumed shortly after harvesting. Some lend themselves to preservation through drying, especially beans, peas, and lentils. Others, like onions of various varieties, can also be stored. Methods of storage were explored and the various types of containers discussed.

Market gardens surrounded the great cities of ancient times as they do today. The peasants brought their goods to the market. Workers and slaves were fed vegetables to keep them healthy. The nobility used vegetables to provide variety. Transportation was discussed.

Although the variety of vegetables was less than in modern times, it was much larger than we might have expected. More than two dozen vegetables were grown for this special exhibit. Vegetables played a significant role in the ancient diet and were prized. *Dining with the Ancients*, a book of recipes from ancient Egypt, Greece, and Rome, had been especially prepared by Karen Herzog. It was an instant success.

As we wanted to appeal to a contemporary set of concerns we turned to "Botanical Symbols in World Religions" for 2001, and in 2002 "Botanical Symbols in Ancient World Religions." These shows presented several dozen plants that have symbolic meaning in the world's religions. These plants appear regularly in artistic presentations. They enrich the meaning of the religious figure portrayed and without a written explanation show the viewer what the scene seeks to portray.

Although we may be familiar with some of this symbolism in Judaism and Christianity, it is often overlooked in the religions of the East. They use symbolism heavily. The botanical symbols can bring us a better understanding of other religions.

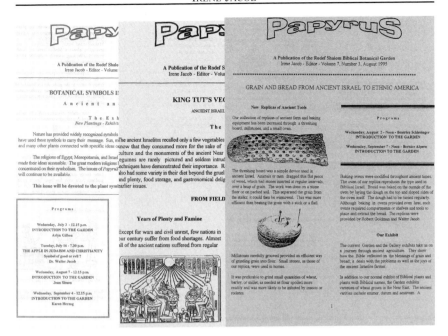

Issues of the *PapyruS* - on the special summer exhibits -
published in June, July and August

A sampling of annual
display and program flyers and pamphlets

This was also the year in which we began a separate venture – the display of replicas of ancient agricultural tools. Our initial set dealt with hand tools of the ancient farmer. We will commission a variety of more complex tools through the years and eventually have a full display of the technology used in ancient Near Eastern agriculture through the long biblical period and the influence of surrounding cultures on the tools.

As we look into the future, there remain a large number of fascinating topics that need to be presented and that will make the world of the Bible and the ancient Near East come to life.

The Biblical Garden presents a vivid illustration of celebrating life and cultivating it. Much of our information has proved useful far beyond Pittsburgh and can be used to supplement biblical curricula both for children and adults. To ensure its wider distribution, the garden continues to publish a newsletter entitled *PapyruS*. The three editions printed during the summer months provide a summary of the special exhibits and the useful qualities connected with them. These exhibits entail a good deal of research. The plants must be found, grown, and naturalized. All of these efforts, along with the publicity that must be generated for the exhibits, mean that although the garden is open only three months of the year, it is a year-round venture that takes hundreds of volunteer hours, and these dedicated volunteers provide lectures and docent talks during the summer. A group of ten docents have led many tour groups. This is a popular venture, and bookings begin in early winter. In addition to the docents there are some forty-five volunteer hosts and hostesses who make visitors feel at home, answer questions, and distribute literature. We are also fortunate to have a number of volunteers for some physical effort of the garden.

Alongside the exhibits, the Garden has published six books. These included (Walter and Irene Jacob) *Forgotten Immigrants – Plant Immigrants to Israel through Three Thousand Years*; (Irene Jacob), *Biblical Plants, a Guide to the Rodef Shalom Biblical Botanical Garden*; (Irene and Walter Jacob) *The Healing Past –*

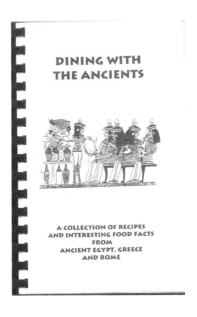

A Sampling of Garden
publications

Pharmaceuticals in the Biiblical and Rabbinic World; (Karen Herzog) *Cooking with Beer*; (Karen Herzog) *Dining with the Ancient*; (Irene Jacob) *Botanical Symbols in World Religions*; (Irene Jacob) *Plants of the Bible and Their Uses*, as well as (Irene and Walter Jacob) "Flora" in the Anchor Bible Dictionary; (Irene and Walter Jacob) "Flora in the Dead Sea Scrolls" in the *Encyclopedia of the Dead Sea Scrolls*.

To the monochromatic black and white print of the Bible, which for too many may remain a drab and closed book, the Biblical Botanical Garden continues to add color and life. We have done so for thousands of visitors each summer and hope that this number will continue to increase.

SOUTHWESTERN DISTRICT OF PENNSYLVANIA JEWISH RELIGIOUS SCHOOLS
A *History of a Noble Experiment in Jewish Education*

Ruth Cooper Reidbord

INTRODUCTION

Perhaps no program developed by Rodef Shalom was as unusual as the one known as the Southwestern District Religious Schools. For over 60 years the Southwestern District of Pennsylvania Jewish Religious Schools Committee provided a unique form of religious education for Jewish children in isolated communities throughout the Tri-State area. It is exactly 30 years since they ceased operation in 1966. Today, when there are sophisticated models for the education of Jewish children from Kindergarten through Confirmation, there are hundreds of people in the Pittsburgh area who still recall with fondness a time when pure devotion and dedication by hundreds of volunteer teachers and Mothers Clubs made possible a network of schools that was unparalleled in its time and perhaps ever after.

IN THE BEGINNING

How did it happen? What and who gave it life? Why was it created? This monograph is one component of the commemorative observances of the 150th anniversary of the founding of Rodef Shalom Congregation so it is appropriate (and historically accurate) to note that initially it was the brainchild of Dr. Lippman Mayer, Rabbi of Rodef Shalom Temple (then called the Eighth Street Temple). In that year, at the first general meeting of the Columbian Council, Dr. Mayer had proposed to the membership that Sabbath Schools be initiated for the education of children of immigrants so that they might learn something of their faith. This religious education, he believed, was an essential ingredient of the Americanization activities the Council was to organize. In a letter from Mrs. Pauline Rosenberg, President of the Columbian Council, to Mrs. S. L. Fleischman, secretary, dated October 24, 1895, she says:

> Dr. L. Mayer [Rabbi of Rodef Shalom] delivered an address in the Synagogue on Washington Street and succeeded in interesting

quite a number of the adult members of that congregation sufficiently to assure their sending their children to the Sabbath School to be taught under our supervision . . . . . It (will) start on November 4, 1894 in their synagogue. I consider this a great achievement knowing the reluctance of that class to anything like enlightenment and their blind antipathy to any member of the Reform Congregation.

She suggested meeting prior to November 4 to confer with Dr. Mayer "who is admirably adapted to cope with the problems these people present to us."

The broad scope of these activities has been documented by archivist Rachel Balliet Colker at the Senator John Heinz Regional History Center. Dr. Mayer believed that children needed to be educated in Jewish history, customs and ceremonials. This mode of education was not normative for many immigrant families, most of whom came from a nominally Orthodox background. It took great courage to propose this concept, but the parents must have been equally courageous to entrust their children to a man whose religious manner differed from anything with which they were familiar.

On the first Sabbath in November 1894, classes began in the Washington Street *shul* (now relocated and known as Beth Hamedrash Hagadol-Beth Jacob). The Columbian Council sponsored and administered the program with instruction provided by volunteer teachers. In a letter to the Sunday School Committee of Rodef Shalom, the president of the Columbian Council asked to have a meeting with the Board of the Temple so that certain policy questions could be posed.

The questions were:

1) To whom should we look for authority when information is desired? Answer: To Dr. Mayer who (also) is Superintendent of the Sunday School.

2) Are Jewish parents who are non-members (of Temple) required to pay to send their children to Sunday School?

Beaver Falls Confirmation Class 1917

Southwest District Confirmation 1945

Answer: If they can't afford it, they aren't taxed by a tuition fee.

3)   Who pays the expenses for the equipment for the Sunday School? Answer: Children (of Temple members) are supposed to buy their books. If they can't afford to do so, the Temple pays.

Soon the program outgrew its quarters in the Synagogue and moved a few times, always in the Hill District environs. Teachers did more than instruct; they washed faces and fixed lunches. The older children were pressed into service to help in "minding the little ones." Religious education was expanded to include socialization activities.

In 1899, one of the older girls, Miriam Schonfield, age 12, started to teach the kindergarten class of the Jewish religious school of what had become the Columbian Council Settlement. Seventy-five children were enrolled in the school. In May 1900, the Settlement was moved to 1835 Center Avenue and, in 1907, at the age of 20, Miss Schonfield was made supervisor of the religious school.

> No history of the Southwestern District could make a pretense to authenticity without (paying) tribute to Miriam Schonfield. Her personality gave light and dignity and love to the work. Her name became a byword, and a password, and a challenge to cooperative effort and understanding and accomplishment. As the chain of the Council's religious schools grew, she nurtured them and bound them together. Before the day of the automobile or bus, she traveled up and down the rivers, organizing, encouraging, laughing, teaching, loving, and loved. And she went about her important work without real teaching material. . . . [Since few] textbooks were available in 1910... she . . .used the oldest textbook of all: the Bible. Interpretative material came...from the Union of American Hebrew Congregations and from. . .creative and enterprising teachers. Miriam Schonfield carried the schools through the years when the American Jewish community was experiencing its early growing and fusion pains.

The foregoing quote is from Mildred Weinberg Kreimer, Field Supervisor from 1942–1946 and author of an article, "Southwestern

Southwest District faculty with Dr.
Freehof. Oscar Harder, a later Supervisor,
is in the left row three - late 1930s

Southwest District faculty 1940s

297

District Religious Schools Celebrate 60th Year." It was published in 1953.

The religious school she directed quickly grew. Even the mothers had a Bible class. In 1908 the National Council of Jewish Women (the name was changed in 1904) decided to carry its religious school work into other parts of rapidly expanding Pittsburgh and its neighboring communities.

A Religious Schools Committee was formed with Mrs. Moses Ruslander as Chairman. She organized the mothers of the McKees Rocks community, and together they founded the McKees Rocks Religious School. This model of organization was to serve the District well throughout its history. Next to be organized was Beth Jehuda on the North Side, with Donora following soon after. During World War I there were eighteen schools, with an average attendance of over 1,000 pupils and 100 voluntary teachers and superintendents.

THE GROWTH YEARS

In 1915 the first confirmation program was held and met with such enthusiasm that Confirmation was incorporated in all the schools thereafter. Students from Carnegie and Lawrenceville made up the confirmation class, with the service being held at the Arcade Theatre. The program was arranged by Lawrenceville superintendent, Oscar Harter, who would become Field Supervisor in 1946. A report published in the *Jewish Criterion* of that year stated that:

> [T]he Religious Schools. . . . will this year make rapid headway in being able to gather in all the Jewish children in our District, so that every child can be inspired by knowing the beauties of their faith. Whilst up to this date all of the parents are not manifestly as much interested in the schools as we would like, we already notice a vast improvement over last year in this respect.

1916 saw Confirmation extended to 20 religious schools, 18 of which held joint (union) services at the Nixon Theater. During that

Stanley Levin, Principal of the Rodef Shalom Religious School (1952-1973) advised and helped the Southwest District, as did his predecessors

Southwest District field trip of several schools 1940s

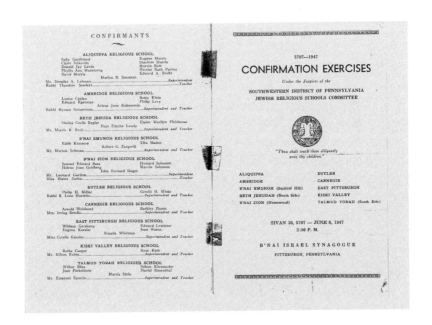

Southwest Confirmation Class 1947

299

year Rabbi Mazure of the Tree of Life Congregation spoke to a meeting of principals and teachers and advocated the founding of a teachers institute. This occurred in the fall of 1916 and thrived until the Second World War.

Following the model established by Mrs. Moses Ruslander, chairman of the Religious Schools Committee, every new school was established concurrently with the organizing of the mothers of that community into a Mothers Club. This Mothers Club was encouraged, from the beginning to ensure financial responsibility for the upkeep of the school. In many cases it took a community several years to become responsible for its portion of the expenses. In such cases the Council Religious Schools Committee bore the necessary expenses. Sometimes, as local Councils of Jewish Women were formed in small towns, they assumed the responsibility for the religious school. In other communities Hadassah groups, sisterhoods, brotherhoods or B'nai B'rith chapters were responsible for sponsoring the schools. But always the Mothers Group was the preferred model. In most cases the local groups were assessed a fee of $1.00 per child. However, the Committee in Pittsburgh would "help out" if this assessment was too burdensome for a community.

Textbooks were purchased and lent to schools that could not afford to buy them. The Religious School at the Irene Kaufman Settlement (which evolved from that first Columbian Council School), known in the records as the Center Avenue Religious School, was always supported in full by the Committee. The office of the Field Supervisor (as the top administrative post was called) was in the home of Miss Schonfield.

In the May 1921 annual report of the Pittsburgh Section of the National Council of Jewish Women, published in the *Jewish Criterion*, Mrs. Louis Amshel, Committee chairman notes that there are 25 schools including those at Morganza and Thornhill (correctional institutions). Teachers' institutes were held every month at Temple Rodef Shalom. Many of the schools organized by Miss Schonfield became the nucleus of new synagogues. The Council president felt this phase of the Council's work was:

> invariably intensely interesting as well as extremely beneficial to both the children and to the members of the Council who have availed themselves of the privilege of attending these (Confirmation) exercises and witnessing for themselves the very great work of the Sabbath School Committee. In Braddock, 175 children were enrolled with a Mothers Club of 75 organized by Miss Schonfield. Several plays were put on [by the children in that] community in the course of a year. The splendid talent displayed by some of [them] was a revelation to the people of Braddock. The attendance at one of these plays at the Carnegie Music Hall [in Braddock] was approximately 1,500.

Schools in operation at this time included South Side, Charleroi, Penn Ave., McKees Rocks, Kittanning, Canonsburg, Beechview, Monongahela, Ford City, Butler. By the middle 1920s nearly 60 schools were enrolled at one time. Added to the list were Ambridge, Bentleyville, Carnegie, Fayette City, Hazelwood, Homewood, Irwin, Jeannette, Johnstown, McDonald, Mt. Pleasant, New Kensington, Vandergrift.

During this period of growth the Pittsburgh Jewish community's population was about 56,000 according to Jacob Feldman, author of *The Jewish Experience in Western Pennsylvania, A History: 1755–1945*. The Jewish population of some of the outlying communities was as follows:

McKeesport	5,000	Carnegie	450
Braddock	2,000	Donora	300
Homestead	1,100	McKees Rocks	250
New Kensington	650	Mt. Pleasant	200
Washington	575	Canonsburg	150
East Pittsburgh	500	Vandergrift	85
Greensburg	450	Leechburg	63

301

During this period Miss Schonfield traveled extensively to the individual schools, sometimes reaching 3 communities on one Sunday, using public transportation. During the year 1923 she visited 20 communities, organized 7 new schools, coordinated a total of 32 schools and instructed, individually, in classes and in monthly Teachers Institutes, 33 superintendents and 154 teachers, with a total pupil enrollment of 1,629.

RODEF SHALOM SISTERHOOD BECOMES COSPONSOR

In 1923 the National Federation of Temple Sisterhoods incorporated into its program the education of unaffiliated Jewish children. Rodef Shalom Sisterhood decided it would be most appropriate for them to join with NCJW since many of the women in the Sisterhood had been working through NCJW on the Religious Schools Committee. The Temple, including its Rabbis were very much involved with the program.

Before the two groups formally joined together there was a period of time between 1923 and 1925 when NCJW endeavored to enlist women from other movements in the effort. In 1924 there was an all day meeting of the Mothers Clubs of the various communities and the Southwest District Council. Mrs. Louis Affelder spoke for Rodef Shalom Sisterhood, and Mrs. Aaron Vitman for the Women's League for Traditional Judaism.

By 1925, however, Mrs. J.de S.Freund, President of NCJW in her annual report, stated:

> Just a year ago in accepting the...cooperation of the Rodef Shalom Sisterhood, the Pittsburgh Section has been the instrument through which the Pittsburgh Jewish Women's Religious Schools Committee was formed and which has developed a unique combined movement of sisterhood and council for the extension of religious schools throughout the Southwestern District of Pennsylvania. Thus for the first time have the Council and Sisterhood united in a definite piece of work and in

302

concentrating on religious schools they have found a project worthy of their mettle. If the tenets of our faith are to be carried on to future generations there is no better way than through the religious training of our children.

After a year's trial the two groups have decided to continue their association, thus marking a great forward step in Jewish women's work as it proves that such union of forces is not only possible but highly desirable. It is hoped that at some not too distant day the local Religious School Committee, which has grown into a districtwide group will become a statewide work covering completely the religious schools needs of our Pennsylvania Jewish children. . . . In order that Council Sections, of which there are 25, sisterhoods, auxiliaries and mothers clubs may have equal credit they will change the name to *Southwestern District of Pennsylvania Jewish Religious Schools Committee.*

The budget will be as follows: $1,875 each from Rodef Shalom Sisterhood and National Council of Jewish Women; the balance to be raised by quotas assigned to communities on the basis of $1.00 per child. Expenditures will fall between $4,300 and $5,200 per year, providing for the first time a full -ime secretary to the Field Supervisor.

The foregoing material was published in the *Jewish Criterion* in May 1925.

Thus was the new entity born. As the president of NCJW said in her 1925 annual report:

This District (of NCJW) is best known for its 43 religious schools, 325 teachers and superintendents and 3,000 students under a well-coordinated system of which the Pittsburgh Section is an important part. Some have asserted that this is the function of the synagogue or sisterhood, but not Council.. *But it must be borne in mind that this (program) reaches all phases of Judaism.* [emphasis added] It does not advocate (R)eform, (C)onservative or (O)rthodox. It offers Judaism in whatever form the community desires–our only stipulation is that the teaching be in English. However, Hebrew instruction can be and often is supplementary. In connection with the well-organized religious school there has developed subconsciously a phase often overlooked.

While little children are led along religious lines, youth at college age are apt to drift. Most of our teachers are drawn from the ranks of students at local colleges and receive personal instruction from the Field Supervisor. There is stimulation towards things essentially Jewish and spiritual.

And so many schools developed, each with a unique history. The opening of the Hilltop School in 1925 is recalled by Grace Fivars in a letter and subsequent interview, her family having played a central role in its establishment:

> Among the many schools served by the Southwestern District was one in an area of Pittsburgh known as Beltzhoover, a tiny neighborhood several street-car zones away from the rest of the Pittsburgh Jewish community. The Beltzhoover initiative was spearheaded by (my parents) Morris and Irene Fivars, who operated a small grocery store at 715 Estella Street. It was Morris Fivars who walked in all directions within a five-mile radius to contact Jewish families in Beltzhoover, Mt. Washington, Knoxville and Mt. Oliver. In 1925 the Hilltop Religious School opened at Weil's Dance Hall on the third floor at 239 Climax Street. The space was donated by Henry and Hattie Weil, founding members of the Hilltop Jewish Community. Morris Fivars had recruited about 25 families. He became the pivotal figure in the congregation. He arranged to borrow a Torah for special occasions; he organized High Holiday activities and he sponsored the Reverend Herman Mermelstein who conducted the services. Irene Fivars was the first president of the congregation. She served for 10 of the 15 years the Hilltop Religious School provided services for the Jewish families in Beltzhoover.

Miss Fivars is one of many former students and teachers who remember Miriam Schonfield with great respect and affection.

> She had a way of drawing people to her that subsequent administrators lacked. Those who knew Miss Schonfield never forgot her. To be in her presence was a rare privilege. She cared about everyone she touched and remembered everyone's name. The Teachers Institute she organized was virtually the only opportunity for young people in outlying areas to meet other young

Jewish people. She provided young teachers (and most teachers were as young as 16 to 21) with an opportunity to grow. She was so inspiring that these young teachers worked for no pay, receiving only the money for carfare.

Miss Fivars remembers leaving her home at 7:00 A.M. on Sunday to reach her teaching assignment. She used two streetcars to get to her school at 9:30. She did not mind this long journey, however, because of her dedication to Miss Schonfield and her program.

Another young teacher, Sarah Bachrach Mishelevich, was 16 years old in 1926 when she taught in the New Kensington Beth Jacob Religious School, where her father was the rabbi. That year she attended the Teachers Institute held in Miss Schonfield's home on Forbes Avenue.

In a telephone interview with Ms. Mishelevich, she recalled Miss Schonfield instructing the teachers in appropriate methods of communicating with students. During the course of this instruction Miss Schonfield asked the teachers, rhetorically, what they would do if a student were to raise her hand with a question during an instructional session. Ms. Mishelevich, thinking she was asking for volunteers to answer a question, raised her hand. Immediately she perceived her error and was very embarrassed. But Miss Schonfield graciously and quickly replied, "Now this is a response that shows you were paying attention." This moment has stayed with Ms. Mishelevich for 70 years.

Much has been written in weekly reports in the *Jewish Criterion* of those years, but nothing is as eloquent in portraying the philosophy and the fervor as the following report by Miriam Schonfield.

MISS SCHONFIELD'S ANNUAL REPORT

The only report written by Miss Schonfield extant is the annual report for 1927/1928, an excerpt of which follows:

In giving a report of the Religious School work for the Southwestern District, one hesitates to know just what would be most interesting to our members, but as there are so many different phases of our work and the time is so limited, I will try to point out the most outstanding features.

What the coming generation is to accomplish depends in no small measure on the type and amount of religious education that it is enabled to acquire; it has therefore been a grave responsibility that has rested upon our religious department under whose training the children have been placed. We all know that the religious training of the child comes under two channels, the home and the religious school. The school gives the children the theory, and in the home, they find the practical application of their religion. In Judaism, ethics and religion are dissolubly bound together. The root of a Jewish ethical life being profoundly religious, the belief in one God, the moral creator of the world, and the Father of mankind. The crowning character of our religion is that it consists not of an immutable torpid system of dogmas, but is in constant process of growth and development. As a mighty stream hastens ever onward in its course, and accommodates itself in the channel in which it flows, so is Israel's religion – a living stream that incessantly pursues an onward and forward path.

If we have deserved the reputation of being most generous in charity, to our religion is due the credit. If we have encouraged learning, it is because our religion enjoins study. If our home life has been beautiful and family relationships admirable, it is again due to the stress our religion places upon filial piety. If we are loyal to our country it is only because our prophets taught us to pray for the land in which we dwell and to seek its welfare. And where we have failed to do these things, it is not because we were true Jews, but untrue Jews, disloyal to the best in our faith.

In our schools this year, we have tried not only to impart knowledge, but to deepen faith. We have taught the children history and the ideals and principles and ethics of our religion, so that they could translate it into life. To say "Love thy neighbor as thyself" and to really express it in action. We have tried to build up a character in the children that will bring them nearer to God. We have asked our mothers in our districts to teach the children to pray and to recall the lesson to the children during the week, thus helping the children to remember what they have learned.

306

When I returned home in September, I discovered that in most districts, a change in staff was desired for many reasons, among which they cite that the injection of a new superintendent in the school tends to give it new life, and prevents undue familiarity between superintendents and pupils. They also claim that after awhile, the superintendents lose interest in that district, and a change always works for the better. A great many of my boys had graduated from school and gone to different cities, so that it was necessary to retrain old boys to assume new duties in new districts, where they must learn to understand the psychology of the Mothers in that district and the children in that school.

Of the 41 schools now in progress, there has been a change in superintendents in every school with the exception of four. There has been a change in the teaching staff of all the schools, in some, the entire corps of teachers was replaced, whereas in others, a few new teachers have augmented the old group. This transfer meant reteaching the old group, and training the new. Our corps of teachers consists of boys and girls from nine different fraternities and two sororities. We find in our midst lawyers, school teachers, business girls, business men, and high school students.

I have found this change and transfer of teachers and superintendents from one school to another a necessity every year. Our entire staff numbers 275 regular teachers, 37 substitutes, 41 superintendents, 11 substitute superintendents, and 14 coaches. The substitutes have also been trained to take up the work . . . and are ready at a few hours' notice to step in wherever they are needed. The teachers are trained individually in my home.

What exactly do I mean by a night's instruction in my home? Let me give you a cross section of an evening spent in my home in the training of a boy or girl. First I talk with them personally, to find out their reaction, background, become acquainted with the type I am dealing with, and learn how much academic and Jewish education they have had. After ascertaining these things, I am ready to teach pedagogical methods of putting over the lesson, by presenting model lessons of psalms, proverbs, commandments, history, ethics, Midrash and the sayings of the Fathers.

I teach them how to use the material I have given them (outlined curriculum) for their particular work, and stress above all,

307

the responsibility of the teacher to his class, the necessity of applying himself, and of knowing his work so well, that he can present it without books or papers. I demand that all preparation be done outside the class. The instruction given to our teachers and superintendents, in one evening, if divided up into parts and presented, as is done by the Institute or Normal Schools (note: forerunner of teachers colleges or schools of education) would take a long period of time, and then the teacher is given only one phase of the work at a time.

Whereas I, by devoting three or four hours at one stretch to the individual, present the problem from all angles, so that the teacher may go directly to a class and has a thorough idea of what he is supposed to get across. We give him a typed curriculum, containing the work for each week's lesson clearly outlined, and have appended model lessons of psalms, proverbs, commandments, moral lessons, prayers, an a list of books pertaining to his work, to be used for reference, so that he may be able to present his work with a broadened point of view. If problems arise, which are very serious or perplexing to him, he comes back for instruction and advice as often as he needs it. The superintendents hold teachers' meetings once a month, where the work is gone over, and the problems of the school are discussed.

The teacher also has an opportunity to attend the monthly Institute meetings where Rabbis and Educators give lectures and Open Forums, which are a great help in solving problems and explaining more intensively the work that we are doing. We conduct three Institutes, one in Johnstown, known as the TriCounty, for Nanty-Glo, Portage, Windber, Altoona, Barnsboro, and two schools in Johnstown; The Valley Institute for Scottdale, Greensburg, Latrobe, Mt. Pleasant and Connellsville, and one in Pittsburgh for 33 schools. As an example of what we are doing in the Institute, this past month Rabbi Irving Levey of Cincinnati, addressed the Tri-County meeting on "The Interpretation of Jewish Ceremonials."

Rabbi Goodman A. Rose of Pittsburgh (Beth Shalom) gave one of the most inspirational lectures at the Valley Institute on the subject of "Facing our Jewish Obligations." And in our Pittsburgh Institute, which was the finest we have had this year, Rabbi Charles E. Shulman of Wheeling, W. Va. gave a most enlightening discourse on "Religion and Youth." After the lecture, Rabbi Shulman came to my home with a number of students and

308

until the wee hours of the morning, answered questions, inspiring and informing them of the many movements in Judaism which have occurred in the past century.

We conduct four Roundtables for Superintendents during the year. This year Mr. Chester Bandman and Rabbi B. A. Lichter (B'nai Israel) addressed two meetings and inspired the boys in their work. I myself addressed a third meeting giving instruction and advice. The purpose of the Roundtable is to present problems which confront the superintendents in the various districts as a whole, for solution, and an interchange of ideas and suggestions.

In addition to these meetings, we also conducted three Confirmation Roundtables, with a special Confirmation committee, to draw up the questionnaires for Confirmation, to mark the papers on their return to our office, and to make plans for the different Confirmation services.

Our curriculum embraces a course of studies from the Kindergarten Age through Post-Biblical History. No child is confirmed unless he is 15 or over, and has the proper attitude. If perchance there is an exceptional case, where a child is only fourteen and has been in the work for eight years, and has developed the proper attitude, then, and then only, do we confirm him. The Rabbis say that it is the attitude rather than the age which counts.

Our curriculum is quite comprehensive. This year we have Post-Confirmation classes in many schools where the boys and girls study the history of the Jewish race in China, Spain and other European countries, and current events. I visited one of these classes the other evening with a former superintendent. This class which meets in the evening is composed of twenty boys and girls from the ages of 17 to 20. They are a very eager and enthusiastic group, ready for all the information I could possibly give them. I helped them choose a name for their organization and after much discussion, decided to call themselves the "Torchbearers." In addition to the Post-Biblical work, they are discussing Jewish Current Events, reading books written by Jewish authors. This class in the West End is indeed an example for other districts to emulate.

Our curriculum because of its elasticity and broadness is in great demand. We have sent it, this year, to Washington, D.C.;

Youngstown, Ohio; Omaha, Nebraska; New York City; Warren, Ohio and Williamsport, Pa. and besides, have helped many other districts throughout the United States by sending out materials and suggestions.

Our Assembly takes the form of service, Bible reading and a story, songs, and reports. For each holiday there is an appropriate service, both for Jewish and secular patriotic days. Each Jewish holiday is fittingly celebrated with plays, programs and parties.

The Center Avenue Religious School, which is under my personal supervision, I use as a training school for young, inexperienced teachers who are not sufficiently equipped to go out to teach on Sunday mornings. After a year or two directly under me, they are fitted [sic] to enter into any school and take up the work.

I have organized six new schools this year, West End, Rankin, Beth Hamedrash Hagodol, McKees Rocks Progressive, Brownsville and Torath Chaim. In West End there had not been a Religious School for ten years. One of the Mothers came to me and asked me to come in and organize their district. I was amazed to find a group of 45 children. These people are so interested and enthusiastic in their work, that they have been able to pay for all their materials. There is splendid cooperation from teachers and superintendents, each teacher having come for instruction to my home. The boys and girls from the ages of 17 to 20 have organized a night club, which I have described above. For this class of 20 students, we have been successful in securing a young Jewish art student from Tech (Carnegie Institute of Technology), a graduate of Rabbi Philo's school, to teach this class. The boys and girls themselves pay their instructor.

In Rankin, the Rabbi with a committee of women, came to my house and spent an evening, persuading me to come to his district. We have organized a school which is most successful, and which has the full cooperation of the Sisterhood. The teachers, who are mostly local girls, came to my home for instruction and are taking their work very seriously. The cooperation of the Rabbi in that district is indeed a delight.

A committee of ten men, backing the Beth Hamedrash Hagodol Religious School asked our organization to enter and

310

organize a school. The teachers were taught in my home, then I went to the school, taught the children in the different classes, instructed the teachers in putting their work across. Fortunately I was able to secure one of my old superintendents to take over the school.

The children of the McKees Rocks Progressive School, with few exceptions had never attended a Religious School. This district felt that they needed a school, asked the permission of committee to organize and with their consent the school was opened. So far we have met with success, and the teachers come often for instruction.

Brownsville, another new school this year, was handed over by the local people as it had been a miserable failure. Since we took it over, we have met with phenomenal success. I visited Brownsville but once to organize and grade the school. I instructed the teachers. The staff of this school come all the way from Brownsville to attend our Institute meetings. They are very enthusiastic.

This past month has witnessed the opening of the sixth district, that of the Torath Chaim Religious School, at 728 North Negley Avenue, East End, Pittsburgh. This school already has a splendidly equipped community house, with well ventilated rooms for each class, pianos, and all necessary facilities for both physical and spiritual advancement of the child.

Besides my visits, my secretary visits a school each Sunday morning. This official visit from the office brings back the strength and weakness of a particular district. Although at the time she cannot do any doctoring, yet it means much to me to know just what is going on. Whether or not the teachers are putting the material across in the right way; whether or not they have the proper materials, if they are following my curriculum, if the superintendent is putting pep into his assembly and conducting it along the right lines, if the children and teachers come on time, and whether or not the interest of the children is sustained br the teacher. My secretary never interferes with the work, she only observes.

A visitor from our Committee going to our town schools would be of the same service. Some may ask "How can the committee be helpful?" It is not necessary for anyone to teach, for that is the duty of the Field Supervisor. We would like to have them visit the Assembly, visit the classes and if they see that the superintendents and teachers come in late, are ill prepared, ... It is indeed pleasing to see visitors sufficiently interested to come to the plays and entertainments, and I feel that at least two visitors from our committee should attend the confirmation exercises, especially in the town schools. . . . During my work throughout the year, I have tried to sum up some of the strengths ...and weaknesses of our schools and I have decided on the following – the strength of the school lies in the fact that physical conditions are as they should be and that the Mothers; Club, Sisterhood, or Council section has a strong vital President to push things along in that particular community, and the committee is willing to follow out the advice of the Field Supervisor, and to sacrifice both time and money in order to help this particular piece of work.

Where the club President or committee is inefficient, where they count everything in dollars and cents, where Mothers allow the children to stay away from Sabbath School, or permit them to oversleep, or keep them home on account of weather conditions, and are prone to criticize each little mistake of a teacher or superintendent and to enlarge on any little thing which may happen in the district, instead of trying to understand, that school is bound to fail.

My work is not limited to the Southwestern District alone, but extends to all parts of the state of Pennsylvania, as well as to the coast. Recently I was invited to come to Pennsylvania State College to address the Jewish student body at a meeting of the Society for Advancement of Judaism. This was indeed a source of great joy and inspiration to me.

I organized the girls at State College into a club for Jewish Culture, to be sponsored by Dr. Theresa Cohen, a member of the faculty, and also secured the cooperation of a number of boys in assisting with Jewish Religious work. The meeting was very well attended and the student body was so enthusiastic and pleased with my address, that I was extended a very cordial invitation to return very soon. I visited the Phi Epsilon Phi house and had a heart to heart talk with the boys, and at the Beta Sigma Rho fraternity house we discussed the Bible.

I was also asked to come to Williamsport to conduct with Rabbi Cronbach of Cincinnati a three-day Religious Education

Conference for Williamsport, Lock Haven and Sunbury. . . . When I arrived in Williamsport, I was informed that I was to occupy the pulpit that evening in Sunbury . . . .As I saw a great many men and young boys in the audience, I emphasized the relationship of parents to the synagogue and the duty of the father to the growing boy. I was enthusiastically received.

The next day, many Sunbury people accompanied me to Williamsport where I conducted a children's service at the Saturday morning service in the Temple. I told the children stories and spoke on a few of the past heroines in the Bible. In the afternoon I spoke on "Religious Training in the Home" before a groups of adults from the surrounding towns.

Several of the colored preachers from Williamsport attended and thanked me for some of the information I had given them. In the evening I addressed the group on "General Principles for Teachers and Parents" discussing the subject from three different angles – How to Prepare a Lesson, How to Present a Lesson and What to expect of the Parents. On Sunday morning at the Religious School session at the Jewish Community Center, I gave several model lesson demonstrations using the children from Sunbury, Lock Haven and Williamsport and environs for pupils in the classroom.

I put on an experimental Kindergarten lesson with those of the lowest grade, and the lesson on Ruth was demonstrated in Grades 3-4, before the entire assembly. In the afternoon I gave an address on "Responsibility of the Parent and Responsibility of the teacher and one Phase of Child Psychology." In the evening I gave several model lessons on Psalms and Proverbs for teachers and superintendents in Rabbi Mantinband's home. Dr. Cronbach also gave four lectures . . . .

Besides our regular schools we conduct a school for the Jewish Children of the Western Pennsylvania Institute for the Deaf . . . . We also conduct a school for the Jewish boys in the Western Pennsylvania Training School at Morganza and Thornhill. The children who unfortunately are incarcerated in these institutions look forward with eagerness to the visits on Sunday of the Sabbath School Teachers. They know the psalms and proverbs off by heart and the teacher has only to give the real interpretation and explanation of the work covered. Mrs. Bacharach, myself and a teacher, Mr. James Hendel visited the school when the boys took

313

part in an operetta. It was an interesting experience for all of us.

[I]t is indeed pleasing and gratifying to know how far reaching our work has become. . . the case of a young Jewish boy who had become disillusioned and discouraged through his environment and family. He called me on the phone one evening and asked if he might come over to visit me. Before he left ..he was interested enough to. . .take a class at the Center Avenue Religious School. I am sure he will . . .gain back his confidence and have a more optimistic view of life. . . . .An interesting incident is that of a....sophomore at the University who was very lonesome until he met a Jewish group at the home of the Field Supervisor.

He had decided that Pittsburgh was very drab and uninteresting and after he had found a center where he could pour out his joys and troubles, he became happier. It is indeed pleasing to know that we can reach just such boys through our work and help them find an interest . . . . My work has been very pleasant as the rabbis always unselfishly are willing to cooperate . . . .Never can we let down for a moment or rest on past laurels, for as Ruskin says, "We must not lower the level of our aim that we may more surely enjoy the complacency of success."

REMEMBRANCES OF THINGS PAST

In her report Miss Schonfield refers several times to her "boys." These were the superintendents of the schools and she admired them. We are fortunate to know what at least one of "Miriam's boys" thought of her and of the operation through the personal reminiscences of Bernard Steinberg, a member of Rodef Shalom, in an interview conducted in June 1996.

At the end of 1928 I was a freshman at the University of Pittsburgh. I received a telephone call from Miriam Schonfield , whom I had met before. She told me that her nephew, Bob Lowe, her sister's son, who lived in Erie, was coming to Pitt as a freshman. She wanted me to meet her nephew. I agreed to come to her home on Forbes Avenue and meet Bob. When I visited Bob at Miriam's home for the second time. Miriam talked to me about the possibility of becoming a teacher in the Southwestern District religious school system.

I was about 18 and a half and had never given such matters any thought although I was a 1925 confirmand of Rodef Shalom Congregation. Miriam felt I would do well. I began my first assignment as a teacher in the fall of 1929 at the Beth Jehuda Synagogue on the North Side. Abe R. Cohen was the superintendent and was also a law student at the University of Pittsburgh. He subsequently became a prominent attorney. I taught the pre-confirmation class. Abe retired at the end of that school year and suggested that I become the superintendent.

During my year as a teacher I was not paid; however I did receive money for carfare. When I became superintendent I was paid $5.00 per session, which meant per week. The reason I knew Miss Schonfield was that my sister, of blessed memory, was one of the first persons to teach for Miss Schonfield. She taught at the Center Avenue School where Miss Schonfield was the superintendent. Miss Schonfield had many wonderful attributes; a good administrator, a good organizer, a good stimulator of people to get involved. In the period when she served there weren't too many people who were competent in the field of Jewish education.

She was the Southwestern District, 100%. She had an ability to motivate people to serve. She was a dynamic person in an era when there weren't too many women involved in such endeavors. The male teachers and all of the superintendents were known as "Miriam's boys." I was very happy to be known in this way because I remember Miriam with great fondness.

My first assignment as a superintendent was at the Hilltop School. Just recently I saw Grace Fivars who told me that she remembers me as the superintendent of her school, the Hilltop School. [See Interview with Grace Fivars] Then in 1931 I became the superintendent in Carnegie. The next year I was sent to Coraopolis. I had to take the train to get there. In 1932 was the superintendent in Greensburg. My duties were to conduct the assembly before classes began and substitute for any teacher who might be absent. I received all of my teaching materials from the District office.

Once a month I attended a teachers' institute at Rodef Shalom. In fact in 1932 and 1933 I was the president of the Teachers Institute. My service to Southwestern ended in 1933, and the next year Miriam passed away. I felt privileged to have served under her tutelage.

Another person who remembers Miss Schonfield from this time period is Dr. Paul Forman, who was interviewed in June 1996.

My memories are focused mainly at the Center Avenue Sabbath School, as it was known when I began as a young child in 1929. My memories are clear, vivid and warm. I eagerly anticipated attending each session. The director, the atmosphere was [sic] warm and welcoming. It was a large school. Physically, the Irene Kaufmann Center was a very comfortable facility.

The individual most responsible for this warm, inviting atmosphere was the superintendent, Miriam Schonfield. She opened each week's session with an assembly, which included a Sabbath service led by her. The service was almost entirely in English with the exception of the *Sh'ma, Kedushah,* and *MiChamocha*. The part I loved best were the beautiful stories that Miss Schonfield used to tell. Thinking of her now as I relate my memories makes me feel very emotional.

She was a warm, inspiring leader. She incorporated homilies from *Pirkei Avot* into her stories. She was a story teller, par excellence. She had favorite expressions when telling these stories that I still remember, such as "This too will pass" or "everything in moderation, nothing in excess," "what is distasteful to you do not do unto others." Years later I learned that the latter phrase was one of Hillel's sayings, but I didn't know that at the time. This was true teaching and learning at its best. The subject I loved best was Jewish history. It was a good base upon which I continued to learn throughout my life.

This exposure to Jewish history helped me to understand the world in which I was living, how I was to fit into it and why I experienced the things that I did in the outside world. These memories are in sharp contradiction to the memories I have of Hebrew School, which I attended just a few blocks away on Center Ave. Although it is only within the past 15 years that I have been a regular Sabbath worshiper at my Conservative synagogue, those early services remain strongly in my memory.

We used the Union Hymnal for our services and for the music we sang. We had a piano accompaniment and everyone participated. As students were confirmed, many of them became

316

teachers in the Southwestern system. My brother, Herman, of blessed memory, and my sister Ann, as well as myself all taught. My brother and I both became superintendents. I served as superintendent in the Carnegie, South Side and Homewood schools while my brother served in the Ambridge and Carnegie schools. Many field supervisors followed Miss Schonfield, and while they were good, no one could match her.

Another student at the Center Avenue School remembers Miriam Schonfield with fondness. Allen Goppman, president of Adath Jeshuren, an Orthodox synagogue in Pittsburgh, began his Jewish education in 1931. He remembers Miss Schonfield as the "lady in charge" and "quite nice to know." He was interviewed in June 1996.

Social life for many of the teachers and superintendents was enhanced by activities sponsored by the District. Fund-raising balls were held yearly during this period. According to the *Jewish Criterion*, a December 1930 Benefit Ball held at the Fort Pitt Hotel with Bernie Armstrong, organist at the Stanley Theatre playing with the Gibby Lockhart orchestra was a "brilliant social success." A 1932 special "live program" featured Dick Powell, Bernie Armstrong, Dorothy Bushey and Rody Klaman at the Schenley Hotel.

In 1932 several Purim plays were produced. Purim and Chanukah plays in many of the schools in the District were directed by people who served the District as coaches. The Jewish Criterion for March tells of two plays performed at the Center Avenue School coached by Mrs. Samuel Lichter, a member of Rodef Shalom Congregation. The *Criterion* article goes on to say that "the Committee notes that since the successful Purim play at the Center Avenue School, many new children have enrolled in the school and more mothers are coming regularly to services conducted by the School." Mrs. Lichter is still a member of Rodef Shalom and recalls the plays and other performances which she directed under the aegis of Miss Schonfield.

The Torch Passes

1933 was Miss Schonfield's last year as Field Supervisor. Unknown to all but a few close associates, she was ill with cancer and January 25, 1934, at the age of 45, she died. This woman who had no formal education beyond high school created a system of Jewish education that was without parallel and influenced the lives of thousands of people, only a few of whom are mentioned in this report.

Miriam Schonfield's legacy of Jewish interdenominational education continued for 30 years after her death. The *Jewish Criterion* articles of the period note programs at Poale Zedeck, which was part of the District. Rabbi Shapiro of Poale Zedeck officiated at the confirmation exercises of Beth Jehuda on the North Side in 1935. I.A. Abrams of Hebrew Institute addressed the Teachers' Institute on the topic, "Orthodox Judaism" while Rabbi Herman Hailperin of Tree of Life Synagogue addressed the teachers on "Conservative Judaism." During this period Abe R. Cohen was Field Supervisor.

By 1937 it was becoming more difficult to recruit teachers, and so an article was published in the *Jewish Criterion* (September 24) making an appeal for volunteers:

> In order to continue to render Jewish education in those communities where means of Jewish education are lacking this organization, which has been established over 25 years, is claimed to be the only one of its kind in the United States.
>
> There are already 140 teachers in the service who give their time voluntarily and make an earnest attempt to serve youth and the Jewish cause. Since a number of schools have applied for admission to this organization, the Southwestern District is in urgent need of a number of volunteer teachers who have had a formal Jewish education.

The article referred to a statement by Dr. Solomon Freehof of Rodef Shalom Temple:

The fact is, the Southwestern District is unique in
American Jewish life. It is a network of Jewish schools teaching a
variety of religion, history and Hebrew subject. This network of
schools is maintained conjointly by the Council of Jewish Women
and the Sisterhood of Rodef Shalom Temple and by whatever help
any other group is willing to give. The teaching has hitherto been
entirely voluntary. Hundreds of young Pittsburgh men and women
serve the cause of Judaism at great inconvenience to themselves,
but nevertheless willingly and ably. One of the greatest problems
of Jewish education in America is how to reach the people in the
smaller towns where there are frequently seven or eight or ten
Jewish families and who because their numbers are few, generally
have not the ability or even the initiative to establish a congregation
and a school. Through the Southwestern District such isolated
communities are given an opportunity for modern education.

Through the end of the 1930s the schools continued to
flourish. Saul S. Spiro became the Field Supervisor in 1938. At that
time there were schools in 30 communities serving 1,000 children who
were taught by 200 volunteer teachers. In January of 1939 the
Teachers Institute held at Rodef Shalom featured Professor Hugh
Wing of the University of Pittsburgh, who presented a talk entitled:
"The Nature of Fascism in America." "To end the evening in a lighter
vein" as the *Jewish Criterion* said, the social committee arranged for
their "Learned Ladies" to meet the "Gentlemen and Scholars" of the
Institute in a "Battle of the Sexes – a Six Round Bout." This was
followed by the Field Supervisor Saul S. Spiro, who presented plans
and projects for school celebrations of Chamisho Oso[sic] B'Shevat,
Lincoln and Washington's Birthdays and Purim.

Dr. Spiro, building on the informal curricula used by previous
supervisors, developed a comprehensive, copyrighted curriculum in
1941. It was supplemented by Mrs. Mildred Kreimer and Mr. Oscar
Harter, field supervisors in the '40s and '50s and contains an
introduction by Dr. Solomon Freehof, which is included here:

> The problem of Jewish education in America is complex
> and difficult. It involves, first of all, a problem of philosophy.
> What are the principles, what are the fundamental intentions of our
> education in the changing world? Second, its is a question of

curriculum. Which subjects shall we teach so as to carry out the intentions of our educational philosophy? Third, there is the problem of textbooks. We must write and publish books which will be the proper vehicles for education and will interpret the curriculum to the modern American Jewish child. Fourth, there is the problem of a faculty. Where can we find, or how shall we train teachers who will have not only the technical knowledge of professional educators, but sufficient acquaintance with the actual material which we desire to teach? All of these problems are serious ones and have been dealt with to an increasing degree of success by many organizations, nation and local, engaged in the great enterprise of Jewish education in America.

There is, however, a fifth problem which is not generally discussed and which is a vital one, namely, the problem of geography. Our system of education must be so organized as to cope with the geographical fact that Jews are not only concentrated in large masses in the great cities but are also scattered in small groups in small towns all over the United States. How can these scattered groups be reached? What opportunity can be provided to them and to their children for the Jewish education for which they often long more ardently than Jews in the great cities?

This problem is not a new one. Many serious attempts have been made to cope with it. . . . The Southwestern District of Pennsylvania . . .is the most practical solution of the problem so far proposed. By uniting the enthusiasm of the (National) Council of Jewish Women under whose auspices the District was founded, and the enthusiasm of the Sisterhood of Rodef Shalom Temple, and by directing this emotional and mental current into the channel of Jewish education, organizing over a score of schools around the Pittsburgh district into one group, this method is small enough in scope to be manageable and large enough in achievement to be encouraging. The Southwestern District may be looked upon as the example which eventually the entire country will follow, Some day great congregations in New York and Chicago and San Francisco and St. Louis will, in collaboration with the Council of Jewish Women, establish similar districts in the neighborhoods around their respective cities. If these new districts will achieve what our Southwestern District has already achieved the geographical problem of Jewish education in America will be largely solved.

Indeed, Dr. Freehof figured prominently in the life of the District.

According to Helen Finkel Eger, office secretary to Chester Bandman, Administrator of Rodef Shalom (and field supervisor of the District for a few months following Miriam Schonfield's death in 1934) and staff assistant to Saul Spiro, field supervisor from 1939 until 1942, the curriculum was developed jointly by Rabbi Freehof and Mr. Spiro.

It was modeled on the curriculum then in use at Rodef Shalom but was adaped for use in small communities with limited resources. More than once throughout the years, Mrs. Eger said, Rabbi Freehof urged the Southwestern District Committee to continue its good work even in the face of competing programs and changing demographics.

Many of the superintendents in the District also looked to Rabbi Freehof for assistance. Harold Soltman, superintendent of the Swissvale Religious School and secretary of the Superintendent's Roundtable in 1938, wrote a letter to Dr. Freehof that has been preserved by his son, Herbert, in which he states that the superintendents discussed the problem of effectively teaching the Bible:

> One superintendent stated that he had successfully used your recent publication on the Psalms as the basis for teaching appreciation and understanding of the Psalms in particular and of the Bible in general. Some of our superintendents, however, indicated that neither they nor their respective communities could afford the purchase of your book. Mr. Spiro mentioned that he had had a conversation with you regarding the possibility of furnishing . . . one copy. . . to each of the District . . . .schools..in order that all the schools might have the benefit of instruction from your highly valuable book. I, personally, have made excellent use of your book and have found it very inspirational, both to myself and to the students whom I have instructed from your writings. In these troubled days, it is increasingly important to us as Jews to be possessed of spiritual courage and hope to face the trouble that besets us, and there can be no doubt that the Psalms afford one of the greatest sources of inspiration to which we can turn and from which we, as teachers, can hope to impart to the youth under our care...and spiritual hope which will serve to carry Israel through the present crisis just as our forebears passed through crises in the last.

The War Years And Beyond

The "trouble that besets us" of course became World War II. While the destruction of European Jewry was taking place and while thousands of young Jewish men (and some few women) were serving in the military, the District schools carried on. Mrs. Mildred Kreimer replaced Dr. Spiro as field supervisor and most of the male superin tendents were replaced by women. No longer did the Pittsburgh Teachers Institute meet nor did the Superintendent's Roundtable. But the schools survived and in many cases thrived.

One such school, the Kiski Valley Religious School, provided this writer with an excellent, personalized education in what can only be called spartan surrounding. Operational from 1938 until 1959, the two people who served as superintendents live in Pittsburgh now and were able to recall the highlights of that tiny school.

The first superintendent, Sylvia Breman Braun, tells her story:

> I married in 1936 and set up housekeeping in Leechburg. Noticing that Jewish children in the Kiski Valley (Leechburg and Apollo in Armstrong County and Vandergrift in Westmoreland County) were devoid of the opportunity of obtaining a Jewish education, I called Milton Sussman, a Pittsburgh attorney, and asked for his advice. Mr. Sussman came out on a cold, wintry night and got so lost he ended up in Saltsburg before proceeding to Vandergrift. We met with him in the B'nai B'rith headquarters, which consisted of an apartment on the second story of a car dealership building. This space ultimately became the space for the Religious School as well as the B'nai B'rith.
>
> I was Superintendent from 1938 until 1950. I also played the piano for the assemblies, which included the worship service. There was an atmosphere of cooperation throughout my years of service. For the first few years the parents taught all the classes, but after that we hired teachers through the District. They came out from Pittsburgh and taught a variety of subjects, including Hebrew. The District took care of sending materials for the students and teachers. We only had to pay for the teachers. The District made all plans for confirmation and even arranged for the female

confirmands to carry bouquets of flowers in the processional. (Note: It was Mrs. Helen Finkel Eger who made these arrangements in the first years).

There is another aspect of which I am proud. We had a Jewish family in Leechburg consisting of a mother, father, and three sons. The father was what would be considered today legally blind. His only livelihood was collecting scrap iron for resale. The mother had T.B. and was in a sanitarium. The boys were sent to our religious school but were poor students and quite disruptive in class.

I decided these boys needed love and attention so I got them to come to my home every Wednesday afternoon for years so I could tutor them. We would study in our breakfast room and on the table were sandwiches, cookies and chocolate milk.. In time they mellowed and all of them were confirmed at our school. One boy went to work for a Jewish merchant in our town and in time opened his own store in another town. The second son became president of a small college in Ohio, while the third son became a teacher in one of our local schools. I felt very rewarded by their achievements.

The classes at that tiny school were conducted in one room. At no time were there more than 12 students in the entire school, but that did not diminish the quality of instruction. This writer remembers having homework assignments in the higher grades that took most of a Saturday afternoon to complete.

And how could one face one's teacher, Jack Rubin, if the work was not done to his satisfaction? Or one's Mother, the Chair of the Mothers Committee, who worked tirelessly for the school even as her family was being destroyed in the Holocaust. This monograph is inspired by her devotion to the future of Judaism, which occurred even as her personal world was crashing. Anne Schiff Cooper, worked tirelessly to keep the school going.

The lessons learned in that tiny school seem even more significant as time has passed. And the most outstanding teacher of my religious school life was able to recall some of these moments in an interview on May 1 of this year.

Jack Rubin has lived in Squirrel Hill since 1959. Prior to that for over 25 years he lived in Vandergrift, where he and his brothers operated clothing stores in the three valley communities. Known as the Kiski Valley because they are situated on the banks of the Kiskiminetas River, the towns had small Jewish populations beginning in the '20s. Jack, born in Russia, came to this country as a small boy, lived with relatives in Brooklyn, and received a thorough Jewish education. He is fluent in and knowledgeable about Jewish texts. He taught in the Religious School almost from its inception, becoming principal in 1950. He served until the school was closed in 1959. At the time the school closed there were only 8 children in the religious school. He made arrangements for them to go to schools in neighboring towns which by now were more accessible because of improved roads.

> The primary reason for establishing the school and for my long commitment to it was to insure Jewish continuity. In the late 30's statistics showed that about 4% of Jews nationally and in Pittsburgh were involved in interfaith marriages. At that time the intermarriage rate for the Kiski Valley was 45%. Young Jewish people were growing up without a Jewish education and with very little prospect of meeting young people their own age. The school was a major effort by some of the parents to insure Jewish survival. I am very proud of these accomplishments because the goal of reducing the rate of intermarriage was met. The vast majority of the graduates married Jewish people and are maintaining Jewish homes. However there is no more Jewish community in the Kiski Valley. There are only two families in the entire valley who identify themselves as Jewish.

But those he reached were touched forever. He had numerous challenges. By the time Jack became superintendent he had to use his own resources to find teachers. Sometimes there was a problem. Some of the teachers he was able to recruit from Pittsburgh were Orthodox and they began to instill a view of Jewish observance that was inconsistent with the practices of most of the students' parents. These parents complained to Jack.

Even through Jack himself was comfortable with traditional observance, he realized he had to accommodate the diverse views and practices of the local community. So he lectured the young teachers about how to instruct the students regarding customs and practices. They were told to devote equal time to a discussion of the three movements in Judaism and to present the information in a non-judgmental manner that no movement was favored over another. At first he worried that the teachers would be unable to fulfill his instructions, but to Jack's knowledge they complied with his wishes.

Jack tells an amusing story that highlights the prevailing practice of the District to hire very young people as teachers and superintendents. One Sunday he and a fellow teacher traveled in snowy weather from Vandergrift to Pittsburgh with the intention of attending a Teachers Institute, a first-time experience for these men, both of whom were in their thirties. After a difficult two-hour trip over icy roads they arrived at Rodef Shalom, where the Institute was already in session. They walked down the hall to the room where it was being held and peered through the glass portion of the door. They saw a room full of young people of college age. Immediately they felt very uncomfortable; in fact Jack's friend refused to enter the room. What to do? They had traveled so far and were reluctant to turn back immediately. So they indulged themselves and went to a Turkish bath!

Jack Rubin and his counterparts in the various schools in the District were following the curriculum prepared by Rabbi Freehof and Dr. Spiro. In his preface to the first edition of the Curriculum in 1941, Dr. Spiro said:

> We have charted out a course of action which is offered to Jewish youth of all complexions: Orthodox, Conservative, and Reform. The present form of the curriculum is no longer in the experimental stage. If certain subjects have not been outlined to

the satisfaction of the Supervisor, it is due to the fact that the Jewish book market, especially the juvenile is still wanting many adequate textbooks.   Great emphasis has been laid upon the teaching of history. It correlates the present and the past, it arouses in the child the pride of its source and heritage, and it stimulates the student to solve present day problems in the light of past experiences.

There followed instructions to teachers as to their responsibilities, directions for class procedures and a guide to teaching Jewish history, including an extensive bibliography.   The teaching guide was age specific with weekly lesson plans for each grade. There were suggestions for extracurricular activities excerpted from materials prepared by Rabbi Abraham N. Franzblau of Hebrew Union College.

This curriculum and the education that resulted from it impressed many graduates of the District schools. Several graduates have told this writer that their education was superior to that received by their own children, many of whom have attended large, well-staffed religious schools in Reform and Conservative congregations.

One person who remembers her religious school experiences of the late '40s and early '50s is Marian Neustadt Hershman. Marian attended the East Hills School from the time she was three or four, because she accompanied her mother, Reva Levenson Neustadt, z'l, who was chairman of the Youth Committee of the Sisterhood and Superintendent of the School. Mothers taught many of the classes, a somewhat different model from other schools.

One of her teachers was Fredda Levy Stang, a past present of Temple Sinai. Marian also taught in the East Hills School for three years. She remembers attending Teachers Institutes but by now they were held three or four times a year, mainly to give out materials and discuss plans for upcoming events.

Others who remember the '40s with great affection include Howard Suffrin and Cecil Bruder Grodner.   Howard and Cecil

326

attended Beth El Congregation, which at that time was in Beechview. Howard's mother was the superintendent for a while. Classes were held in the balcony of the synagogue. Cecil has lived away from Pittsburgh for 40 years but keeps in close contact with people and subscribes to the *Jewish Chronicle*. She was confirmed at Beth El, organized a post-confirmation class, and taught at the school. She remembers teachers Zelda Rubinstein Limsi and her brothers, Sidney and Isadore..

By the end of the '40s many changes had taken place. One traumatic event was the closing of the Center Avenue School in 1944. From an enrollment high of 700 in 1919, attendance dropped to 150 in the mid '30s and to 100 by 1940. The population, of course, had moved from the "Hill" and new communities were forming. Likewise many of the small schools and congregations in the City closed as other population shifts occurred. After the late 1940's there were no schools in the West End, North Side, Homewood and Hilltop. As more people began to drive and as roads were improved people could send their children to schools that were farther away.

By 1961 there were only 11 schools and in 1963, 8: Mt. Pleasant, Latrobe, Punxsutawney, Indiana, Clearfield, Charleroi, Donora and Jeanette. Mr. Maurice Levy, field supervisor from 1961 until the program was discontinued in 1966, recalls these last years:

> The schools were dropping off because the Jewish communities they served were disintegrating. Fewer and fewer Jews remained in these communities. There were a handful of students in each community, with most schools having no more than 10 or 12 students.

> In 1962 National Council of Jewish Women withdrew their support. I talked to Rabbi Freehof and he implored the Rodef Shalom Sisterhood to continue their support, which they did for a few years. At this point my position was a part-time one. I came in once a week. My secretary worked a few hours a week. My salary was underwritten by the SWD Committee.

327

At this juncture the District did not get involved in hiring teachers or superintendents. That was left to the individual communities. I organized a Teachers Institute, which met once a year for a whole day. I held it at Rodef Shalom and I brought in speakers on topics such as teaching methods, crafts, music. One of my first projects after becoming Field Supervisor was to rewrite the curriculum, which had not been revised to any great degree since it was written by Dr. Spiro in 1941. The curriculum was primarily historically based.

I tried to supplement it by doing research on innovative ways to celebrate the holidays in these tiny schools. I would prepare guides based on my research and send it out to the schools. While I would send out the curriculum; the actual textbooks were the responsibility of the individual community.

Another duty which I enjoyed was visiting the schools. There wasn't enough money in the budget to visit them as often as I would have liked, but I did manage to visit each school at least once a year. On a typical morning when I would visit a school, I would first talk with the superintendent of the school. Then I would observe the classes.

Then I would participate in the assembly or service. Many times I would ask the children how they felt about being Jewish. Most of them professed not to think about it very much. They knew they were in the minority. They were enthusiastic students because they realized their parents cared so much about the schools and about their education. I tried to teach them more than history.

I used a book by Lillian Freehof on ethics entitled *The Right Way*. The parents were very dedicated and far more involved than in the larger congregations or communities. The success of the schools was in very large part dependent on the commitment of the parents. I particularly remember the dedication of the Clearfield superintendent, Mrs. Silverblatt, who never missed a Teachers Institute in Pittsburgh even though the trip from her community to Pittsburgh was over three hours at that time.

I also officiated a the confirmation services which at this time were held in the constituent schools. Sometimes I did two services in one day, one in the morning and one in the evening.

In my opinion, the end of the Southwestern program coincided with the end of an era in family cultural values. What was possible to achieve in those years in those small towns may not have been possible in the '70s and '80s. The effort of the District and, by definition, of the Rodef Shalom Sisterhood and the National Council of Jewish Women, was a noble one. They reached out to small communities and helped them to educate their children. They felt a responsibility to help to ensure the survival of Judaism in those small communities.

I tried to do as much as possible with the modest budget that was available. As a professional educator who taught in the Pittsburgh Public School system for 33 years, I feel that I was able to offer a professional approach to the position. I thoroughly enjoyed my tenure with the District. To say that the services provided by the District were commendable doesn't begin to describe how important it was [*sic*].

The Southwestern District program was a classic example of Jews who had more opportunities wanting to share what they had with Jews who had fewer resources because of their geographic isolation. It was a noble experiment.

The Committee disbanded after the close of the school year in 1966. A few of the schools survived. In most cases students were transported to the closest town that had a Religious School. Yet, thirty years after the last Confirmation, these little schools live on in the memory of hundreds of people in the Tri State area.

They and their classmates who may have moved to all parts of the country remember with great fondness their unique experiences in those tiny isolated schools. This noble experiment contributed greatly to the survival of Jewish people in Western Pennsylvania.

APPENDIX

Schools enrolled by the District at one time or another: City of Pittsburgh: Adath Israel (Oakland); Adath Jeshurun (East End); Beth Hamidedrosh Hagadol (Washington Street, Hill District); Beth El (Beechview); Beth Israel (North Side – Woods Run); Beth Jehuda (North Side--Manchester); B'nai Emunoh (Squirrel

329

Hill/Greenfield); Center Ave. (Irene Kaufmann Settlement, Hill District); Hazelwood; Hilltop (Beltzhhoover, Arlington area); B'nai Zion (Homewood); Kehilath Jeshurun (Schenley Heights); Penn Ave; Lawrenceville; Ohev Zedeck (Oakland); Poale Zedeck (Squirrel Hill); South Side Talmud Torah; Torath Chaim (East End); West End.

Outside the City of Pittsburgh: Aliquippa, Ambridge, Barnesboro, Beaver Valley, Bentleyville, Braddock, Brownsville, Butler, California, Canonsburg, Carnegie, Charleroi, Clearfield, Connellsville, Coraopolis, Donora, Dubois, Duquesne, East Pittsburgh; East Liverpool, Ohio; Edgewood (Western Pennsylvania School for the Deaf); Ellwood City; Etna; Ford City; Glassport, Greensburg, Homestead, Huntington, W. V.; Indiana, Irwin, Jeannette, Johnstown; Kiski Valley (Leechburg, Vandergrift, Apollo); Kittanning, Latrobe, McDonald, Masontown, McKeesport, McKees Rocks, McKees Rocks Progressive; Midland, Monongahela, Morganza Correctional School, Mount Pleasant, Nanty Glo, New Castle, New Kensington, Portage, Punxsutawney, Rankin, Scottdale, South Fork, Steubenville, Ohio; Swissvale, Tarentum, Thornhill Correctional School, Uniontown, Washington, Weirton, W. V.; Wilkinsburg, Woodlawn

FIELD SUPERVISORS

Miriam Schonfield (1907–1934); Chester R. Bandman (1934–4 months); Abe R. Cohen (1934–1937); Saul S. Spiro (1937–1942); Mildred Kreimer (1942–1946); Oscar I. Harter (1946–1961); Maurice Levy (1961–1966)

COMMITTEE CHAIRPERSONS

Mrs. A. Leo Weil (Columbian Council); Mrs. Moses Ruslander (CJW); Mrs. Fannie Weinhaus; Mrs. A.J. Marx; Mrs. Louis Caplan; Mrs. Louis Amshel (SWD); Mrs. Joseph Jackson; Mrs. Carl M. Bachrach; Mrs. Julian Kimmelsteil; Mrs. I. H. Levin; Mrs. Jay Goldstein; Mrs. J. Robert Kalish; Mrs. Edgar L. Hirsch; Mrs. Joseph Goodman; Mrs. Sigmund Arnold; Mrs. Merle Spandau; Mrs. Benjamin Schecter; Mrs. Lester Strauss; Mrs. Andrew Citron; Mrs. A. L. Cohen; Mrs. Jean Shugarman.

PEOPLE INTERVIEWED

Maurice Levy, Herbert Soltman, Sarah Mishelevich, Allen Goppman, Genevieve Rubenstein Bliwa, Cecil Bruder Grodner, Zelda Rubenstein Limsi, Howard Suffrin, Bernard Steinberg, Bea Lichter, Grace Fivars, Marian Neustadt Hershman, Sherman Hershman, Barbara Berns, Harry Seltzer, Leonard Schneider, Estelle Belkin, Ruth Gross, Jack Rubin, Sylvia Braun, Helen Finkel Eger, Paul Forman.

THANKS TO

Estelle Belkin, Librarian, Rodef Shalom Religious School, for assisting in examining the volumes of the *Jewish Criterion*; Rachel Balliet Colker, Archivist, Western Pennsylvania Jewish Archives, Historical Society of Western Pennsylvania; David Rosenberg, Director, Archives of Industrial Society, Hillman Library, University of Pittsburgh; Sharyn Rubin, Program Director, Jewish Community Center of Pittsburgh who facilitated the interview with her father-in-law, Jack Rubin; Barbara Bailey, secretary to Dr. Jacob and Mardi Jackley, Events Planner, at Rodef Shalom for their gracious assistance; Sam Balk for help on the history of Western Pennsylvania Jewish communities; Faye Lebovitz, former archivist, Historical Society of Western Pennsylvania, for suggestions on research; Marvin S. Reidbord, who provided encouragement and support throughout the project.

Special thanks to Dr. Walter Jacob, Rabbi, Rodef Shalom Congregation, who suggested the undertaking of this project and who offered advice and assistance.

Notes

1. Volumes of the *Jewish Criterion* from 1915 to 1959 were reviewed. These volumes, housed at Rodef Shalom Temple, provide a rich source of history of the District and its forerunner organization.

2. The Jewish Archival Survey Collection, 1912-1990, Library and Archives Division of the Historical Society of Western Pennsylvania was reviewed. The only relevant material was in the file of the former Ohav Shalom congregation in Donora which contained the complete curriculum of the Southwestern District prepared by Dr. Saul S. Spiro, published in 1941 and updated until 1953.

3. Historic files of the National Council of Jewish Women are located in the Archives of Industrial Society, Hilllman Library, University of Pittsburgh. The files on Religious Education are contained in Box 17, files 1 through 14. They are divided into two parts: A. Historic correspondence on religious education, 1894-190? and B. Southwestern District Of Pennsylvania Jewish Religious Schools Committee. This part has 8 sections one of which contains the annual report by Miriam Schonfield for 1928, the most extensive report in the collection.

4. Background material on the period was derived from *The Jewish Experience in Western Pennsylvania: A History:1755/1945*, by Jacob Feldman, published by the Historical Society of Western Pennsylvania.

5. Personal and telephone interviews were conducted with people who responded to articles in the Rodef Shalom newsletter and the *Jewish Chronicle*. Additional information not cited in the report includes the following:

Grace Fivars provided a list of the founding families of the Hilltop Religious School. Bea Lichter noted that she was born on

Dinwiddie Street and then lived on the South Side. Her mother was instrumental in establishing the South Side school; however, Bea was taken to Rodef Shalom Temple at an early age and received her religious education there. She coached plays in Homestead, South Side, Carnegie, and other towns for Purim and Chanukah. She remembers Miriam Schonfield as a strict disciplinarian who moved teachers and superintendents around frequently so that they wouldn't become stale in one setting. She remembers Miss Schonfield not permitting teachers to date superintendents. After her stints as drama director she served on the Southwestern Committee for several years. Harry Seltzer, a member of Temple Emanuel, attended the South Side school. His confirmation, in the early '30s was held at the Tree of Life Synagogue. He remembers paying a nickel a week for donation to the religious school. Leonard Schneider is a member of Rodef Shalom. He attended a religious school in Beltzhoover (Hilltop) in the early 30's. He particularly remembers the plays they put on at Purim. Barbara Berns is a member of Rodef Shalom from which she was confirmed in the early '50s. Her family then transferred their membership to Temple Sinai so that her brother could become a Bar Mitzvah. She wanted to teach religious school at Sinai and talked to her rabbi, who suggested she contact Oscar Harter, at that time field supervisor of the Southwestern District. He assigned her to the Homestead religious school. All classes met in the sanctuary of the synagogue. The children sat in pews, and each group of students was scattered so as not to disrupt the teaching and learning of a nearby class. Homestead had a vibrant Jewish community at that time and the parents were quite involved in the synagogue's activities and were extremely supportive and appreciative of their children's teachers. She taught there for two years before going on to teach at Temple Sinai.

Estelle Begler Belkin was confirmed from the Beth Jehuda school on the North Side as was her sister. She has saved confirmation certificates and programs from 1945 (her own) and 1947 (her sister's). Herb Soltman, a member of Temple Emanuel, has saved extensive materials from his father's files, including voluminous study guides and examinations that he prepared in connection with his service as superintendent of the Swissvale Religious School. The material includes a program for the closing services of the school year; confirmation program of the Southwestern District for 1938; sample of a confirmation exam, copy of directions given to confirmands instructing them to memorize several pages of material, a paper prepared by Mr. Soltman, Various Methods in

Jewish Education, class notes for the year 1937-1938, a paper by Dr. Freehof: The Synagogue and the Disintegrated Jew" a program entitled, "Conference on Jewish Education" under the auspices of the Rodef Shalom Faculty Association in 1937 to which teachers in the Southwestern District were invited. Also in these files is a letter from one of his students, dated June 23, 1938, which says: "This is just a little note to express thanks to you from your confirmation class. It has been a real privilege and pleasure to have you as our teacher. Your unfailing patience, never ending stream of knowledge, and supreme willingness to help us in every way is deeply appreciated. We sincerely wish that we may become worthy of all your efforts. You will always stand in our hearts as someone who brought out the finest, purist, highest ideals from within us, someone who has added a beautiful touch to our lives by instilling within us the sacred sweetness and beauty of religion. May God bless you and good luck be with you always. Please accept most sincere thanks from your confirmation class, including your pupil, Jean Silberman."

Ruth Gross grew up in Brownsville and was confirmed from the Orthodox synagogue in that town. She has fond memories of her school years. She also remembers Rabbi Lichter, z'l , of B'nai Israel officiating at her confirmation service. Helen Finkel Eger came to Rodef Shalom in 1939 after graduating from Margaret Morrison Carnegie College of the Carnegie Institute of Technology, now Carnegie Mellon University. Mrs. Edgar H. Hirsh was the chairperson of the Southwestern Committee while she worked there and she considered her outstanding. At the time she worked there the fee for a community to be affiliated with the District was calculated at $2.00 per student. She planned the confirmation program and took care of all arrangements for the service. She attended the meetings for the teachers and superintendents that were held every few months. These meetings provided a good opportunity for teachers to socialize and a few romances occurred as a result of these meetings. Mr. Spiro would attend the meetings of the Southwestern District Committee. Sometimes these meetings were quite tense. Some of the ladies wanted Mr. Spiro to raise the fees charged to the schools because they did not begin to cover the costs of operation, but Mr. Spiro knew that these communities were strapped financially and couldn't pay more. Allen Goppman remembers helping the field supervisor, Mr. Spiro, after he was confirmed in 1941, by mimeographing materials at the District office at Rodef Shalom. His wife, Ethel, was confirmed in 1942 from the South Side

Talmud Torah which was part of the District. Shalom. One of the "benefits" she received upon being confirmed was a year's membership in the Y in Oakland. Genevieve Rubenstein Bliwa attended school in Allentown (Hilltop). Her sister, Tillie, taught at Beth El in Beechview.

SOME WERE RESCUED
MEMOIRS OF A PRIVATE MISSION*

David Glick

Early in the year 1936, Mr. Max Warburg of Berlin and Hamburg, Germany, communicated with his brother Felix Warburg in New York telling him that conditions and circumstances under which the Jews of Germany were compelled to exist had reached a point where it was necessary to attempt to have an American citizen come to Germany and act as a liaison between the German Jews and the officials of the large German cities.

By decrees issued by the Nazi government, all Jews had been discharged from all civil service. After that, there slowly followed more decrees forbidding the employment of Jews as professors in universities, as lawyers, as physicians, and as jurists. Benefits in sick funds and health insurance were canceled. In private enterprises, management had been dragooned into discharging all Jewish employees. Finally there was the beginning of property. A decree had been issued that denied a Jew the right to call upon any German official unless ordered to do so. Furthermore, the Jews of Germany were not permitted to meet with Jews of foreign countries, nor were Jews of foreign countries permitted to meet with Jews of Germany. Because of these decrees, official and unofficial, the Jews were classed outlaws as well, as outcasts.

My brother, Peter (who had been Secretary of Labor in Pennsylvania), met with Messrs. Felix Warburg and Paul Baerwald in New York City and volunteered to go to Germany and make the attempt to act as liaison. They dissuaded him when they learned he had five children. My brother Peter then called me and I went to New York and met with Messrs. Warburg and Baerwald. My wife was as deeply concerned over the tragic plight of the Jews in Germany as I was and supported my decision to make the effort and assume the risk. If I went to Germany, it would be my task to try to bring to the attention of the Nazi officials any suggestion, recommendation or assistance I thought should be given the Jews that would enable them

* Reprinted by permission from the *Harvard Law Review*

to migrate to other lands. I suggested to Messrs. Warburg and Baerwald that my first objective should be to meet with Mr. Himmler, who was the Chief and Head of the Gestapo. The reason was obvious, for within a few days, the Secret Police would pick me up, ask my purpose in coming to Berlin and any attempt to explain would only result in my being told to leave the country. Both men agreed with my suggestion.

I left for Germany early in April 1936. When I arrived in Berlin, I registered at the Esplanade Hotel, which was directly across the street from the United States Consulate. After I was settled at the hotel, I called upon Mr. William F. Dodd, our Ambassador to Germany, a truly patriotic American and a remarkable man, who took advantage of every opportunity in speaking to the small group of Americans in Berlin, stressing the nature and significance of democratic institutions. This, of course, had made him unpopular with the Nazi officials. I explained to Mr. Dodd the purpose of my coming to Germany. He wished me well in my work and told me that he, as Ambassador, could not be of any help; that it would be the task of the American Consul to arrange a meeting with Mr. Himmler. I then called upon Mr. George S. Messersmith, the United States Consul General, an outspoken and fearless representative of our country, and his First Assistant, Raymond H Geist, the United States Consul. I explained to both these officials the purpose of my visit to Germany and requested that they try to arrange an interview with Mr. Himmler. They reacted enthusiastically and immediately phoned Himmler without disclosing to him the purpose of the call, simply asking for an interview. The interview was granted, and a few days later I drove with Mr. Geist to the headquarters of the Gestapo, at No. 8 Prinz-Albrecht-Strasse.

I recall vividly that on the main entrance to the headquarters, there was posted this sign, "JUDEN HABEN HIER KEIN EINTRIT" (Jews cannot enter here). Geist snarled at this sign. I just "wondered." Even though I was with an American Consul and therefore under complete protection, I am sure that, at that time, I must have been tense and nervous, for during the previous few days,

David Glick

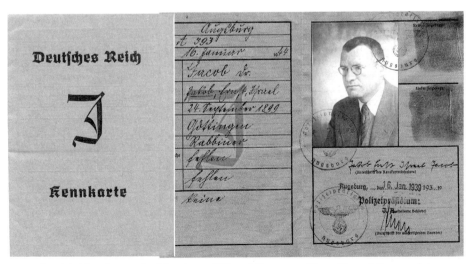

Jewish identity card with a large "J" and the name "Israel" and fingerprints
added - following the release of Ernst Jacob from Dachau, January 1939

337

I had seen the parades of the Brown Shirts, the Black Shirts, the thousands of swastikas and flags flying from all buildings in Berlin and could feel the oppression of a totalitarian government. Mr. Geist suggested that he do all the talking, that I was to give no indication to Himmler that I could speak German fluently. Geist was to tell Himmler my purpose in coming to Berlin in German, then relate to me Himmler's reply in English, and I would speak to Geist in English. This arrangement worked satisfactorily and gave a kind of semi-official appearance to my visit. Geist told Himmler that I was in Berlin at the request of two men; that there had been no publicity given to my trip to Berlin; that no publicity was intended; that my work would be done quietly; that I would make no speeches or propaganda upon my return to America, nor write any articles. My purpose was specifically to give help to the Jews of Germany to assist them in leaving Germany for other parts of the world with as much of their property as possible under the laws of Germany. He also told him that arrangements for the Jews to migrate could be accomplished, but that they must take with them some property in order that they would not become a charge on the community to which they migrated.

After considering the matter, Mr. Himmler consented to the arrangement and called in Reinhard Heydrich, explained the situation to him, and Heydrich then took me to the office of the Deputy in charge of the "Juden Fragen" (Jewish Problem), whose name was Dr. iur. Karl Haselbacher. I spent considerable time with Haselbacher, for he knew the important Jews in every large city in Germany. He had a filing card system that contained the names, addresses, activities, and occupations of thousands of the important Jews in Germany. Haselbacher was good enough to give me his calling card with his private phone number so that if I needed to call him for any reason, I would have no difficulty. He also furnished me with a list of leading Jews in the large cities of Germany. Geist and Messersmith were both amazed that permission was granted so quickly. News of the granting of permission was never disclosed to the public. At that time there were in Germany great and important newsmen such as Louis P. Lochner, Pierre J. Huss, and William L. Shirer. But my word had been given to the Gestapo that my work was to be accomplished without

338

publicity, and these men were never apprised by Geist or Messersmith of that interview and, so far as I know never learned of my presence in Germany, although I crisscrossed Germany from Hamburg to Breslau and from Stuttgart to Königsberg in East Prussia, visiting nearly all the important cities and hundreds of smaller towns and villages.

I remained in Germany a full year and returned to America and reported to Messrs. Warburg and Baerwald. They were already quite satisfied with the work from reports that they had received from Mr. Max Warburg. They requested that I return for a second year.

When I returned in 1937, and again began to visit cities outside Berlin, I was stopped at intervals by Secret Police and questioned at Frankfurt and Munich. I returned to Berlin and met with Mr. Geist, told him that I was being annoyed and questioned by the Gestapo and suggested to him that I perhaps should meet with Heydrich again. Mr. Geist arranged for a visit, and at that time, Heydrich called in Dr. Best, Deputy Leader of the Secret State Police, who was also an attorney, to sit in on the conference. When I explained the purpose of my call to Mr. Heydrich, I suggested that since I had violated none of the original agreement that I had made with him the laws of Germany and was carrying out the purpose ofmy task, that I would like to have a letter from the Gestapo which I could show to any of the Secret Police in Germany, as I intended to visit a great many small Cities in Germany and was particularly interested in visiting East Prussia, where the Jews were completely isolated. East Prussia at that time was separated from Germany proper by the City of Danzig and the Polish Corridor. Heydrich and Dr. Best consented, and within a few days after my visit I received the letter from the Gestapo. When I visited East Prussia in June of 1937, I called upon the head of the State Secret Police in Königsberg and he too gave me a letter. I carried both these letters with me at all times.

With the help and advice of the Reichsvertretung der Juden in Deutschland (National Committee for German Jews) it is estimated that 90,000 Jews were able to migrate to other lands during the years that I worked in conjunction with the Reichsvertretung in Germany. The vast majority were able to obtain visas to South America; Argentina accepted the largest number.

It was necessary to meet with representatives of these South American countries to acquire visas, arrange for transportation and for liquidation and transfer of property. The story of the migration of Jews from Twentieth Century Germany to Sixteenth Century Bolivia (La Paz) is almost legendary in its details, but absolutely true, as I can affirm.

Bolivia, a landlocked country whose inhabitants were 80% Inca Indians and into which country there had been practically no white migration since the days of Pizarro, suddenly finds 3.000 refugees seeking a home, visas having been granted by Bolivian representatives in Germany. Housing, food, blankets, had to be furnished in a city (La Paz) 12,000 feet above sea level. The only approach to La Paz from Arica, Chile, was either by small aeroplane (1939) or by train, which took 1½ days to reach La Paz — a train without any of the modern conveniences of utilities or supplies of food and water in quantities. Try to picture these men, women and children who had been living in the most modern scientific country in the world, with all the physical comforts of modern science, suddenly faced with the difficulties of a pioneer life in a country as strange to them as the planet Mars, confronted with the problems of employment, altitude, language and customs of the country, and with none of the benefits of modern social agencies to assist them in the problem of integration.

Well, a legendary figure did appear in the form of Don Mauricio Hochschild of tin mine fame, a citizen of Argentina and a resident of La Paz, Bolivia. He converted himself into a one-man Community Chest and arranged for the settlement of these bewildered families and did it without Madison Avenue publicity. Through his vast economic empire, he brought to these refugees the financial assistance and benefits of what we in America extend through the Community Chest.

340

It would be interesting to relate in great detail the manner in which these refugees settled in the various countries of South America and began to contribute to the welfare of the country through their knowledge and abilities. Among these refugees were scientists, engineers, social workers, tradesmen, and teachers, and over the years they have become healthfully integrated into their new homelands, but all that would require a story of great length.

I hesitate to begin a recitation of my experiences and the work accomplished, for old soldiers never die; their memories fade and their imaginations grow. During the two years, I could see the effect of the power and cruelty of the tyrannical half-mad dictator. I never met Hitler or Goebbels or Goering, but heard them speak often and saw them in parades and at the annual meeting of the Nazi party in Nuremberg, which was referred to a "Der Partei Tag," although it continued for a full week. Each day was devoted to a specific branch of the Party service: one day devoted to the acts of the Brown Shirts; another day for the Workers' Service; Hitler Youth; Young Girls' Organization, and the Army. At each of these daily events, which were held in the vast stadium in Nuremberg, Hitler would deliver his fanatical tirades against the Jews in Germany, who, according to him, were responsible for the Treaty (Chains) of Versailles, for the rise of Bolshevism in Russia, for decadent capitalism, for the control of the press, the cinema, education, law, medicine, banking, for the corruption of art and for Germany's economic collapse and its unemployment. All the ills of Germany were due to a handful of Jews.

I recall in one of my talks with Hasselbacher that I pointed out to him that out of the population of 65 million Germans, just 1% were Jews, and that of this 1%, approximately half were male, and half were female; that of the male and female, some were children and many were aged, and it was irrational and unreasonable to try to convince me that the small remaining fraction could control so much. He said he would furnish me with an answer but he never did and I never pressed him at later meetings. I recall another incident with Haselbacher. The Berlin-Rome Axis was the power that was to rule the world because that Axis represented Aryan supremacy. Later,

Japan was taken in and the Axis became Berlin-Rome-Tokyo. When I wondered at the Japanese becoming part of the Aryan Axis, Haselbacher replied that Hitler had issued a decree making the Japanese Aryans. Goering's First Deputy of the Air Corps was made an Aryan by decree of Goering, as was the Great Director of the Berlin Opera. I believe, although I am not certain, but there was a rumor that since Goering's wife was purchasing her fine outfits at "Braun's," Unter den Linden, Goering decreed that the Brauns were Aryans.

Only when a lover of liberty lives in a totalitarian state can he understand and fully appreciate the full significance of our Bill of Rights. When one man controls absolutely the Secret Police, the military, the press, radio, cinema, then freedom vanishes like the morning mist.

My wife came to Germany for a brief stay and we visited together some of the glory of medieval Germany in Bavaria, along the River Main and the Rhine Valley. From the city of Kehl, we crossed the International Bridge to Strasbourg to see that beautiful cathedral with its unsurpassed single spire woven in stone. We were to be gone just for the day, so we traveled without baggage. At the German end of the bridge, I declared my finances (for under Schacht, exchange was strictly controlled – "devisen Falschung" was a serious crime) and nothing else. At the other end of the bridge, the French Inspector asked the customary question, "Avezvous quelque chose à déclarer?" "Oui," replied my wife. I was frightened. Had she something that violated Nazi law that would have serious consequences when we returned to Germany that evening? When the Inspector asked "Quoi?" she proudly replied "Je déclare ma liberté." She was the recipient at that moment of a true "poilu" embrace.

Having spent two years under Hitler, I know the meaning of the words liberty and freedom, even though I cannot define them. Such names as Rabbi Leo Baeck, Otto Hirsch of Stuttgart, and Julius L. Seligsohn are well known because of their heroic efforts in behalf of that ancient, cultured Jewish community of Germany which Hitler destroyed, but I cannot refrain from mentioning the names of those men and women, who, in their native cities and towns, worked bravely in behalf of their beleaguered co-religionists during the period when beasts were governing Germany. These men and women were not mentioned in the books; no tablets were erected in their memory, but they were so courageous in their quiet and successful work; such men as Emil Oettinger of Frankfurt, Leopold Levi of Stuttgart; Dr. Nathan Stein of Karlsruhe, Julius Beck of Danzig, Wilfred Israel of Berlin, Sally Eichengrün, Rabbi Baerwald, Justizrat Dr. Oestreich, all of Munich, Prof. Dr. Hugo Falkenheim of Königsberg, Prof. Dr. Eugen Mittwoch and Prof. Dr. Ismar Elbogen of Berlin, Lola Warburg Hahn (Youth Aliyah) and Cora Berliner. Their memory, at least to me, has been a blessing and I end with a tribute to the effective and generous help I received from every U. S. Consul in Berlin, Stuttgart, Munich, and Danzig. I never met up with "The Ugly American."

I returned home in the summer of 1938 and in March 1939, with Frederich Borchardt, a former director of the Reichsvertretung an Deutsche Juden, made a survey of the needs of the German Jews who had migrated from Germany to South America during the previous three years, in order to determine what financial help could be given them in order to enable them to integrate themselves economically and culturally in a land altogether strange to them in language, custom and tradition. We visited by air every capital in South America and reported our findings and recommendations upon our return to New York.

SUPPLEMENT

I hope you did not expect something conspiratorial, a sort of cloak-and-dagger tale, some clever and cunning pulling of wires – well, I could dramatize the story. I could describe the room in which we met with Himmler, how Geist approached the subject and the spirit of the conversation, and describe Himmler and Heydrich. Himmler, at first glance, appeared like an experienced title searcher in the office of the Recorder of Deeds of a country county seat. No pomp, no table thumping, no attempt to make an impression. He sat there with three SS men around him, but those eyes of his; those beady, button eyes, cruel as he was cunning and cunning as he was cruel. When Heydrich entered the room, my first thought was, "What a tackle he would make on a professional football team." He was a blond gorilla – big shoulders, long arms, powerful legs.

I could relate many of the tragic tales; conversations with fathers who had been informed against by sons, and sons informed against by fathers; the knock at the door followed a few months later by a box of ashes from the crematorium; humble and poor Christian families who risked all to provide food for their Jewish neighbors under cover of night in the small villages: how I was tailed by the "Kriminal Polizei" in the Deutsches Museum in Munich, But all this has been told over and over again. I am a lawyer and lawyers can read between the lines.

My temper does rise, however, when a German who was between the ages of, say, 16 to 90, and who lived in Germany between the years 1932 to 1939, tells me or tells the world he did not know what treatment we meted out to the non-Aryans (Jews). The country was plastered from the North Sea to the Bavarian Alps, from the Rhine to the Polish Border, with posters attacking the Jews. Every country crossroad in Pomerania, Mecklenburg, Saxony and Bavaria had billboard posters attacking the Jews. The leading newspapers in Germany were the *Völkischer Beobachter,* owned by Hitler, *Der Angriff,* owned by Goebbels, and *Der, Stürmer,* owned by the leader of the Arbeitsfront, Julius Streicher, and they were devoted almost entirely to attacking the Jews. The radio filled the air defaming the Jews. There was not a German in Germany from Dr. Schacht, the financial director, down to the ordinary tavern keeper, who was not aware of the treatment of Jews. The Nuremberg Parteitag was publicized all over Germany, spectators and participators in the activities and events came from all parts of Germany and the cry was "Juden sind unser Unglück" (Jews are our misfortune). We must rid the Reich of the Jews to maintain the purity and sacredness of "Blut und Boden" (Blood and Soil). Hundreds of villages, and I visited hundreds of villages, proudly displayed signs as you entered: "Wir sind Juden rein" (We are rid of Jews).

344

I repeat, when one who lived in Germany from 1932 to 1939 and between the ages of 16 to 90, tells me or the world that he did not know of the ghastly martyrdom of the Jews, he is either witless or a downright fabricator of falsehoods. These are strong words, but I stand by these words.

APPENDIX

I

SKETCH OF THE PROGRESS OF THE RODEF SHOLEM

CONGREGATION

PITTSBURGH, PENNSYLVANIA*

The inception of Public Divine Services among the Israelites of Pittsburgh and vicinity commenced in the year 1847, prior to that time there were not sufficient members here to organize a service. In the year 1847, the following well-known persons held the first religious services: Eph. Wormser, David Strassburger, Wm. Frank, Nathan Gallinger, Jacob Klein, Eml. Klein, Moritz Kraus, Eiseman Kahn, Reis Bros., Stein Bros., Louis Morganstern, Henry Silverman, Alex. Fink, (there were a few others here, but they did not identify themselves by helping along or supporting the congregation.) They engaged the Rev. Manheimer as Chasan, (Cantor) and their first meeting place was in a room on Penn street, near (Walnut) now Thirteenth street. The Israelites in those days were few in this part of the country and coming here strangers without any means, it required time and perseverance to establish a permanent place of worship, and those that did come and locate here at that time came to promulgate their religion for themselves and their posterity, because most of them had been living in small villages, isolated and no opportunity of worshiping God according to their religion, and this was the principal reason of gathering in a large city.

* *History, Constitution, By-Laws and a List of Members of the Rodef Sholem Congregation* (Pittsburgh: 1898). This brief history of the Rodef Shalom Congregation may be attributed to Dr. Lippman Mayer or Judge Josiah Cohen. Until we have more than the sparse samples of the writing of both of these leaders, the problem of authorship is unlikely to be solved. This piece was published as a small booklet at a time when many of the founders and early members were alive. Although it was widely distributed, few copies have survived.

About 1847 they removed their place of worship to Liberty Street, where the Jenkinson Cigar Factory now stands and changed their Chasan by electing the Rev. Mr Sulzbacher, who officiated until the year 1853, there were a few members added during the time: Isaac and Chas. Bierman, Jos. Meyers, C. D. Arnsthal, L. Hirschfeld, Louis Fleishman, Jacob Silverman, Jos. Morganstern, Michael Streng, Mr. Sheyer, Mr. Alexander, Ben. Oppenheimer and a few others whose names are not accessible. After the year 1853, the place of worship was transferred to the Hall over the Vigilant Engine House on Third Avenue. The Rev. Mr. Marcuson was engaged in place of the Rev. Mr. Sulzbacher, he officiated about two years; up to this time the congregation underwent many changes, as hair splitting doctrines of dogmas and reforms created more or less strife and other congregations were formed.

The organization was not known then as "Rodef Sholem." It came later - it was organized about the year 1856, a majority of the members of the first organization constituting the mainstay of this; then about this time the Frauenfeld Bros., A. Guckenheimer, Wertheimer Bros. Louis Myer, Alex. Greenwald, M. Hanauer, Simon Zugsmith, M. Rosenthal, Klee Bros., Simon Kaufman, I. Kahn, H. Rosenbaum, Henry and Moses Oppenheimer, G. Kann, J Rothschild, Simon Marks, S. Trauerman, S. Prager, Moses Good, L. Berkowitz, Jaroslawski Bros., Z. Eisner, G. Grafner, Jacob Rosenthal, Max. Arnold, Chas. Zeugschmidt, H. Rosenbach and some others became members of the new congregation. Max Arnold was elected the first President and assisted the Chasan during the Holiday services. The Rev. Wm. Armhold was chosen Chasan and German Teacher and the place of worship was again removed to a hall on Third Avenue, opposite the Vigilant Engine House, where they worshiped about two years; from there they went to (St. Clair street,) now Sixth street in the hall of the Irish Building. In 1860 Josiah Cohen was elected English Teacher by the congregation, he remaining with them in this capacity until his admission to the bar in 1866.

In 1860 efforts were first started to build the present Temple on (Hancock) now Eighth street. After hard struggles the small band of reformers striving for improved and modern ritual succeeded, and we have been worshiping in our own Temple since 1865. Rev. L. Naumberg was elected after Rev. Wm. Armhold resigned, and he officiated in the Temple until the present officiating Rabbi, Rev. Dr. L. Mayer was called in 1871. There have been many improvements and the congregation alive to the wants and necessities of modern progress have made the changes as required, and there has been a steady growth in membership and wealth among the supporters of the congregation since the building of the Temple, and the outlook in the near future is that a larger and more commodious Temple will have to be erected to accommodate the membership and patrons. The religious instruction developed this, the Sabbath Schools conducted by the officiating Rabbi and his able assistant are a credit to the progress of the Reform Israelites of Western Pennsylvania and beneficial to Reform Judaism, inculcating in our children the doctrines of our ancestors, in fostering and maintaining in an intelligent manner the belief in the worship of the ancient Mosaic Religion that the pioneers earnestly strived for.

II

AN INTERVIEW WITH SOLOMON B. FREEHOF*

Walter Jacob

S olomon B. Freehof and I have now worked together for almost twenty-five years. It is surprising how active he remains at the age of eighty-seven after many years of retirement. Since Dr. Freehof's withdrawal from the leadership of Congregation Rodef Shalom, he has devoted himself exclusively to studying and writing. He speaks to the congregation on rare occasions, including the anniversary of his *bar mitzvah* and as part of an educational seminar on Yom Kippur. His writing has kept him occupied during the major part of the year, which he spends in Pittsburgh. Since his retirement in 1966, Dr. Freehof has produced popular commentaries to Isaiah, Jeremiah, and Ezekiel, all published by the Union of American Hebrew Congregations. In addition, he has continued to answer numerous halachic queries, although a major portion of the questions now go directly to the CCAR Responsa Committee. His responsa have accumulated into several volumes during these years, and the seventh of these volumes is scheduled for publication in 1980.

In 1978 Dr. Freehof began a new project that will seek to introduce the average Jewish reader to the world of our classics. This book will take the form of brief selections from the Mishnah, Talmud, and later classics relevant to each Torah portion. It will represent a modern version of Hayim Vital's *Hok L'yisrael*.

Between his reading and writing, Dr. Freehof has continued to bind books and has taken special delight in rescuing books from abandoned synagogues across the country. He would be very happy to receive such Hebrew volumes for loving restoration and distribution to colleagues and students, with an occasional volume going to the library of the Hebrew Union College. Dr. Freehof and his wife, the author Lillian Freehof, have set a fine pattern of active

*Reprinted with the permission of the Central Conference of American Rabbis, from *Journal of Reform Judaism*, Summer 1980, pp 16-20.

retirement. Although he does little reminiscing, he agrees to engage in the following interview, which begins with a preliminary statement of his own before his responses to my questions.

SOLOMON B. FREEHOF: King Solomon must have intended the warning for himself, as well as for us all, when in his old age he said: Do not ask why things were better in the old days; there is no wisdom in such a question. That is, indeed, an unwise question, because in our old age much that happened in our youth becomes suffused with a golden glow. Therefore, I shall be careful in answering the questions you ask about my early days at the Hebrew Union College, in the Conference, and in the Reform movement.

WALTER JACOB: Who was your favorite professor at the College? How did he influence you?

SOLOMON B. FREEHOF: Most of us who were students in the years between 1909 and 1915 did not realize what the professors of the time really meant to us. They were all foreigners by birth, and we thought that there would be much better pedagogy at the College when, at last, there would be American-born professors. But we were all mistaken. These great foreign-born scholars left a permanent impress on us. Jacob Marcus grew up under the influence of Gotthard Deutsch; Abraham Feldman carried on the preaching moods of Kaufmann Kohler; Maurice Eisendrath continued the prophetic idealism of Moses Buttenwieser. And the favorite teacher who influenced my own life was Jacob Z. Lauterbach.

WALTER JACOB: What was the nature of the CCAR when you joined it?

SOLOMON B. FREEHOF: It was in the year 1915, and we younger members felt that we had come into the presence of giants. Some of us admired the organizational skill and loyalty of David Philipson. All of us were deeply impressed by the rabbinical learning and fiery eloquence of Samuel Schulman. and whenever Hyman Enelow got up to speak, we were entranced by his cultured English. In spying out the "Promised Land" of our future, we felt that there were friendly giants in Canaan.

WALTER JACOB: What were the main conflicts and problems in the CCAR at that time?

SOLOMON B. FREEHOF: Two great fields of disagreement divided the minds and hearts of the Conference in those days. One was Jewish nationalism, and the other was social action. Jewish nationalism was represented by the small party of Zionists and, in spite of the general disagreement with the doctrine in Jewish nationalism, an outstanding pioneer Zionist, Max Heller was elected president of the Conference. Both issues faded away with the establishment of the beloved State of Israel and the social action question disappeared with the New Deal and the establishment of such programs as Social Security.

WALTER JACOB: How has the Conference changed during these decades? How has Reform Judaism changed?

SOLOMON B. FREEHOF: I believe that the main change is from the external to the internal. The Conference seems now to be concerned mostly with the relationship of Reform to Jewish history and the great Jewish cultural achievements of the past. In my early years in the CCAR we sought independence; now we are reaching out for comradeship.

This also applies to the main changes of Reform in the United States. Intergroup contacts have led to numerous changes both in the Reform and in the non-Reform Jewish world. Particularly important in achieving these changes was the close cooperation of Reform, Orthodox, and Conservative rabbis in the military chaplaincy and in the Synagogue Council of America. We know now that we can cooperate, even though it is wiser to avoid halachic disagreement. As for the status of Reform in the world: With the shifting of the World Union headquarters from England to the United States, the various small Reform movements have been strengthened by their union with a strong, powerful brother, the American movement, with its seven hundred congregations and more than a thousand rabbis. Due to this new family bond, world Reform is more confident of its status and more sure of its future.

WALTER JACOB: Since you were originally interested in prayer and liturgy, how did your interest shift to Jewish law?

SOLOMON B. FREEHOF: The change was due to what might be called a political accident. When the united States entered World War II and we organized the Chaplaincy Commission with eight Orthodox, eight Conservative, and eight Reform leaders, we were governed by an unvoiced caution to avoid the touchy problems of Jewish law. But very early in our work we received a question from Iceland as to what hour should be the hour for Friday night worship there, where the sun does not set for six months of the year. Simultaneously, we received a question from the Coast Guard: How shall a soldier observe *Yahrzeit* for his father when he is on a three-day Coast-Guard patrol with two (Gentile) fellow-soldiers? So we were forced to take up the questions of *halachah*. A committee of three was appointed. It was understood that the chairman of the committee would write the responsa and the other two members would agree or disagree. I wrote about two hundred responsa, and in only one of them, and that for an understandable reason, was any objection raised by one or the other members of the community. Since I had this duty, I accumulated a library of responsa, studied the methods, classical and modern, and learned to write responsa.

WALTER JACOB: How would you characterize the men who headed the CCAR Responsa Committee before yourself, Kohler, Mann, Lauterbach, Bettan?

SOLOMON B. FREEHOF: All of them were similarly motivated, namely, to use the treasures of Jewish legal thought as a guide to solving modern problems. But there was the difference between these great predecessors and myself: They gave their annual reports consisting of two or three responsa to the Conference, but they must have received at least fifty more during the year which they saw no reason to publish. However, I felt that many of these unpublished questions would have served to reveal the changing moods in Reform Judaism and, therefore, they should have been published. Besides, I believe it would be useful for other reasons to build up a body of Reform responsa. So I obtained permission from the Conference to publish those responsa which I wrote and which were not included in the annual Conference report. Some questions, of course, came from overseas, and not from Conference members. Thus, six volumes of my responsa have appeared and a seventh is waiting publication.

WALTER JACOB: What do you consider to be your main contribution to the ideology behind the responsa?

SOLOMON B. FREEHOF: Living and working in the present day in America, my attitude was necessarily different from the founders of Reform who lived in Europe a century or so ago. They were

354

confronted with rigid Orthodoxy in which the rabbis were judges and could virtually control religious life. At that time it was necessary to achieve a revolution for freedom or conscience. But by now Reform is a great, independent movement. We need no longer look over our shoulder nervously at what Orthodox rabbis think of us (as, unfortunately, Conservative rabbis tend to do). Also, we live in an open society and therefore can reestablish close contact with the *halachah* without fear of our life being controlled by Orthodoxy. Besides, I was sure that the Christian theologians were wrong when they taught that the influence of the great prophets died out in Judaism, that it was destroyed by Jewish legalism. I believe, as we all believe, that the influence of prophetic idealism has never died out and lives in the entire Jewish literature and constitutes the essential spirit of the *halachah*. Therefore, since we are free, and since all of Judaism breathes the prophetic spirit, I was able to sum up my attitude to the *halachah* in the phrase; "The *halachah* is not our governance but our guidance."

WALTER JACOB: As preaching has been so much part of your life. Would you like to comment on preaching in the Jewish tradition? Advice do you have for the modern preacher, particularly for the young preacher just out of the seminary? And what balance would you create between structure, idea, and delivery of a sermon?

SOLOMON B. FREEHOF: Regular Sabbath preaching was one of the chief contributions of Reform to modern Jewish life. So valuable is it that it is now a regular part of the Conservative movement and also of modernized Orthodox congregations. It is a grand successor to the work of the itinerant *maggid* and the two halachic lectures that used to be given by the traditional rabbi during the year. So it is in the Reform movement that the technique and mood of the modern sermon were developed.

There has been a great change in modern preaching and, in spite of King Solomon's warning mentioned above, I will say that I consider it an unfortunate change and that our modern preachers are not to be blamed for it. There has been a change in the general public mood. The age of eloquence has, for the moment, died. The present is an age of matter-of-fact talks and colloquies. But anyone who heard Dr. Kohler preach in the Hebrew Union College chapel would understands the words of the prophet, "My words are a flame, a hammer smashing the rock." Until a generation of listeners and a generation of speakers who respond to the art of eloquence and who are willing to be exalted through the medium of public speech arise again, the sermon must wait for its resurrection.

As for the content of the sermon, my unforgettable classmate, Abba Hillel Silver, phrased the purpose of the sermon when he said: "It is to bring the timeless to bear upon the timely." We all know what is timely. The newspapers and the media keep us informed. But what is timeless must be achieved and reachieved in the classic Jewish way, through continuous study on the rabbi's part. This is especially necessary today. Most of our people no longer read Scripture regularly. Their only knowledge of the Bible itself, the only texts they hear, come from the sermon. This puts a very heavy responsibility on the rabbi. He dare not be trivial.

WALTER JACOB: Do you view the Reform movement with hope?

SOLOMON B. FREEHOF: I do, indeed. Its influence on American Jewish life is all-prevading. The changes that are occurring in all branches of Jewish religious life show the massive influence of Reform.

WALTER JACOB: What is you feeling about the future of American Jewish life, especially of American Jewish religious life?

SOLOMON B. FREEHOF: Who can foretell the future? Much of the future depends upon what the presently active generation achieves. I can say at least one thing about the future of American Jewish religious life, and that is that we need a new dimension in Jewish education. The educational effort of Reform and other modernist movements in Judaism has been confined chiefly to the area of child education, and much has been accomplished in this field. But this achievement has left unrestored the great uniqueness in Jewish education. Ours is the only religious tradition which required of all its followers a continuing, life-long religious self-education. This was actually exemplified in the past. Therefore, when we can re-win our people to regular Jewish self-study, our future will be as bright as our past was heroic.

III

THE BROADER ROLE OF THE RABBI*

Walter Jacob

All American rabbis continue to play a role in the broader community and serve on a variety of communal boards. Some have been catalysts of new ventures; other have gone further and been the founder of new organizations and gotten them underway. The best example was Isaac Mayer Wise who established two national newspapers, *The American Israelite* and *Die Deborah,* the Hebrew Union College, and the Central Conference of American Rabbis – or in Pennsylvania, Joseph Krauskopf of Philadelphia, who established the National Farm School. This role of the American rabbinate is unique in our long history. The unusual opportunities presented by the North American setting along with the changing character of the modern rabbinate have made it possible; yet there is more to it than that. Such efforts have appealed to me and led to my becoming the founder or co-founder, on a lesser scale, of four organizations here briefly described.

HORIZON HOMES

The first of those is Horizon Homes, now Mainstay Services. It began out of the personal need to find a suitable setting for our daughter, Claire, who was born with a variety of problems including cataracts, and cerebral palsy, etc. By age ten the existing institutions in which she spent her weekdays were no longer appropriate, and Irene and I began to search for a proper setting not too far from home, so that she could continue to spend weekends at home. What we found was between poor and appalling even when we searched further afield. We, along with Helen Chamowitz, and Mrs. Harry

---

* This is a portion of a larger essay devoted to an exploration of this aspect of the American rabbinate which places it into a broader framework. This excerpt has been adapted for this volume.

357

Clapp, and the enthusiasm of Murray Levine, looked into the possibility of creating a group home as had been done in Connecticut, but not in Pennsylvania.

We began this effort in 1968; as president, it was my task , together with our small inner board group, and especially Irene, to simultaneously move our group of five, along with a few less active board members, to seek advice from the State and local agencies, discover a site, and seek financing from foundations, individuals, as well as governmental sources. From incorporating and persuading well known individuals to form an advisory board, this was a major task that involved seeing several hundred people, arguing with government officials on many levels, and fighting a vigorous zoning battle for three years. In the end that involved getting hundreds of individuals to write to City Council to overturn a zoning decision. The four of us who were persistent and primarily involved were joined by others somewhat later as we formed a working board.

Even at that point the task remained difficult, as we needed to modify the house we had selected, find an administrator, and put together a staff for twenty-four-hour care. We wanted to be innovative, and so immediately developed a system of respite care– a place where families who cared for their handicapped children and young adults throughout the year, could leave them during a family emergency or just to take a well-earned vacation with the rest of the family. We promised to provide long term care so that families did not need to hunt for another site after a few years with us.

We opened Horizon Homes on North Negley Avenue in the summer of 1972, and I remained as president for the founding years. As the need was great, after a few years, we expanded to other sites that served the same purpose. Later, we merged with another facility and created Mainstay Services, which provided some economies of scale without losing the personal attention for all the residents and their families which is so important.

358

THE ASSOCIATED AMERICAN JEWISH MUSEUMS

As no one was doing anything for Jewish art exhibits outside the major Jewish museums, I established the Associated American Jewish Museums in 1972 with some broad goals in mind. The Associated Jewish Museums is an organization of Reform, Conservative, and Orthodox synagogue museums. It seeks to achieve the following purposes:

1. Encourage the development and exhibition of synagogue collections of Judaica, archival, photographic, and historical material.
2. Encourage exhibits of a broader nature such as The Ancient Near Eastern, Jewish Life in the Diaspora, and Inter-Religious Understanding.
3. Provide practical advice on exhibits.
4. Describe what other synagogues are doing.
5. List exhibits that may be borrowed; all exhibits would be free.
6. Provide information on how to generate exhibits.
7. Publish brief studies in the field of Jewish art, and related fields.
8. Produce a regular newsletter, three times each year.

This was to be a nonprofit (501 [c] 3) organization of synagogue and Jewish Center museums that would prepare and circulate exhibits, engage in studies, and publish an informational newsletter. The exhibits were to be free and designed to travel to sites with limited or no professional staff.

At first I thought it would be possible to mount exhibits by borrowing from various small collections. For this purpose I asked a friend to design idiot-proof portable display cases, but this proposal collapsed under the weight of insurance costs.

After a decade and a half of playing only an advisory role, I began to organize traveling exhibits and to publish a regular journal, *Gallery*. Our membership increased to more than sixty institutions and the exhibits as well as symposia we sponsored have been well received. Through the late 1980s to the present time the following exhibits have circulated nationally, some seen by as many as 50,000:

Synagogues Around the World (Photographs by Burton Hirsch). Presents a highly personal view of sixty synagogues in all parts of the world. The exhibit is not a survey of synagogue architecture, but presents an insight into the variety of Jewish houses of worship throughout the world.

Synagogue Interiors Through the Centuries (Photographs Burton Hirsch). This exhibit of thirty pictures focuses on the worship space of the synagogue rather than the exterior architecture and also tells us something about the community that created it.

Ketubot - Ketubot - Ketubot - The largest display of *ketubot* to be circulated in North America. Twenty-six artists are represented by one or two original works. Techniques of painting, cut-outs, water color, lithographs, and overlays have been used by these artists which illustrate a fascinating variety.

Off the Beaten Path - the Neglected Museums of Israel - The exhibit features the smaller Israeli museums with their astonishing variety of specialized collections.

Survivors - Eastern European Synagogues Now - (Photographs of Burton L. Hirsch). Remnants of a proud and creative Jewry which was destroyed by the Holocaust. Only a small number of buildings remain in use as synagogues for the tiny, re-established communities.

We have sponsored a number of national symposia, including *Small Town Synagogues of Western Pennsylvania* (1997) with Dr. Lee Shai Weisbach, University of Louisville, *Roots of Our Rural Synagogues;* Dr. Edward Muller, University of Pittsburgh, *The Western Pennsylvania Background;* Dr. Walter Jacob, *Architectural Influences - European and American.*

Museums and Ideas (1998) with Nancy M. Berman, Director, Skirball Cultural Center, *The Power of Images;* Rabbi Cooper, Associate Director, Wiesenthal Center, *Our Work and Its Implications;* Rabbi Richard Rosenthal, Tacoma, Washington, *Minhag Books and Artistic Expression.*

Art and the Ancient and Medieval Rabbis (1999) with Irene Jacob, Director, Rodef Shalom Biblical Botanical Garden, *Plants and Synagogue Mosaics;* Elizabeth Agro, Carnegie Museum, *Nature and Symbolism;* Diane Samuels, Pittsburgh artist, *A German Town*

Chooses a Jewish Artist; Charles Rosenbloom, Carnegie Mellon University, *American Synagogue Architecture 1900 - The Case of Henry Hornbostell.*

We also presented the following exhibits locally:
Haggadahs through the Centuries
The Ancient Near Eastern Farmer
Papyrus to Paper - Jewish Books through the Centuries
The Clothes We Wore - Exotic Jewish Costumes
Our Crowd - Four Generations at Rodef Shalom- An Exhibit of 1500 Photographs

THE SOLOMON B. FREEHOF INSTITUTE OF PROGRESSIVE HALAKHAH

In the late nineteen eighties after a decade and a half as Chair of the Responsa Committee of the Central Conference of American Rabbis, which dealt with *halakhah* I wished to concentrate more on specific issues. I also wanted to provide a more systematic background for the modern problems that confront us, through position papers along with practical guidance for the modern Jew. A new committee of the Conference seemed like an appropriate vehicle. It was appointed but proved difficult as the organizational nature of the Conference imposes restraints. Moshe Zemer, an Israeli colleague, came to Pittsburgh with similar thoughts which would meet the needs of Israel and perhaps others as well. We were both very much on the same track and decided that an independent institute would be the proper route, as it could move quickly, with a minimum of structure and no bureaucracy. Moshe Zemer would be our "Director" in Israel and would take care of Israeli matters, while I as "President" would take care of North America and Europe. As Solomon B. Freehof, who had done so much for Reform *halakhah*, had died recently, we sought and received permission to use his name for the Institute, founded in 1989, selected an advisory board, and held our initial seminar in London.

We have sponsored one or two seminars subsequently each year in North America, Israel, and Europe. Most of the symposia, regularly held since 1989, have been planned jointly. The thirteen volumes, a volume each year, have, however, been edited and subsequently set up for printing by me. In addition to the editorial process, publication and distribution, I undertook the organizational, financial, and membership tasks, with the generous aid of Nancy Berkowitz, who copy-edited many volumes, and the kind help of my secretary, Barbara Bailey. I have also written and edited *HalakhaH*, our journal, which appears three times each year.

Our membership, continues to be international as are our contributors, and interest in the Institute among colleagues and lay people continues to grow. Our purpose is clearly summarized in a brief statement:

The Freehof Institute of Progressive *Halakhah* is a creative research center devoted to studying and defining the progressive character of the *halakhah* in accordance with the principles and theology of Reform Judaism. It seeks to establish the ideological basis of Progressive *halakhah* and its application to daily life. The Institute fosters serious studies and helps scholars in various parts of the world to work together for a common cause. It provides a continuing forum through symposia and publications, including the quarterly newsletter, *HalakhaH*, published under the editorship of Walter Jacob in the United States. The foremost halakhic scholars in the Reform, Liberal, and Progressive rabbinate, along with some Conservative and Orthodox colleagues as well as university professors, serve on our Academic Council.

The following volumes have appeared: *Dynamic Jewish Law, Progressive Halakhah- Essence and Application* (1991), *Rabbinic-Lay Relations in Jewish Law* (1993), *Conversion to Judaism in Jewish Law* (1994), *Death and Euthanasia in Jewish Law* (1995), *The Fetus and Fertility in Jewish Law* (1996), *Israel and the Diaspora in Jewish Law* (1997), *Aging and the Aged in Jewish Law* (1998), *Marriage and Its Obstacles in Jewish Law* (1999),

Crime and Punishment in Jewish Law (2000),
Gender Issues in Jewish Law (2001),
Re-examining Progressive Halakhah (2002),
The Environment in Jewish Law (2003),
Beyond the Letter of the Law - Essays on Diversity in the Halakhah (2004).

These volumes are part of a series whose subjects are as diverse as the approaches taken by the authors. We wish to encourage wide-ranging discussions of contemporary and historic themes.

ABRAHAM GEIGER COLLEGE

An invitation from the World Union of Progressive Judaism, which I had served as Vice-President, to speak at a Liberal Jewish meeting in Vienna in 1995 introduced me to the leadership of the small central European Reform movement. Clearly Liberal Judaism had a lot to offer the expanding Jewish population of Central Europe, especially as the older "Traditional" community was becoming more Orthodox and less tolerant at the same time as the communities experienced major growth through immigration from the Soviet Union. The future of Liberal Judaism was stymied by the refusal of the official central Jewish governing bodies, to provide recognition or financial support and by the lack of interest and support from the American Reform movement. We also suffered from a lack of new lay and rabbinic leadership. A few of us began to discuss the possibilities of changing this situation. On the lay leadership issue, I decided to organize and sponsor a pilot educational program for the month of August, 1999 in Pittsburgh for prospective young lay leaders. Students had to possess a working knowledge of English and provide their own transportation to the United States. We would house, feed, and provide educational programs for a month. Members of Rodef Shalom opened their homes to the students, the Sisterhood set aside funding for a trip to the Social Action Center and related sites in Washington. The Jr. Congregation helped with the leisure and social life of the group. I organized a full morning of classes, generously taught by all my Reform colleagues in Pittsburgh and afternoon presentations by most of the major Jewish organization in the city as well as an introduction to the music of the service by Mimi Lerner. The program was successful and all of the students have become leaders in their communities or in the youth movements of Central Europe.

Rabbinic leadership presented a greater challenge; as less than a handful of older American rabbis fluent in German were able to commit time and energy to the task of congregation building, this was not an answer. Sending prospective candidates to North America was also problematic as such students would lose contact with their home congregations and would probably remain in the United States. Nor was the Leo Baeck College in London able to add more than a few students to its program.

During these years, Walter Homolka with whom I had developed a friendship years earlier and who had studied at the Leo Baeck College was working as chief of staff of Bertelsmann in Munich; he helped to reorganize that congregation and created the Union of Progressive Jews which united the Liberal congregations of Central Europe, not an easy task and one which required considerable effort and diplomacy. This led to new Reform congregations along with *havurot* throughout Central Europe. I helped the lead congregation in Munich by becoming its pro bono senior rabbi. A little later I was invited to teach a course for the Mendelssohn Institute of the University of Potsdam which provided some contacts there. As the need for rabbinic leadership was urgent, Rabbi Homolka and I began to look seriously into the possibility of a rabbinic seminary in Germany. We took the curricula of the Hebrew Union College-Jewish Institute of Religion and of the Reconstructionist Rabbinic College as our model. Faculty and facility costs appeared daunting, but Rabbi Homolka discovered a less expensive solution through utilizing the excellent Jewish studies programs at various German universities. The University of Potsdam, with which we developed and agreement, offers a wide ranging Jewish studies curriculum through its departmental faculty of twenty-two. It

364

has a good Jewish library. Other major universities in Berlin with their Jewish studies programs were also available. We saw that we needed to assemble only a small additional faculty and would not be burdened by expensive buildings.

Chartering the school, organizing the board, office space, as well as the details of an agreement with the University was accomplished by Dr. Homolka who was at that time fully employed as the Director of the Cultural Foundation of the Deutsche Bank; each of these tasks required presence in Germany a knowledge of the people and broad contacts. I worked on American contacts, both academic and organizational. Both of us together worked out the curriculum, faculty needs, student standards, etc. and dealt with the opposition from various sources. We reached decisions jointly and were in touch by e-mail and telephone almost daily. The World Union of Progressive Judaism supported our efforts. Rabbi Homolka became the Rector of the College while I serve as its President.

I worked on obtaining American support - both the help of American Jewish organizations and those of the Reform movement. The Union of Reform Judaism, the Hebrew Union College-Jewish Institute of Religion, the Central Conference of American Rabbis, and the Reconstructionist Rabbinic College as well as the Reconstructionist Rabbinic Fellowship quickly became supportive. Unfortunately it was much more difficult to obtain any assistance from American Jewish organizations which had established themselves in Central Europe; they remained cautious and despite a pluralistic stance in North America, refused to apply it to Europe. All of this took considerable effort .

The *Zentralrat*, the governing body of the German Jewish community through which the government funds Jewish religious life, should have offered its support, but it was dominated by traditionalists who refused. This led me to organize the American Friends of the Union of Progressive Jews, a tax exempt charity and enlist virtually all American rabbis who had been educated in pre-war Central Europe onto its advisory board and formed a small inner board. Then I began to raise the necessary funds. Individuals and foundations in Pittsburgh and the surrounding area responded generously; soon these efforts were expanded to other cities.

By 2000 we were ready to dedicated the College; the ceremonies were attended by leading government and religious figures. In 2001 we accepted our first group of students. A small part time faculty with an emphasis on Hebrew, Bible, rabbinics, pastoral counseling, homiletics, and music, along with Dr. Admiel Kosman as professor of Talmud takes care of the academic needs not fulfilled by the faculty of the University of Potsdam. A simple office in the heart of Berlin provides space for the administration and for our library. Each of our students spends a year in Israel. Immediately upon opening, we saw the need to expand our effort to Eastern Europe as the need for rabbis in those lands is even greater than in Central Europe. At the present time our students come from Russia, Ukraine, Belarus, Germany, Sweden, and the Czech Republic.

Each year we have organized continuing education symposia for rabbis, lay-leaders, and cantors. These forums have brought outstanding scholars from the United States, France, and Israel to the College and provided an ongoing contact with the larger Jewish world. Separately we have published prayerbooks and texts for the Reform movement.

Dr. Homolka has spent several years virtually full time as the Rector of the College, largely pro bono. He has engaged in a difficult struggle to obtain the recognition and financial support of the *Zentralrat*. These complicated efforts have involved court battles as well as political struggles. At the same time I have organized campaigns of American Jewish organizations and individuals to apply further pressure on the German government and its ambassadors to demonstrate that the American Reform Jewish community strongly backs these efforts. Continuing efforts to obtain wider recognition, raise funds for half of our costs, stay in touch with our supporters, and teach a semester each year represent my current efforts. The College will continue to look to the North American Jewish community for help with special projects and student support as we receive more applications from the lands of Eastern Europe..

The establishment of this new rabbinic seminary, the first in Central Europe since the Holocaust has demanded considerable effort. It has always been a pleasure for Rabbi Homolka and me to work with Rabbi Uri Regev, the Executive of the World Union of Progressive Judaism, Rabbi Eric Yoffie, the President of the Union of Reform Judaism, Dr. David Ellenson, the President of the Hebrew Union College, Rabbis Menitoff, Stevens, and Marder, of the Central Conference of America Rabbis along with the various lay leaders of our American and European movements, such as Dr. Jan Muehlstein, who has been most helpful. All of us are looking forward to the first rabbinic ordination in 2006.

CONTRIBUTORS

Barbara Burstin is a Lecturer in Jewish studies at the University of Pittsburgh. She is past president of the American Jewish Committee (Pittsburgh Chapter), the Pittsburgh Jewish Student Center, and Chair of the United Jewish Federation of Pittsburgh.

David Glick (1887–1964) was a senior partner of the law form Glick, Berkman and Engel, past president of the Allegheny County Bar Association, the Foreign Policy Association, the Visiting Nurses Association, and on the board of numerous organizations including the Western Pennsylvania Historical Society. He spent 1936, 1937, and part of 1938 in Germany to facilitate the emigration efforts of the *Reichvertretung der Juden in Deutschland* of Jews to South America. Subsequently he visited South America to encourage further immigration.

Frances Aaron Hess is a governor of the Hebrew Union College-Jewish Institute of Religion, and honorary governor of the American Jewish Committee, and an honorary vice-president of its New York Chapter, a trustee of Congregation Emanu-El of New York, of the World Union for Progressive Judaism, and serves on numerous educational and cultural boards.

Irene Jacob is the founding director of the Rodef Shalom Biblical Botanical Garden. She has taught economic botany at Chatham College and initiated a docent program at Phipps Conservatory. She is the author or editor of five books including *Gardens of North America and Hawaii – A Traveler's Guide* (1985), *The Healing Past, Pharmaceuticals in the Biblical and Rabbinic World* (1993), *Botanical Symbols in World Religions* (2000), and *Plants of the Bible and Their Uses* (2003).

Walter Jacob is Senior Scholar of Rodef Shalom Congregation, Pittsburgh, Pennsylvania; President of the Abraham Geiger College in Berlin/Potsdam, Past President of the Central Conference of American Rabbis, President of the Freehof Institute of Progressive *Halakhah* and the Associated American Jewish Museums. Author, editor, or translator of thirty-two books including *Christianity through Jewish Eyes* (1974), *American Reform Responsa* (1983), *The Changing World of Reform Judaism* (1985), *Liberal Judaism and Halakhah* (1988), *The Second Book of the Bible: Exodus interpreted by Benno Jacob* (ed., tr.) (1992), *Rabbinic - Lay Relations in Jewish Law* (1993), *Not By Birth Alone, Conversion to Judaism* (1997), *Die Exegese hat das erste Wort* (2002), *Beyond the Letter of the Law* (2004).

Susan Friedberg Kalson serves as President of the Board of Trustees of the Rodef Shalom Congregation. She is a graduate of Harvard University, the University of Kent, Canterbury, England, and has a law degree from the University of Pittsburgh.

Eileen Lane earned a BA in American Studies from Goucher College and did graduate work in history and religious studies at the University of Pittsburgh. In part her interest in immigration stems from the personal experience of emigrating to England in 1968 and "repatriating" to Pittsburgh ten years later with her English husband and children. Active in many civic, educational, community service and philanthropic endeavors, she is a past president of Rodef Shalom Congregation.

Ruth Langer is Associate Professor in Theology at Boston College with a special interest in Jewish Liturgy and Christian Jewish Relations. She is Associate Director of the Center from Christian Jewish Learning there. She has written extensively in both fields, including *To Worship God Properly: Tensions between Liturgical Custom and Halakhah in Judaism* (1998). She has served as book review editor of the *CCAR Journal: A Reform Jewish Quarterly.*

Ruth Cooper Reidbord is a Planning Consultant was Planning Director for Mount Lebanon, Pa. and has served as president of the Pittsburgh Regional Chapter of the American Planning Association. She is a past president of Synagogue Council of Greater Pittsburgh and the Tri-State Region of the Pennsylvania Council of the UAHC and is currently a trustee of Temple Sinai and teaches at the CMU Academy for Lifelong Learning. She attended a school affiliated with the Southwest District

Richard Rosenzweig is a lawyer in Pittsburgh with an interest in local history. An article based on the subject of his paper appeared in *Western Pennsylvania History*. He teaches at the CMU Academy of Lifelong Learning.

Rina C. Youngner is an art historian with a Ph.D. and has contributed to catalogues at the Carnegie Museum of Art and the American Jewish Museum of Pittsburgh. She has curated an exhibit on Gorson at the Frick Museum of the University of Pittsburgh. Earlier she taught English in Pittsburgh high schools.